The Changing Vietnamese M[anagement]

Vietnam has emerged from long periods of colonization, wars and ideological conflicts to become an important economic force within Asia and a promising destination for international business ventures.

The latest book in the popular Working in Asia series, *The Changing Face of Vietnamese Management*, draws on the experiences of Vietnamese experts to offer a unique perspective on the opportunities, challenges and issues facing managers and organizations operating in this fascinating emerging market. The book:

- contextualizes political, economic and social traditions
- discusses Vietnam's competitiveness within the global economy
- analyzes key functional areas, including Human Resource Management, marketing, finance and strategy
- examines key issues and new developments in management and business.

This key text includes illustrative case studies and vignettes to provide broad coverage and content that will serve the needs of students and managers alike.

Chris Rowley is Professor of Human Resource Management and Director of the Centre for Research in Asian Management at City University, UK. He is editor of the leading journal *Asia Pacific Business Review* and has published widely in the area of Asian business and management with more than 300 publications.

Quang Truong is Professor of Organizational Behaviour and Human Resource Management at Maastricht School of Management, the Netherlands. He has written extensively in local and international journals on development matters in Vietnam.

Working in Asia

General Editors:
Tim G. Andrews
University of Strathclyde
Keith Jackson
School of Oriental and African Studies, University of London
and **Chris Rowley**
Cass Business School, City University, UK

This series focuses on contemporary management issues in the Asia-Pacific region. It draws on the latest research to highlight critical factors impacting on the conduct of business in this diverse and dynamic business environment.

Our primary intention is to provide management students and practitioners with fresh dimensions to their reading of standard texts. With each book in the *Working in Asia* series, we offer a combined insider's and outsider's perspective on how managers and their organizations in the Asia-Pacific region are adapting to contemporary currents of both macro- and micro-level change.

The core of data for the texts in this series has been generated by recent interviews and discussions with established senior executives as well as newly fledged entrepreneurs; with practising as well as aspiring middle managers; and women as well as men. Our mission has been to give voice to how change is being perceived and experienced by a broad and relevant range of people who live and work in the region. We report on how they and their organizations are managing change as the globalization of their markets, together with their business technologies and traditions, unfolds.

Drawing together the combined insights of Asian and Western scholars, and practitioners of management, we present a uniquely revealing portrait of the future of working and doing business in Asia.

Titles in the series include:

The Changing Face of Multinationals in Southeast Asia
Tim G. Andrews, Nartnalin Chompusri and Bryan J. Baldwin

The Changing Face of Chinese Management
Jie Tang and Anthony Ward

The Changing Face of Japanese Management
Keith Jackson and Miyuki Tomioka

The Changing Face of Korean Management
Chris Rowley and Yongsun Paik

The Changing Face of Management in South East Asia
Chris Rowley and Saaidah Abdul-Rahman

The Changing Face of Women Managers in Asia
Chris Rowley and Vimolwan Yukongdi

The Changing Face of People Management in India
Pawan S. Budhwar and Jyotsna Bhatnagar

The Changing Face of Management in Thailand
Tim G. Andrews and Sununta Siengthai

The Changing Face of Vietnamese Management
Chris Rowley and Quang Truong

The Changing Face of Vietnamese Management

Edited by Chris Rowley and Quang Truong

Routledge
Taylor & Francis Group

LONDON AND NEW YORK

First published 2009
by Routledge
2 Park Square, Milton Park, Abingdon, Oxon OX14 4RN

Simultaneously published in the USA and Canada
by Routledge
270 Madison Avenue, New York, NY 10016

Routledge is an imprint of the Taylor & Francis Group, an informa business

© 2009 Chris Rowley and Quang Truong

This edition first published in paperback 2010

Typeset in Times New Roman by
RefineCatch Limited, Bungay, Suffolk
Printed and bound by MPG Books Group, UK

All rights reserved. No part of this book may be reprinted or reproduced or utilised in any form or by any electronic, mechanical, or other means, now known or hereafter invented, including photocopying and recording, or in any information storage or retrieval system, without permission in writing from the publishers.

British Library Cataloguing in Publication Data
A catalogue record for this book is available from the British Library

Library of Congress Cataloging-in-Publication Data
The changing face of Vietnamese management / edited by Chris Rowley and Quang Truong.
      p. cm.
   Includes bibliographical references and index.
   1. Management—Vietnam.   2. Organizational change—Vietnam.
   3. Corporate culture—Vietnam.   I. Rowley, Chris, 1959–   II. Truong, Quang.
   HD70.V5C43 2009
   658.009597—dc22

2009014956

ISBN10: 0-415-47604-6 (hbk)
ISBN10: 0-415-59564-9 (pbk)
ISBN10: 0-203-86840-4 (ebk)

ISBN13: 978-0-415-47604-1 (hbk)
ISBN13: 978-0-415-59564-3 (pbk)
ISBN13: 978-0-203-86840-9 (ebk)

For Andrea, for understanding and caring.

For Thuy-Loan, a so faithful companion.

Contents

Figures	xi
Tables	xiii
Text boxes	xv
Case studies	xvii
Abbreviations	xix
Contributors	xxi
Acknowledgements	xxv
Map of Vietnam	xxvi

1 Setting the scene for the changing face of management in Vietnam   1
CHRIS ROWLEY AND QUANG TRUONG
- Introduction   1
- Key contexts within which management and business operate   3
- The issue of competitiveness   13
- Structure and content overview   14
- Coverage of cases   19
- Common themes   19
- Conclusion   21

2 The changing face of human resource management in Vietnam   24
QUANG TRUONG AND BEATRICE I.J.M. VAN DER HEIJDEN
- Introduction   24
- Key issues and new developments   25
- Case studies   37
- Challenges   43
- Conclusion   45

3 The changing face of marketing management in Vietnam — 50
PIERRE DIETRICHSEN, WITH CONTRIBUTIONS BY
ELIZABETH ERASMUS AND THANH PHUNG PHUONG
- Introduction — 50
- Key issues and new developments — 52
- Case studies — 72
- Challenges — 81
- Conclusion — 85

4 The changing face of financial market management in Vietnam — 93
OLIVER MASSMANN AND CHRIS ROWLEY
- Introduction — 93
- Key issues and new developments — 94
- Case studies — 107
- Challenges — 115
- Conclusion — 125

5 The changing face of strategy management in Vietnam — 128
QUANG TRUONG AND THIEM TON THAT NGUYEN
- Introduction — 128
- Key issues and new developments — 130
- Case studies — 141
- Challenges — 151
- Conclusion — 153

6 The changing face of foreign direct investment management in Vietnam — 158
CLEMENS BECHTER, CHRIS ROWLEY, KATHARINA KÜHN
AND OLIVER MASSMANN
- Introduction — 158
- Key issues and new developments — 159
- Case studies — 171
- Challenges — 177
- Conclusion — 182

7 The changing face of public sector management in Vietnam — 187
TRUONG XUAN DO AND QUANG TRUONG
- Introduction — 187
- Key issues and new developments — 188

- Case studies 202
- Challenges 210
- Conclusion 215

8 The changing face of women managers in small and medium sized enterprises in Vietnam 221
ANNE VO AND CHARLES HARVIE
- Introduction 221
- Key issues and new developments 222
- Case studies 236
- Challenges 242
- Conclusion 246

9 The changing face of Vietnamese management revisited 251
CHRIS ROWLEY AND QUANG TRUONG
- Introduction 251
- Major findings revisited 252
- Implications and future trends 254
- Conclusion 257

Index 261

Figures

1.1	The strategic mismatch in Vietnam	11
4.1	US$ versus VND exchange rate, 1 September 2008 to 1 July 2009	95
4.2	Year-on-year GDP growth	96
4.3	Year-on-year inflation (%)	97
4.4	VN Index fluctuation, 2000–2007	106
6.1	Vietnam FDI – registered vs implemented, 1998–2007	162
6.2	Types of FDI in Vietnam	165
7.1	Relationship between the CPV and executive and the legislative branches	189
8.1	Highest education level achieved by population aged 15 and over in 2002 (%)	230
8.2	Labour force participation rates (million people)	232
8.3	Unemployment rate in urban areas by sex, 2001–2003 (%)	233

Tables

1.1	Geographic and topological indicators of Vietnam	4
1.2	Development and key milestones in Vietnam	5
1.3	Key economic indicators in Vietnam, 1995–2008	9
1.4	GDP in Vietnam, 1976–2008	9
1.5	Population and Patterns of living in Vietnam, 1995–2007	11
1.6	Cultural indicators in Vietnam, 2008	12
1.7	Ease of doing business in Vietnam (N = 181 economies)	14
1.8	Starting a business in Vietnam	14
1.9	List of case studies: Organizations and managers	20
2.1	Dimension of the labour market in Vietnam, 2000–07	26
2.2	Human Resource Management practices by type of enterprise across different time periods	28
2.3	Challenges facing enterprises in the post-*Doi Moi* period	31
2.4	Employee vs. employer perceptions as regards issues of satisfaction (in order of importance) (N = 300)	32
2.5	The HR service market in Vietnam	45
4.1	Vietnam's Stock Exchange, 2008	104
4.2	Comparison of balance sheets of SeABank and MHB (VND million)	110
4.3	Comparison of income statements of SeABank and MHB (VND million)	111
5.1	Economic growth in Vietnam, 1986–2010	129
5.2	Vietnam's overall competitiveness ranking (socio-economic indexes)	129
5.3	Vietnam's economic structure, 1995–2007	132
5.4	Investment structure in Vietnam, 1995–2007	135
5.5	Vietnam's top export items in value, 2005	136
5.6	Balance of trade, 1990–2010 (US$ billion)	137

5.7	Growth competitiveness comparison index (GCI), 2000–08	138
5.8	Investment by source (% of GDP)	139
6.1	Vietnam's FDI registered capital, 1988–2007 (US$ million)	160
6.2	Vietnam's top ten investors by country, 1988–2007 (US$ million)	161
6.3	Licensed FDI projects, by major cities/provinces, 1998–2007 (US$ million)	170
8.1	Composition of GDP (%) and industrial production by ownership type (%)	227
8.2	Types of non-farm household enterprise operated by men and women in rural and urban areas (%)	234
9.1	Implications and future trends	255
9.2	HR challenges in Vietnam	256
9.3	Human Resource Management challenges and responses in Vietnam	257
9.4	Human Resource Management as a competitive edge in Vietnam	257

Text boxes

3.1	Buyer behaviour in Vietnam and its impact on marketing	67
3.2	Market research in Vietnam	71
3.3	Household and personal consumer goods – Unilever and others	76
4.1	Vietnam's monetary policy measures and exchange rate regime	115
4.2	The Credit Market in Romania	121
4.3	The Credit Market in the Philippines and Mexico	122
6.1	North Red River new residential area, Hanoi	178
6.2	Amata	179
6.3	Nike	181

Case studies

2.1	Property Development Company (PDCo)	38
2.2	VinaGame Co (www.vinagame.com.vn)	39
2.3	Mrs Nguyen thi Hong-Phiet	40
2.4	Three female HR managers	42
3.1	IBM	73
3.2	Dutch Lady and Nestlé	74
3.3	Ms Thuy Dam, Country Head, ANZ Bank Vietnam	78
3.4	Dr Truong Gia Binh, Chairman and CEO, FPT Corporation	80
4.1	Southeast Asia Commercial Bank (SeABank)	108
4.2	The Housing Bank of Mekong Delta (MHB)	109
4.3	Mr Sandy Flockhart, CEO, HSBC Asia Pacific	112
4.4	Mr Ashok Sud, Chief Executive, Standard Chartered Vietnam (SCV), Laos, Cambodia	114
5.1	An Phuoc Garment Company (APG)	142
5.2	Duoc Hau Giang (DHG Pharma)	144
5.3	Mr Dang Le Nguyen Vu, CEO, Trung Nguyen	146
5.4	Mr Nguyen Thanh My, CEO, My Lan Chemicals (MLC)	150
6.1	DKSH: A Swiss business with strong Asian roots	171
6.2	Organizations in the energy sector	173
6.3	Mr Mark Schiller, Managing Director, Shipbuilder Strategic Marine (SSM)	174
6.4	Mr Takashi Fujii, General Director, Dai-Ichi Life Insurance Company of Vietnam Ltd (DIIVN)	176
7.1	Performance management in HCMC	202
7.2	Hiring CEOs for SOEs	205
7.3	Mr Luong van Ly	207
7.4	Mr Nguyen van Giau	209
8.1	Garment Company (GC)	236

8.2	Printing Company (PC)	237
8.3	Ms A, Owner, GC	238
8.4	Ms B, Owner, PC	240

Abbreviations

AFTA	ASEAN Free Trade Agreement
ASEAN	Association of South East Asian Nations
BCC	Business cooperation contract
BOT	Build-Operate-Transfer
CEO	Chief Executive Officer
CPV	Communist Party of Vietnam; *Dang Cong san Viet Nam*
CRM	Customer relations management
CSR	Corporate social responsibility
EU	European Union
FDI	Foreign direct investment
FIE	Foreign invested enterprise
FMCG	Fast moving consumer goods
FOE	Foreign owned enterprise
GDP	Gross domestic product
GSO	General Statistics Office; *Tong cuc Thong ke*
HCMC	Ho Chi Minh City – the new name for Saigon
HR	Human resource
HRD	Human resource development
HRIS	Human resource information system
IMC	Integrated marketing communication
IT	Information technology
JSB	Joint stock bank; *ngan hang co phan*
JSC	Joint stock company; *Cong ty co phan*
JVE	Joint venture enterprise
LFI	Law on foreign investment
LLC	Limited liability company; *Cong ty trach nhiem huu han*
LOE	Law on Enterprises; *Luat doanh nghiep*
LOI	Law on Investment; *Luat dau tu*

MNC	Multinational company
MNE	Multinational enterprise
MOLISA	Ministry of Labour, Invalids and Social Affairs; *Bo Lao dong, Thuong binh va Xa hoi*
MPI	Ministry of Planning and Investment; *Bo Ke hoach va Dau tu*
NGO	Non-governmental organization
NPL	Non-performing loan
ODA	Overseas development aid
OFA	Ordinance on Foreign Exchange
PAR	Public administration reform; *cai cach hanh chanh cong*
PC	People's Council; *Hoi dong nhan dan*
PE	Private enterprise
PMS	Performance management system
PPP	Purchasing power parity
QWL	Quality of working life
RO	Representative office
SBV	State Bank of Vietnam; *Ngan hang nha nuoc Viet Nam*
SEDS	Socio-Economic Development Strategy
SME	Small and medium-size enterprise
SOCB	State-owned commercial bank; *ngan hang quoc doanh*
SOE	State-owned enterprise
SRV	Socialist Republic of Vietnam; *Cong hoa xa hoi chu nghia Viet Nam*
SSC	State Securities Commission; *Uy ban Chung khoan nha nuoc*
STC	State Trading Commission
T&D	Training and development
VCCI	Vietnam Chamber of Commerce and Industry; *Phong Thuong mai va Cong nghiep Viet Nam*
VGCL	Vietnam General Confederation of Labour; *Tong lien doan lao dong Viet Nam*
VND	Vietnam *Dong* – the Vietnamese monetary unit: 1 US$ = 17,400 VND at January 2009
VNI	Vietnam Index
WB	World Bank
WTO	World Trade Organization

Contributors

Clemens Bechter is Adjunct Associate Professor at the Asian Institute of Technology Center Vietnam (AITCV). Prior to his academic career, he gained solid management experience as Managing Director of the UK subsidiary of Zweckform Büroprodukte GmbH (now Avery-Dennison-Zweckform) and Product Manager at BASF AG. He is founding partner of the US-based travel company Hotelsensation, Inc. and has published widely in the area of international business.

Pierre Dietrichsen has lived in Vietnam since 2002 and is a university lecturer in Hanoi, specializing in strategy, leadership and management. He is a former ambassador and consultant, and holds a master's degree in commerce and a doctorate in business administration.

Truong Xuan Do is a lecturer at the National Economics University in Hanoi. He graduated with a MBA and PhD from the Asian Institute of Technology in Bangkok, Thailand. His main areas of research and consultancy include Human Resource Management in the public sector, public administration reform, and training and development. He has provided consultancy services for several donors such as the Asian Development Bank (ADB), United Nations Development Program (UNDP), Japan International Cooperation Agency (JICA), and Swedish International Development Cooperation Agency (SIDA).

Elizabeth Erasmus, MBA, lives in Hanoi and is a lecturer in buyer behaviour and marketing and a keen observer of consumer trends in Vietnam.

Charles Harvie holds a PhD in economics from the University of Warwick, UK, and is currently an Associate Professor in the School of Economics at the University of Wollongong, Australia. He has published over 150 papers in refereed journals, book chapters and refereed conference papers, 15 edited and authored books on the economies of East Asia, economic integration in East Asia, and SMEs in East Asia. His current research interests include private small business development in Vietnam.

Beatrice I.J.M. van der Heijden is Professor of Strategic Human Resource Management at the Open University of the Netherlands. She is Director of Research and Doctoral Programs at the Maastricht School of Management and Head of the Department of Organizational Behaviour/Human Resource Management. She is affiliated with the University of Twente, Department of Human Resource Management. She holds a MA in psychology from the Catholic University of Nijmegen, and a PhD in management science from the University of Twente, the Netherlands. Currently, she coordinates two European cross-cultural research projects on career success. Her main research areas are career development, employability, and aging at work.

Katharina Kühn is a LLM candidate at the University of Bremen and a *stagiaire* with the Trade Section of the Delegation of the European Commission to Vietnam. She specializes in international economic law and has previously worked as a trainee for Baker & McKenzie in Hanoi, Vietnam.

Oliver Massmann is a partner with Duane Morris Vietnam LLC providing consultancy primarily in the areas of corporate international taxation, power/water projects, and matters related to oil and gas companies, telecoms, privatization and equitization, mergers and acquisitions, and general commercial matters for multinational clients in relation to investment and doing business in Vietnam.

Thiem Ton That Nguyen holds a PhD from the Université Libre de Bruxelles, Belgium, and is currently Professor *cum* Director of the EMBA programme of United Business Institute (Belgium); and Director of the local office of the Nyenrode Business University/Vietnam National University cooperation programme in Vietnam. He has written extensively in the leading journals and published several books on strategy management and branding in Vietnam.

Chris Rowley is Professor of Human Resource Management and Director of the Centre for Research in Asian Management, City University and editor of the leading journal *Asia Pacific Business Review*. He has published widely in the area of Asian business and management with more than 25 books, 140 chapters and entries and more than 130 articles.

Thanh Phung Phuong, MBA, is a market research and business lecturer in Hanoi and was born in Vietnam.

Quang Truong is Professor of Organizational Behaviour and Human Resource Management at Maastricht School of Management, the Netherlands. He holds a PhD from the Vrije Universiteit of Amsterdam, the Netherlands. His research and consultancy concentrate primarily on areas such as human resource management, development process and organizational effectiveness in emerging countries, especially Vietnam. He has written extensively in local and international journals on development matters in Vietnam.

Anne Vo holds a PhD in human resource management from De Montfort University, UK and is a lecturer in the School of Management and Marketing at the University of Wollongong, Australia. She researches in the areas of international and comparative Human Resource Management, the transfer of multinational companies' Human Resource Management policies and practices across borders, the transformation of Human Resource

Acknowledgements

We would like to thank all the organizations and managers who participated in this book.

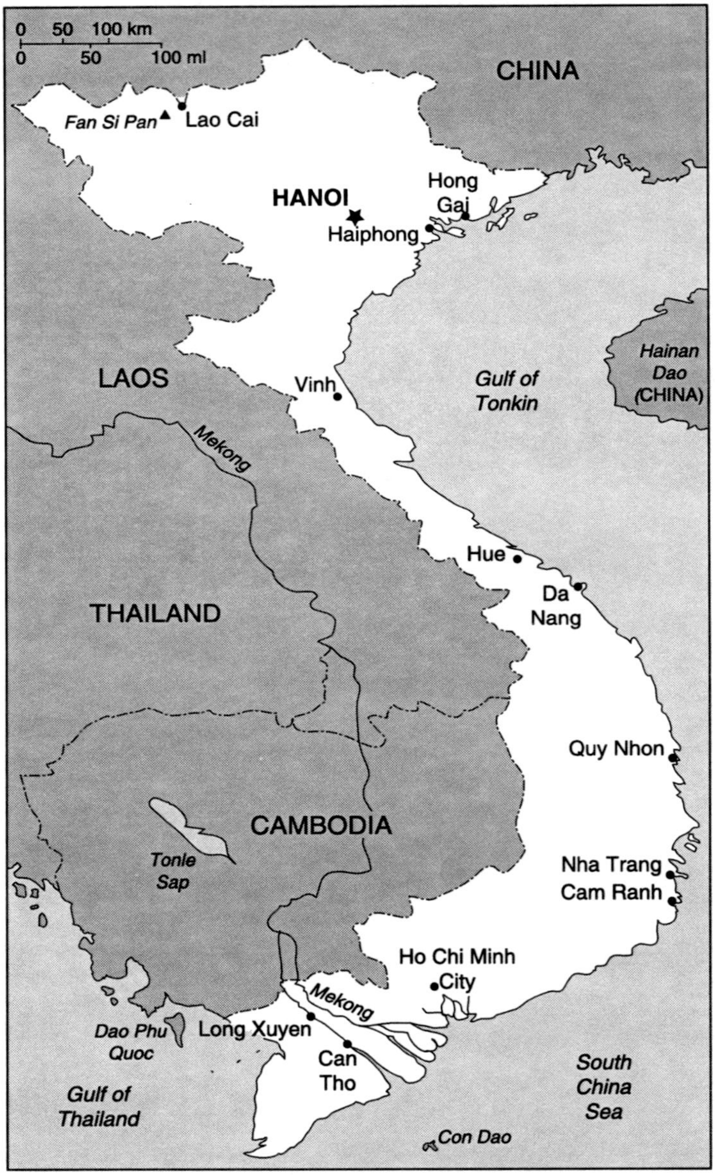
0 50 100 km
0 50 100 ml
CHINA
Fan Si Pan
Lao Cai
HANOI
Hong Gai
Haiphong
LAOS
Vinh
Gulf of Tonkin
Hainan Dao (CHINA)
Mekong
Hue
Da Nang
THAILAND
Quy Nhon
CAMBODIA
Tonle Sap
Nha Trang
Cam Ranh
Ho Chi Minh City
Mekong
Dao Phu Quoc
Long Xuyen
Can Tho
Gulf of Thailand
South China Sea
Con Dao

1 Setting the scene for the changing face of management in Vietnam

Chris Rowley and Quang Truong

- Introduction
- Key contexts within which management and business operate
- The issue of competitiveness
- Structure and content overview
- Coverage of cases
- Common themes
- Conclusion

Introduction

This book on management and business in Vietnam continues in a similar vein to recent texts in the innovative 'Working in Asia' Routledge book series in terms of developing, in some fresh ways, the original purpose and conceptualization of the series. The intention of this unusual series is to provide accessible books that are easy to read and use, written by experts – many local – and critically which give 'voice' to individuals, especially local managers, within organizations. This 'voice' can come via illustrative case studies and vignettes, used to examine and exemplify the changing practices, issues and 'face' of management in Asia. The aims and format of this series in turn require a commensurate downplaying of more research monograph-type content and structure. With the ongoing widespread interest in Asia, the time is ripe for books using such a focus and format.

This book on Vietnam follows the generic rubric of the series and focuses on the broad area of management in the country set within its context and contemporary changes. The aim of the book is to examine a range of key management and business practices, strategies, areas and issues in the framework of the local political, economic and social traditions and the global economy and challenges, and to give 'voice' to local managers and practitioners and illustrative organizational case studies and vignettes. The text not only covers a wide range of management areas, but it does so in a common three-part framework (key issues and new developments, organization and manager cases, and challenges) to create greater consistency across chapters and quicker and easier inter- and intra- cross-chapter comparisons, depending on the reader's particular interests and focus.

The book is useful and important for several reasons. Often, much that is written in the field comes from non-Vietnamese and uses Western perspectives, models and theories, while concentrating on only a single or a few practices, issues or areas. Moreover, much of what we know about Vietnamese management is more commonly drawn from studies conducted at the macro (national) level. Less is known of Vietnamese managers and specific issues at work. This book is more holistic. Furthermore, the book's stance is different: the aim is to allow the 'voice' of local managers, practitioners and organizations to come through more.

Vietnam experienced rapid growth and increasingly became an important destination for FDI, often seen as possibly the next 'Asian Tiger' economy. These developments contributed to greater interest in Vietnam and the study of this fascinating country. However, given such rapid changes, much of what we know about Vietnam needs to be updated and refreshed. In short, this book examines the opportunities and challenges facing managers and organizations while presenting a timely update on management developments using experts with high direct Vietnamese experience and grounding.

This book is also important because the topics and areas have relevance to many different types and levels of qualifications and subjects, researchers and readers. These include business and management (such as international business and cross-cultural management) and functional areas covering Human Resource Management, marketing, finance and strategy, as well as issues such as the public sector, FDI, women managers and SMEs. As such, the book's broad coverage and content will also be of use in fields such as Asian studies and sociology, as well as issue-related areas, amongst many others. Additionally, the diverse range of organizational and management cases can be used in a variety of ways, including teaching and education.

Therefore, many levels and types of educational and T&D programme would benefit from this text. The book has both country-specific and international appeal – especially in other parts of Asia, Australia, North America and among English-speaking and Western-educated managers from Asia and those with an interest in this fascinating country. An additional market includes practising managers, both expatriates and locals, of organizations with a Vietnamese aspect, and those who may be thinking of setting up activities in Vietnam. Furthermore, the chapter readings and bibliographies are important as many students and teachers in this area often find it difficult to locate up-to-date sources of information in respect of the topics and issues covered in this book – in particular, easily accessible texts written by local experts.

The rest of this chapter takes the following format. Next we describe the key contexts within which management and organizations operate, and the critical issue of Vietnam's competitiveness is also discussed. These sections are also useful as they set the context for the rest of the substantive chapters in the book and their areas and issues. An outline of the structure of the book is then given followed by overviews of the chapters, coverage of the case studies and a note of some of the common themes.

Key contexts within which management and business operate

Traditions and developments in the key operating contexts for management and business are important. The areas include the following.

Geographical context

Vietnam is situated at a strategic crossroads in the Asia Pacific region, bordering China, Laos and Cambodia and lying along the western shore of the South China Sea (in Chinese) or the Eastern Sea (in Vietnamese). The country covers an area of about 329,560 square kilometres, stretching over a distance of 1,650 kilometres and is about 50 kilometres wide at the narrowest point. The long thin S-shaped country is filled with many hills and densely forested mountains, with level land accounting for less than 20 per cent of the total. Approximately 30 per cent of the land is under cultivation and the country has a variety of natural resources (see Table 1.1). With a coastline of 3,260 kilometres, excluding islands, Vietnam claims 12 nautical miles as the limit of its territorial waters, an additional 12 nautical miles as a contiguous customs and security zone, and 200 nautical miles as an exclusive economic zone.

Table 1.1 Geographic and topological indicators of Vietnam

Country name	Socialist Republic of Vietnam (*Cong hoa xa hoi chu nghia Viet Nam*)	
Location	South East Asia, bordering the Gulf of Thailand, Gulf of Tonkin and South China Sea, alongside China, Laos and Cambodia	
Area	Total Land Water	329,560 sq km 325,360 sq km 4,200 sq km
Land boundaries	Total China Laos Cambodia	4,639 km 1,281 km 2,130 km 1,228 km
Climate	Tropical in the South, monsoonal in the North with hot, raining season (May to September) and warm, dry season (October to March)	
Natural resources	Phosphates, coal, manganese, bauxite, chromate, offshore oil and gas deposits, forests	

Source: Compiled by the authors

Geographically, the country is segmented into three regions with distinct climates. The North (*Bac bo*) consists of uplands and mountainous areas and the Red river delta; the Central (*Trung bo*) includes the coastal area along the Truong son mountain range and the central highlands; the South (*Nam bo*) embraces the Eastern region and the Mekong river delta. The country has a tropical, monsoon, and very humid climate, with humidity averaging 84 per cent throughout the year. Annual rainfall ranges from 120 to 300 centimetres, annual temperatures vary up to 37° C depending on the region. Climatic extremes in the form of too much or too little rain – which are the rule rather than the exception – have a disastrous effect on agricultural production.

Politico-economic context

A quick overview of key dates and events in Vietnam can be seen in Table 1.2. These have impacted on the operating contexts for management and business and the table indicates how they have changed.

Table 1.2 Development and key milestones in Vietnam

1858	Conquest by France, completed by 1884
1954	Geneva Agreements end French colonial period Divided into two at the 17th parallel: communist North and pro-Western South
1960s	US economic/military aid build-up to bolster the South
1968	Communist forces launched Tet Offensive
1969	US announced gradual troop withdrawal
1973	Paris Peace Accords signed US forces withdrawn
1975	Communists capture the South
1976	Officially reunited Nationalization and centralization of entire economy Campaign against capitalists and agricultural collectivization launched in South
1979	Invaded Cambodia Brief war with China on northern borders
1986	*Doi Moi* economic liberalization launched
1991	Soviet Union, main source of vital aid, collapsed Trade agreement with EU
1994	US lifted trade embargo
1995	Joined ASEAN and AFTA Vietnam–US diplomatic relations restored
2000	Vietnam–US Bilateral Trade Agreement signed Established stock market and recognized private enterprises
2001	CPV 9th National Congress resolution: turn into an 'industrialized' country by 2010
2007	Joined WTO

Source: Adapted from *The Economist* (2008)

The political system in Vietnam is based on consensus and collective decision-making (democratic centralism) following the principal tenets of socialism. The dominance of the CPV and the rule of socialist principles still have a strong influence on all activities in society and business with regard to the structure, culture and HR of enterprises, which will be discussed in more detail in subsequent chapters in this book (see also Vuving, 2008).

Vietnam remains a one-party system, with the CPV in absolute control since 1954 in the North and since 1975 over the whole country (see also Chapter 7). The politburo (*bo chinh tri*) and permanent secretariat (*ban bi thu*) are positioned at the top of the CPV. The CPV Central Committee (*ban chap hanh trung uong dang*) is the all-important decision-making body, under which all local committees, constituted by CPV members, are located. In practice, these top party organs control and guide the NA (legislature), the cabinet (executive) and satellite organizations (i.e. CPV-controlled), such as the Fatherland Front (*Mat tran to quoc*), the trade union (i.e. the General Confederation of Labour (*Tong lien doan lao dong Viet Nam*)) and the Youth/Women/Farmers Associations. This parallel structure goes all the way down to the lowest administrative (village) and production (enterprise) units. Elections are to be understood within this political framework.

In principle, the state organ of power is vested in the NA (*Quoc hoi*) and the state administrative system (*He thong co quan nha nuoc*). In practice, the decisions of the CPV are adopted and implemented by an elaborate and complex system of local and national government. In this context, the NA operates at the central level, while the PC (*Hoi dong nhan dan*) is the main organ at the local level. Both the NA and the PC have the task of supervising the state machinery's actions. So, according to the amended 1992 Constitution, the unicameral NA is the highest representative body and the highest state authority. It is entrusted with wide constitutional and legislative powers (under Articles 83 and 84), which include:

- amending the Constitution;
- issuing and amending laws;
- determining state plans and ratifying implementation;
- examining and approving state budgets;
- setting taxes;

- ratifying or abrogating international treaties;
- electing and removing the President, Vice-President, Chair of the NA and other members of the Standing Committee of the NA, Prime Minister, President of the Supreme People's Court, Head of the Supreme People's Office of Supervision and Control, and other members of the cabinet, etc.

The NA is elected every five years from only one slate of candidates recommended by the Fatherland Front. The NA consists of 493 members of which about 90 per cent are CPV members.

The NA is, therefore, the supreme organ of the state with full legislative, administrative, judicial and controlling powers. Most importantly, the NA can raise and debate issues, and hence may effect the decisions of the CPV Central Committee. However, in practice it is unlikely that the NA would stand in the way of the CPV because the legislators, many of whom are CPV members, would not advocate positions known to be at odds with the CPV leadership (Quang, 1981). Moreover, virtually all of the CPV and government (central and local) leaders are selected to the NA.

The executive branch of the NA is under the direct control of the state President (*Chu tich nuoc*), who acts on behalf of the country in domestic and foreign affairs (Article 101), and the Prime Minister (*Thu tuong*), the head of the government (*Chinh phu*) and the executive body of the NA (Article 109). The President is elected by the NA from among its members and serves a five-year term. The President appoints the Prime Minister from among NA members and the Prime Minister, in turn, appoints deputy Prime Ministers. Apart from the Prime Minister, other members of the cabinet need not necessarily be representatives of the NA (Article 110). The Prime Minister proposes a cabinet, which is then appointed by the President, subject to NA ratification. The cabinet is composed of three deputy Prime Ministers, 18 ministries, four ministry-equivalent agencies and eight other agencies. Again, most of its members hold important positions in the CPV hierarchy, hence ensuring that policy makers can equally oversee the execution of their policies.

At the lower level, the People's Committees (*Uy ban nhan dan*) are the executive bodies of the PCs and are elected by the latter. People's Committees are assisted by a series of mass organizations, notably the Fatherland Front, the Youth Union, the Women's Union, etc., which are concerned with the effectiveness and direction of the state bureaucracy. These bodies, together with the other official control organizations in the state apparatus and the CPV, have become mechanisms of control over various state organs (Quang, 1981).

Since 2005 local government has been divided into three tiers. The first level comprises 64 provinces (*tinh*) and five principal cities (*thanh pho*) of HCMC, Hanoi, Haiphong, Danang and Cantho. The second level covers 25 cities under provinces (*thi xa*), 42 urban districts (*quan*) and 536 rural districts (*huyen*) and towns (*thi tran*). The third level consists of 1,181 precincts (*phuong*), 583 towns under districts, and 9,012 communes (*xa*) (SRV, Government Web Portal, 2008).

The political context is important to the evolving economic context in Vietnam, which can be seen in Table 1.3. This shows not only trends in imports, exports and GDP, but also the shifting composition over time of contributions from different types of enterprise ownership and sectors and their changing importance to development and employment.

Following the end of the war in 1975 the economy had two distinct periods of development. The period up to 1986 was characterized by a centrally planned economy in which the state held absolute control over the whole economy. Under such a rigid system personal interests were disregarded or ignored for the promotion of egalitarian and collective welfare. Economic development was not viewed as a relevant concern. Hence, economic performance was mediocre, with poor GDP growth, supply of goods, foreign trade and inflation. The general population was poor, especially when the country was at war again with the neighbouring countries of Cambodia and China, and after critical sources of assistance from socialist countries ceased with the end of the Cold War and the collapse of communism.

To rescue the country from virtual bankruptcy, the *Doi Moi* (renovation) policy was launched in 1986. This policy was primarily aimed at transforming the command economy into an open and market-oriented system, albeit with 'socialist characteristics'. As a consequence, Vietnam achieved impressive performance enhancement, moving from low growth in the period 1976–80 to high growth phases of more than 8 per cent annually during the period 1991–2005 (see Table 1.4). The two most critical factors in this success

Table 1.3 Key economic indicators in Vietnam, 1995–2008

	1995	2000	2005	2007*	2008**
GDP (US$ billion)	20.7	31.2	53.1	70.0	81.3
GDP per head (US$)	270	405	638	835	1,024
GDP annual growth rate (%)	9.54	6.75–5.5	8.4	8.5	6.23
Inflation (%)	12.7	−0.5	5.3	12.6	24.5
GDP by ownership (%)					
State sector	40.4	38.5	38.4	36.5	NA
Non-state sector	53.5	48.2	45.6	45.9	NA
Foreign-invested sector	6.1	13.3	16.0	17.6	NA
GDP by sector (%)					
Agriculture	27.2	24.5	21.0	20.3	22.0
Industry	28.8	36.7	41.0	41.6	39.9
Services	44.0	38.8	38.0	38.1	38.1
Exports (US$ billion)	5.2	14.3	16.9	48.4	65.2
Imports (US$ billion)	7.5	15.2	18.9	60.8	75.2
Total trade (US$ billion)	12.7	29.5	35.8	109.2	140.4
Trade balance (US$ billion)	−2.3	−1.6	−2.0	−12.4	−10.0
Total population (millions)	72.0	76.3	84.1	85.3	86.1
Total labour force (millions)	NA	37.6	42.5	44.2	47.4
In agriculture (%)	72	62.5	57.2	53.8	NA
In industry (%)	16	23.4	29.9	31.9	NA
In services (%)	12	11.4	12.9	14.3	NA

Source: Compiled by the authors

Notes: Figures can be inconsistent as a result of different sources and lack of consolidated official statistics over time; *preliminary statistics (GSO, 2009); **other sources.

were the restructuring of the state-owned sector and allowing private sector development.

The Vietnamese form of privatization, equitisation (*co phan hoa*), transformed SOEs into companies (mostly JSCs) by issuing or selling proportions of shares to the private sector. The majority of the equity

Table 1.4 GDP growth in Vietnam, 1976–2008

GDP	1976–80	1981–85	1986–90	1991–95	1996–00	2001–05	2006–07	2008
% Growth	0.4	6.4	3.9	8.2	7.0	7.4	8.4	6.2 (8.5)*

Source: Adapted from Quang (2006).

Notes: * plan

was meant to be offered to the SOEs' own management and workers. The restructuring effort led to some improvements in company performance, but most equitised companies and general corporations still faced a number of problems.

Overall, since the beginning of the 1990s, Vietnam entered a transformational stage that dramatically altered the economic landscape (and the social and cultural life of the people – see the next section). High-tech industry and added value service sectors started to gain ground, albeit at a slow pace and concentrated mostly in the areas of semi-conductors and hospitality.

However, despite these developments and achievements (especially in attracting FDI and maintaining GDP growth), the country's economy still largely rested on agriculture and low-end industries. The average GDP per head of US$ 818 (or US$ 2,900 at PPP), put Vietnam in 113th place out of 134 countries and in the 'low stage of development' category (WEF, 2008). Vietnam remains basically an agriculture-based country with more than 70 per cent of the population living in the countryside, although there are some shifts in employment patterns (see Table 1.3). This shows that over the period 1996–2007 the labour force in agriculture fell from accounting for nearly three-quarters (72 per cent) of the total to just over one-half (53.8 per cent); industry's share grew from less than one-fifth (16 per cent) to nearly one-third (31.9 per cent), while that of services grew slightly, from 12 per cent to 14.3 per cent.

Also, a 'strategic mismatch' can be distinguished and outlined (as seen in Figure 1.1). Vietnam needs to focus a great deal on building its competitiveness through HRs and an effective 'safety net' in anticipation of possible social consequences. Several chapters in this book cover this area in more detail, and we return to it in Chapter 9 in particular. In addition, the post-2008 global financial crisis has presented challenges to the economy, which is heavily export-oriented with a high subcontracting base and low value-added content.

Social, cultural and religious context

Vietnam is home to many ethnic groups with diverse social and cultural heritages (see Table 1.6). The ethnic Vietnamese (*Kinh*) are

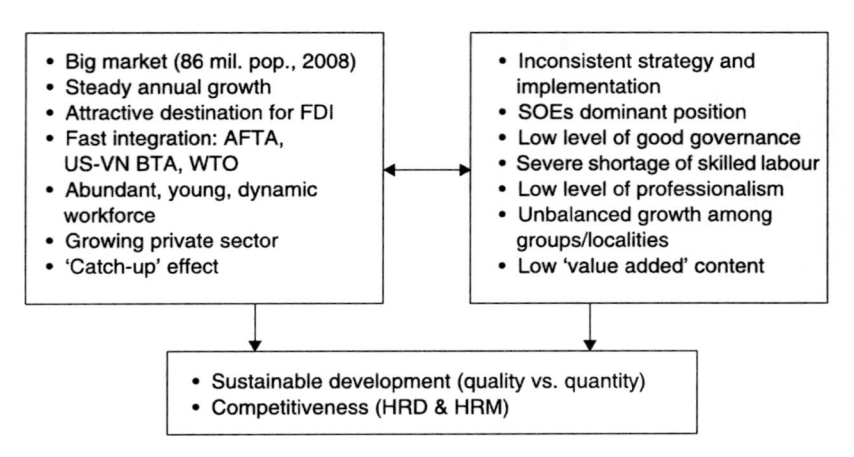

```
┌─────────────────────────────────┐      ┌─────────────────────────────────┐
│ • Big market (86 mil. pop., 2008)│      │ • Inconsistent strategy and     │
│ • Steady annual growth          │      │   implementation                │
│ • Attractive destination for FDI│      │ • SOEs dominant position        │
│ • Fast integration: AFTA,       │◄────►│ • Low level of good governance  │
│   US-VN BTA, WTO                │      │ • Severe shortage of skilled labour│
│ • Abundant, young, dynamic      │      │ • Low level of professionalism  │
│   workforce                     │      │ • Unbalanced growth among       │
│ • Growing private sector        │      │   groups/localities             │
│ • 'Catch-up' effect             │      │ • Low 'value added' content     │
└─────────────────────────────────┘      └─────────────────────────────────┘
                    │                                      │
                    ▼                                      ▼
              ┌─────────────────────────────────────────────┐
              │ • Sustainable development (quality vs. quantity)│
              │ • Competitiveness (HRD & HRM)               │
              └─────────────────────────────────────────────┘
```

Figure 1.1 The strategic mismatch in Vietnam.

concentrated largely in the alluvial deltas and coastal plains. As a homogenous social group, the Vietnamese exert influence on national life through their control of political and economic affairs and their role as purveyors of the dominant culture. It is generally believed that the *Kinh* from the north are more politically able than other groups, while the ethnic Chinese (*Hoa*) are more entrepreneurial.

The majority of the Vietnamese, especially the *Kinh*, practise some kind of ancestor worship (a mixture of Confucianism and home-practising Buddhism). Other main religions coexist along with indigenous religious sects, such as *Cao Dai* and *Hoa Hao*, especially in the southern parts. Vietnamese or *tieng Viet* (in the Latin alphabet) is used as the official national language. Comparatively, the Vietnamese are relatively well educated with a high literacy rate.

Table 1.5 Population and Patterns of living in Vietnam, 1995–2007

Millions	1995	2000	2005	2007 (estimate)
Total population	72.0	77.7	83.1	85.2
Rural	57.1	58.9	60.8	61.8
Urban	14.9	18.8	22.3	23.4

Source: Adapted from www.gso.gov.vn

Table 1.6 Cultural indicators in Vietnam, 2008

Population (2008 estimate)	86,116,560
Age structure (%)	
0–14 years	25.6
15–64 years	68.6
65 years and over	5.8
Population growth rate (%, 2007)	1.188
Life expectancy (years, 2008 estimate)	
Total	71.3
Male	68.5
Female	74.3
Literacy rate (%, 2006)	
Total	90.3
Male	93.9
Female	86.9
Ethnic groups (number)	54
Types (%)	Kinh (Viet) (85.73), Tay (1.97), Thai (1.79), Muong (1.52), Khmer (1.37), Chinese (Hoa) 1.13), Nung (1.13), Hmong (1.11), others (4.1)
Languages	Vietnamese (*tieng Viet*) official language, English (increasingly favoured as second language), some French, Chinese, Khmer, ethnic minority languages
Religions (%, 2007)	Buddhist (85),* Catholic (6.9), Cao Dai (2.8), Protestant (1.75), Hoa Hao (1.5), Muslim (0.076), Baha'i (0.007), others animist religions
Telephones (million, 2007)	
Main lines	18.8
Cellular	32.2
Internet	
Hosts (2008)	84,151
Users (2007)	17.9 million

Source: Compiled by the authors

Note: * Estimated as CPV members required to claim no religion even if they practice, while many others practice a mixed form of worship for ancestors' (**tho cung to tien**) but are not attached to Buddhist organizations.

In relative terms, China, Japan, Korea and Vietnam are considered to be part of the same cultural region under a common Confucian heritage influence (Hung *et al.*, 1999). These cultures tend to be more collectivist and hierarchical than Western cultures. Following Hofstede's (1997) typology, Vietnamese culture is typified as being high in 'power distance' (acceptance of authority), 'collectivism' (value group membership) and 'context', while moderate in 'uncertainty avoidance' (value security and stability) (Swierczek, 1994).

Some studies suggest that contemporary Vietnamese culture is experiencing a subtle change from its traditional values as a consequence of the post-1990s socio-economic developments. For example, the move towards a market-oriented economy from a communist system and Confucian cultural philosophy has resulted in a paradoxical composite embracing both collectivism and individualism (Ralston et al., 1999). Other authors observed that, despite the influence of socialist ideology, Vietnamese employees tended to veer towards individualism in that they had neither common goals nor shared objectives and, therefore, emphasized more on individual achievement (Quang, 1998; Tuan and Napier, 2000).

Nevertheless, the discrepancy in cultures between regions, the shared heritage of long periods of colonization (under the Chinese and the French), and the protracted internal conflicts have all left their mark on all types of organization in terms of strategy development and implementation, leadership styles and management practices (Thang et al., 2007). This blend of behaviours and practices – such as 'the noble person', 'hierarchy', 'mandarin/public service career', 'respect for seniority' and 'middle of the way' (from the Chinese); 'divide and rule', 'elite system', 'formalism' and 'individualism' (from the French); 'grassroots democracy', 'merit system' and 'delegation' (from the Americans); 'egalitarianism' and 'collective decision-making and responsibility' (from socialism) – may still be seen in organizations throughout the country (Quang and Thang, 2004).

The issue of competitiveness

As Vietnam entered a new phase of development in the 2000s it faced several challenges. The foremost was in its complex and unbalanced economic structure, in which all forms of enterprise operate under an imperfect and ineffective legal framework and governance system (see Chapter 4). Some issues in this respect, such as ease of starting-up and undertaking a business can be seen in Tables 1.7 and 1.8. A second challenge is that, in spite of a comparatively high level of growth post-1990s, economic performance remained below potential. The private sector that is the base of the country's 'internal strength' and the engine for growth, had not been fully developed nor allowed to operate on an equal footing with other sectors, such as SOEs and FOEs (see Chapter 8). A third challenge is that overall competitiveness needed to be overhauled at both macro and micro levels with regard to the quality of strategy development and implementation (see Chapter 5), Human Resource Management, HRD (see Chapter 2), management and business environment to improve the country's position in the face of competition as a result of globalization.

Structure and content overview

This book has the following seven substantive chapters, which cover several of the main functional and practice areas and key issues in

Table 1.7 Ease of doing business in Vietnam (N = 181 economies)

Activity	2009 rank	2008 rank	Change in rank
Starting a business	92	87	−5
Dealing with construction permits	108	104	−7
Employing workers	67	64	−3
Registering property	37	38	+1
Getting credit	43	51	+8
Protecting investors	170	168	−2
Paying taxes	140	131	−9
Trading across borders	67	65	−2
Enforcing contracts	42	42	0
Closing a business	124	124	0

Source: Adapted from World Bank (2008)

Table 1.8 Starting a business in Vietnam

Item	Vietnam	Region	OECD
Procedure (number)	11	8.6	5.8
Duration (days)	50	44.2	13.4
Cost (% GNI per capita)	16.8	32.3	4.9

Source: Adapted from World Bank (2008)

management and business in Vietnam. They take a common format to that end, covering key issues and new developments, presenting organizational and management cases and vignettes and discussing future challenges.

Chapter 2 covers Human Resource Management and notes Vietnam's shift in focus to achieve more qualitative growth aimed at balancing economic development and quality of life via Human Resource Management and HRD. Being one of the best performing economies (until the post-2008 global financial crisis) and an attractive FDI destination depended upon the way HRs were managed. Therefore, the evolution of Human Resource Management, its correspondence to changes in political-economic conditions and the need to enhance competitiveness are all analyzed. The labour market's development is outlined, followed by an overview of Human Resource Management practices in the areas of employee resourcing and T&D. Case studies are presented to provide more detail and insight into Human Resource Management practices at both organizational and individual levels. As Vietnam is striving to become an industrialized country, Human Resource Management is perceived to be a leading issue that requires solutions at both macro and micro levels. Consequently, the chapter presents a summary of critical challenges. These areas include:

- an unbalanced workforce;
- lack of attention to HRD and the management of the workforce;
- social tensions between expatriates and locals;
- under-utilized stocks of highly valued overseas Vietnamese professionals in all fields;
- the need for the Human Resource Management function to be further developed in order to become more professional.

Chapter 3 covers marketing within a range of organizations and issues. These include SOEs, wholesalers and distribution channels, market sectors and segments. Cultural differences in consumer behaviour are also analyzed. Vietnam's growth significantly impacted on consumer spending patterns and retail business, including in relation to fast-moving consumer goods. These issues, and the role of FIEs which played leading roles in advertizing and developing the marketing function, are also reviewed. Case studies are presented and analyzed in the context of CSR, public relations and corporate communications practices. Marketing practices closely related to CSR are reviewed and contrasted with a foreign company adapting its marketing practices to local customer profiles, while maintaining regional and global corporate branding strategies. Key issues impacting on the marketing function and its quest for greater professionalism are identified. Adopting a more integrated marketing approach, the value of integrated marketing communications, the need for marketing to be seen as a senior management task and strategy concern, and better branding awareness are all advocated. Local enterprises have adopted a more entrepreneurial spirit and enterprise has flourished more in the SME sectors, yet regulators maintained tight control in many areas. WTO commitments are, nevertheless, progressively opening sectors, such as retail and distribution, to foreign firms. Although businesses face challenges in obtaining reliable data and market intelligence, market research firms are increasingly targeting Vietnam, resulting in more readily available information. However, fast growth and inadequate educational standards have caused a shortage of qualified and experienced skilled HR which threatens the ability of firms to implement marketing plans effectively.

Chapter 4 covers finance and explores key issues with regard to the speedy, substantial and structural changes undertaken. In the first part the central aspects of the financial environment are analyzed; these include currency and monetary policy, the banking system, the development of a subnational debt structure and stock markets. The second part of the chapter provides case studies comparing banks under different ownership – state and private – which are beginning to compete in the financial market. While some differences are found, both banks have more similarities than expected given the differences in their origins and positions in the banking system. Cases of individual managers in the financial system are also outlined. The third part of the chapter provides an analysis of key challenges in the area relating to currency and monetary policy, the banking system, subnational debt and the stock exchange.

Chapter 5 covers strategy and deals with issues at both macro and micro levels. It explains why Vietnam developed despite a set of formidable constraints – for example, central planning, ending of external aid, embargos and poor governance. Some newer problems are also outlined. The chapter first provides a review of the process of development of the economic structure after the *Doi Moi* reforms. The unbalanced development of the SOEs, especially the big corporations (*tap doan*) which, despite privileged treatment from the state, continued to be heavy loss makers, is analyzed. The chapter notes that FIE products generally carry low local content and that the growing private sector remains inferior in capacity, small in size and waiting for a more level playing field. Case studies of companies in some of the most popular and better developed sectors illustrate key issues. These include the importance of enhancing capacity of delivery (hence, competitiveness) by having long-term strategic vision, structural adjustments and organizational development, talent management (domestic and overseas) and consistent management. Management cases are also provided, which highlight various issues such as leadership. The challenges facing this area are also detailed and include administrative and legal system reforms, institutional arrangements and improving competitiveness.

Chapter 6 covers FDI and describes how Vietnam has come a long way from a war-torn and isolated communist country to be a more market-oriented economy. While the reform of the regulatory framework towards a market economy formally began in 1986, it was the beginning of the WTO accession negotiations in 1995 that really started the adoption of substantial changes. The changes undertaken affected a wide number of areas relevant to FDI. The chapter argues that the single most important shift was legislative (the LOI and LOE in 2005), as this change provided a common framework for all investors and put private and public companies on the same legal level. The lengthy WTO accession process of 11 years for a country with relatively little economic power illustrated both the interest of foreign countries in the Vietnamese market and the high level of reform required. In addition, the failure of other countries (especially China), to successfully implement WTO commitments posed additional challenges and led to a number of reforms prior to accession. As a result, the protection of investors improved and the legal framework became more favourable and comprehensive. The growth of FDI was phenomenal and FDI-invested sectors were the most dynamic in terms of generating GDP growth. The most rapidly expanding sector was low-wage, export-orientated manufacturing, such as textiles, garments and footwear. However, attracting FDI on the grounds of cheap labour has caused disputes and is a problematic long-term strategy. Cases are used to illustrate the opening up to FDI, especially in critical sectors, and there are management cases in both manufacturing and services. The challenges faced by management in this area are detailed and include aspects of labour productivity, real estate investment, industrial parks and labour relations.

Chapter 7 covers public sector management and highlights prominent issues and changes in the area. Following accession to the WTO the public administrative system needed to contribute more effectively to the country's transformation into an industrialized and modern country. One route to this was via PAR, the theme by which changes in management have been made. The chapter argues that the capacity and quality of law making are increasingly in accordance with international standards. An overview of the civil service, which is largely organized as a career-based system, is presented. However, poor salaries and working environments in the public sector restricted high-quality job entrants while state agencies faced an increasing 'brain drain'. Furthermore, corruption – in the form of soliciting bribes by creating obstacles, accepting bribes for favours and using public means for personal benefits – is perceived as common. The most cited reason for corruption is a lack of legal regulation, which significantly weakens the efforts to fight corruption. Case studies illustrate some key issues and demonstrate how change is made in the public sector. One study shows how HCMC experimented with a performance management system. Another outlines the government's efforts to encourage more effective SOEs by allowing them to hire CEOs externally. These examples help to explain why reform in the public sector usually progresses more slowly than it does in the private sector. There are also case studies of managers. Challenges in the area are described; they include redefining the government's role, balancing the competing roles of stakeholders, encouraging civil society participation and developing cohorts of competent civil servants.

Chapter 8 covers women managers and SMEs and examines issues in these areas. It looks at the cultural, social, legal, economic and gender dimensions of SME development and identifies challenges for women in SMEs at two levels: family and institutional. Case studies of organizations and managers are presented which focus on the experiences of females working in SMEs in Vietnam. The chapter argues that female SME managers are attempting to combine their new roles as (another) breadwinner with traditional roles of daughter, wife and mother. The main challenge that needs to be overcome to achieve recognition and success is the stereotypical perception of women's unsuitability to own and run businesses, which is widely held in society. The old system of a division of labour based on gender is still maintained in the majority of families; this leads to limited school opportunities, a disproportionate burden of unpaid housework and hinders women from taking up employment opportunities outside the family. In terms of business-related issues, both female and male entrepreneurs face a number of problems and challenges in managing their businesses. In particular, the following are problematic: an understanding of the legal framework and laws relating to business, access to land, finance, markets, government support, technology and use of IT. However, it is argued that female entrepreneurs have even more problems with access to finance, market information and opportunities than do men.

Coverage of cases

The diverse range of case studies and vignettes used in this book provide a wealth of interesting and useful examples. The case studies are divided into two categories: the first group covers a wide range of organizations by ownership, size and industrial sectors; the second group provides a profile of managers (foreign and local) in their functions and roles. This variety can be seen in Table 1.9 below.

Common themes

The chapters contain several themes running through them. One common issue concerns the area of so-called 'best practices' and is seen, for example, in the chapters on Human Resource Management and marketing. HR and the need for T&D is another concern, for example, in the chapters on Human Resource Management, marketing, finance and strategy. Some concern for the increasing need for functional professionalism occurs as, for example, in the chapters on Human Resource Management, marketing and strategy. Another example of common concern is customer relationship management, for example, in the chapters on strategy and marketing. There is also

Table 1.9 List of case studies: Organizations and managers

Chapter 2. Human Resource Management	
Case 2.1	Property development company
Case 2.2	VinaGame Co
Case 2.3	CEO, Huu Nghi 2 Garment Co Ltd
Case 2.4	Three female HR managers
Chapter 3. Marketing	
Case 3.1	IBM
Case 3.2	Dutch Lady and Nestlé
Case 3.3	Country Head, ANZ Bank Vietnam
Case 3.4	Chair and CEO, FPT Corp
Chapter 4. Finance	
Case 4.1	Southeast Asia Commercial Bank
Case 4.2	The Housing Bank of Mekong Delta
Case 4.3	CEO, HSBC Asia Pacific
Case 4.4	CEO, Standard Chartered Bank, Indochina
Chapter 5. Strategy	
Case 5.1	An Phuoc Garment Co
Case 5.2	Duoc Hau Giang
Case 5.3	CEO, Trung Nguyen
Case 5.4	CEO, My Lan Chemicals
Chapter 6. FDI	
Case 6.1	DKSH
Case 6.2	Organizations in the energy sector
Case 6.3	Managing Director, Shipbuilder Strategic Marine
Case 6.4	General Director, Dai-Ichi Life Insurance Company
Chapter 7. Public Sector Management	
Case 7.1	HCMC Administrative Reform
Case 7.2	Hiring CEOs for SOEs
Case 7.3	Ex-Deputy Director, HCMC Planning & Investment Department
Case 7.4	Governor, SBV
Chapter 8. Woman managers and SMEs	
Case 8.1	Garment company
Case 8.2	Printing company
Case 8.3	Owner, garment company
Case 8.4	Owner, printing company

the area of good governance, for example, in the chapters on Human Resource Management, public sector and finance. The need for more of a 'level playing field' for enterprises and business is often mentioned as in, for example, the chapters on strategy, FDI, public sector and women and SMEs. Finally, strategic competencies (vision, formulation and implementation) are a common theme, for example, in the chapters on Human Resource Management, marketing and strategy.

Conclusion

This chapter has provided an overview of Vietnam, one of the emerging economies in Asia, coming from a background of long periods of colonization, wars and ideological conflicts. On the path towards development the country has overcome enormous difficulties to achieve considerable results. This is an important context for management and business in Vietnam and its 'changing face'.

Nevertheless, as will be discussed in the following chapters which deal with specific functional areas and issues, Vietnam is facing a strategic dilemma while integrating itself into the world economy. On the one hand, the country enjoys the advantages of a sizable market, attractiveness as a FDI destination, an abundant and young workforce and a growing entrepreneurial private sector. On the other hand, Vietnam's drive to reach a higher level of development has been hampered by its low delivery capacity – in particular, inconsistent strategy and implementation, the dominant position of SOEs, poor levels of public governance, shortages of skilled HR, limited professionalism, unbalanced growth among groups and localities, and low 'value added' content of products and services (as seen earlier in Figure 1.1).

A deeper look into the areas and issues of management in Vietnam will demonstrate that, in order to continue the scope and pace of its development, the country needs to boost competitiveness at both macro (country) and micro (enterprise) level. This, in turn, has implications for the changing face of management in Vietnam in all its dimensions of functions and dealing with issues.

Bibliography

ADB (Asian Development Bank) (2008) 'Asian Development Bank and Vietnam'. Available at http://www.adb.org/Documents/Fact_sheets/VIE.pdf, (March).

Cima, Ronald J. (1987) (ed.) 'Vietnam: a country study'. Washington: GPO for the Library of Congress. Available at http://countrystudies.us/vietnam.

Economist, The (2008) 'Vietnam: Asia's other miracle', 24 April 2008.

GSO, General Statistical Office (2009) 'Statistical data'. Available at http://www.gso.gov.vn/default_en.aspx?tabid=467&idmid=3, (accessed 19 March 2009).

Hofstede, G. (1997) *Culture and Organizations: Software of the Mind*. New York: McGraw-Hill.

Hung, L.N., Appold, S.J. and Kalleberg, A.L. (1999) 'Work attitudes in Vietnam: Organizational commitment and job satisfaction in a restructuring economy', *Journal of Asia Business*, 15, 3, 41–48.

IMF, International Monetary Fund (2008) 'Vietnam and the IMF'. Available http://www.imf.org/external/country/vnm/index.htm?type=9998, (updated 17 March 2009).

Indexmundi (2008) 'Vietnam GDP (official exchange rate)'. Available http://www.indexmundi.com/vietnam/gdp_(official_exchange_rate).html, (accessed 26 March 2009).

Quang, T. (1981) 'Political Development and Leadership in the Socialist Republic of Vietnam (1975–1981)', Doktoraal-Scriptie Politicologie, Vrije Universiteit, Amsterdam.

Quang, T. (1998) 'A case of joint venture failure: Procter & Gamble vs. Phuong Dong in Vietnam', *Journal of Euro-Asia Management*, 4, 2, 85–101.

Quang, T. (2006) 'Human resource management in Vietnam', in A. Nankervis, S. Chatterjee and J. Coffey (eds.), *Perspectives of Human Resource Management in the Asia Pacific*, pp 231–52. Sydney: Pearson Education Australia.

Quang, T. and Thang, L.C. (2004) 'Human Resource Management in Vietnam', in Pawan S. Budhwar (ed.), *Managing Human Resources in Asia-Pacific*, pp 173–99. London and New York: Routledge.

Quang, T., Thang, L.C. and Rowley, C. (2008) 'The changing face of human resource in Vietnam', in C. Rowley and S. Abdul-Rahman (eds.), *The Changing Face of Management in South East Asia*, pp 185–220. London and New York: Routledge.

Ralston, D.A., Thang, N.V. and Napier, N.K. (1999) 'A comparative study of the work values of north and south Vietnamese managers', *Journal of International Business Studies*, 30, 4, 655–72.

SRV (Socialist Republic of Vietnam) (2008), Government Web Portal. Available http://www.chinhphu.vn/portal/page?_pageid=439,1&_dad=portal&_schema=PORTAL.

Swierczek, F.W. (1994) 'Cultures and conflicts in joint-ventures in Asia', *International Journal of Project Management*, 12, 1, 7.

Thang, L.C., Rowley, C., Quang. T. and Warner, W. (2007) 'To what extent can management practices be transferred between countries: Human Resource Management in Vietnam', *Journal of World Business*, 42, 1, 113–27.

Tuan, V.V. and Napier, N.K. (2000) 'Paradoxes in Vietnam and America: Lessons earned', *Human Resource Planning*, 23, 1, 7–10.

US Department of State (2009) 'Vietnam'. Available http://www.state.gov/r/pa/ei/bgn/4130.htm, (accessed 30 March 2009).

Vuving, A. (2008) 'Vietnam arriving in the world – and at a crossroads', *Southeast Asian Studies*, 375–93.

VVG (2009) 'Current reports of Vietnam's economic indicators'. Available at http://www.vvg-vietnam.com/economics_cvr.htm#Rates, (updated 21 March 2009).

WEF (World Economic Forum) (2008) 'Global Competitiveness Report 2008–2009 @ 2008 World Economic Forum'. Available at www.wef.org.

World Bank (2008) *Doing Business 2009: Country Profile for Vietnam*. Washington DC: The International Bank for Reconstruction and Development. Available at http://www.doingbusiness.org/Documents/CountryProfile/VNM.pdf (accessed 23 February 2009).

2 The changing face of human resource management in Vietnam

Quang Truong and Beatrice I.J.M. van der Heijden

- Introduction
- Key issues and new developments
- Case studies
- Challenges
- Conclusion

Introduction

After an extensive period of quantitative growth, Vietnam is now focusing on achieving qualitative growth aimed at balancing economic development and quality of life for its population. Human Resource Management and HRD have been chosen to be the key areas for an effective implementation of the current strategy (Nguyen and Truong, 2008).

Vietnam has been widely regarded as 'one of the best performing developing economies in the world' (IDA, 2007: 1), and as 'the world's most attractive new investment destination' (Ishii, 2008: 1). After two decades of *Doi Moi* (renovation), Vietnam has basically succeeded in transforming an inward-looking economy to one that is more market-based and globalized. Since 2000, the country has managed to grow by, on average, 7.5 per cent per year (Hookway and Nguyen, 2008; Ishii, 2008). On a comparative basis, Vietnam has achieved impressive results in a number of key areas of the United Nations-sponsored 'Millennium Development Goals' campaign launched in September 2008 with regards to poverty reduction, enrolments in primary education, gender equality, child mortality, and maternal health (Swinkels and Turk, 2003). More specifically, the number of poor households has declined from 58 per cent in 1993 to 15 per cent in 2007, with a reduction of 2 per cent on average per year (IMF,

2006; Scribd, 2007; Ishii, 2008). Vietnam's integration into the global economy has made quick progress by its joining the WTO in 2007, as well as by reaching other Free Trade Agreements (FTA) enabling Vietnamese products to enter large markets, such as North America and the EU. The country's integration and its economic transformation have made it more resilient and responsive to external conditions.

As the economy has become more developed and sophisticated, its continued success will largely depend on how well its HRs are managed (King-Kauanui *et al.*, 2006). Analogous to other emerging economies, HRs are seen as the most critical assets to develop and sustain the national economy and the competitiveness of Vietnamese enterprises. However, there are still several factors that are impeding the process of upgrading the quality of the workforce and Human Resource Management practices in organizations.

This chapter reviews the evolution of Human Resource Management and its continued changes under political-economic conditions, and analyzes the need for increasing the competitiveness level of Vietnam's workforce. In addition, current Human Resource Management practices will be dealt with and the challenges to be faced will be discussed.

Key issues and new developments

Labour market development

Vietnam has a young, dynamic and abundant working population that, in 2006, made up about half of the total population of 84.1 million (World Bank, 2007). This is distributed unevenly among business sectors and regions (see Table 2.1). Labour mobility is low in the north-west and central Highlands, higher in the densely populated and more industrialized areas in the south-eastern part of the country (see map at the start of the book). The workforce continues to expand into the industry-manufacturing-construction category, and decreases in the agriculture-fisheries-forestry sectors as a result of the drive to industrialize (Table 2.1). The unemployment rate decreased from 6.4 per cent in 2000 to 5.3 per cent in 2005 (Ly, 2006; GSO, 2009), but is expected to rise to 8.2 per cent in 2009 as a

Table 2.1 Dimension of the labour market in Vietnam, 2000–07

	2000	%	2005	%	2007*	%
Total population (million)	**77.6**		**83.1**		**85.1**	
Male	38.1	49.1	40.8	49.1	41.8	49.1
Female	39.5	50.9	42.3	50.9	43.3	50.9
Total working population (million)	**37.6**		**42.5**		**44.2**	
State sector	3.5	9.3	4.0	9.4	4.0	9.0
Non-state sector	33.7	89.6	37.4	88.0	38.7	87.6
Foreign-invested sector	0.4	1.1	1.1	2.6	1.5	3.4
Agriculture	24.5	65.2	24.3	57.2	23.8	53.8
Industry	8.8	23.4	12.7	29.9	14.1	31.9
Services	4.3	11.4	5.5	12.9	6.3	14.3
Unemployment						
Urban area (%)	6.42		5.31		4.64	
Under-employment (% working time/total)						
Rural area	74.16		80.65		81.79	
Inflation (% at year-end)	–0.6		8.4		12.6	

Source: Desk work; compiled data from GSO (2009)
Note: * preliminary data

result of job losses resulting from the global economic crisis which started in 2008 (Loan and Nhat, 2009).

Despite continued efforts in the areas of employment orientation, vocational training and wage adjustment, which are aimed at aligning practices to external conditions, the labour market remains under-developed in many aspects. These include the following:

- a serious imbalance between supply and demand to meet the actual needs of industry at the high-end of the labour market, both in terms of quantity and quality;
- high employment pressure on a relatively young workforce, especially in urban areas;
- a high proportion of the workforce was not professionally trained at the time the country became a member of the WTO (up to 70 per cent of the total population), especially among young people between the ages of 20 and 24 (80 per cent) (Tran, 2007b).

Constant economic growth brought about by the ongoing liberalization and integration of the economy has further exposed the unbalanced composition of the workforce that is still heavily concentrated on agriculture and related industries (see Table 2.1). To cope with the new conditions, the labour market has been adjusted and developed along the following directions:

- gradually moving from a technical/scientific training base (as the basis of socialism) to a more market-supported one, with new management subjects introduced into the curriculum of professional training institutions and colleges;
- reducing the unemployment pressure by exporting manual and poorly qualified workers, especially to Taiwan, Japan, South Korea, Malaysia and the Middle East;
- promoting a subcontracting (*gia cong*) market for low-cost labour production, especially in textiles, garments and footwear industries;
- developing towards an outsourcing capacity base, especially in the IT field; and
- partly allowing foreign workers to immigrate and encouraging overseas Vietnamese workers to take up positions in the high-end of the labour market.

Human Resource Management function

Up to the early years of *Doi Moi*, many Vietnamese managers practised personnel management without much of a theoretical or analytical-based foundation (Pieper, 1990). 'Modern' Human Resource Management concepts and practices, together with other management techniques, were introduced into the country only when it decided to shift towards a free market economy (Quang and Thang, 2004). Nevertheless, the scope of Human Resource Management practices appeared not to be the same across sectors, and also varied greatly from one type of enterprise to another, often requiring some degree of accommodation and adjustment to the specific conditions in which an enterprise was operating. In a comparative study, Thang and Quang (2005) found that the adaptation of Human Resource Management practices reflects the company's ownership traits. Accordingly, FIEs are more developed in Human Resource Management practices than are SOEs. In contrast, local PEs, albeit relatively more entrepreneurial, are often less receptive to adopting Human Resource Management practices compared to SOEs. It was also found that transforming SOEs into equitised enterprises had not brought about any significant change in this regard. Similarly, detailed case studies among enterprises covering a range of ownership types indicated a diversity of Human Resource Management practices, with certain practices being more prevalent in some types of enterprise (Thang and Quang, 2005; Zhu *et al.*, 2008).

In general, the differences in Human Resource Management practices across sectors, over time, can be summarized in Table 2.2.

With the exception of FIEs, the heritage of the 'revolutionary organization' model – that is, one characterized by centralizing all personnel issues at the centre ('power reserved') – is still deeply rooted in the majority of enterprises (state and private-owned alike) across industrial sectors (Ly, 2006). For instance, even the leading JSC, FPT (www.fpt.com.vn), which can be considered as a leading PE, still labels its Human Resource Management function as '*Phong to chuc can bo*' (Organization and Cadres Department) and calls its employees '*can bo*' (cadres) – a general connotation for all those who

Table 2.2 Human Resource Management practices by type of enterprise across different time periods

Time period	1955–1975	1976–1986	1987*–2000**	2001–>
Political orientation	Leninist–Stalinist	Socialist	Mixed	Market economy
Economic conditions	Static	Chaotic	Dynamic	Competitive
Human Resource Management practice level according to type of enterprise				
State-owned	Low	Low	Low	Low
Equitised	NA	NA	Low	Low
Private	NA	NA	Low	Low/Medium
Joint ventures	NA	NA	Medium/High	Medium/High
Foreign-owned	NA	NA	High	High
Human Resource Management focus	Loyalty	Loyalty	Loyalty/ Professionalism	Professionalism

Source: Own analysis
Notes: *1999 Enterprise Law, **2000 Law on Foreign Investment, NA = not applicable

work in the party, mass organizations, government agencies, military and security units, SOEs, and the like. Other enterprises just changed the name of their Human Resource Management function to the *'Phong nhan vien'* (Personnel Department) or to *'Phong nhan su'* (Staffing Department), yet did not alter its key focus into managing HRs instead of dealing purely with numbers of workers. More often than not, most of the heads of these departments were not appointed based on merit, but rather based on other non-professional criteria, such as loyalty and trust, and therefore often lacked the required knowledge and competency in foreign languages, law, social sciences (especially psychology and sociology), and general management principles.

A large majority of Vietnamese enterprises are still in the very first phase of development, and generally lack a strategic Human Resource Management focus and recognition for the crucial role of the HR function (Quang, 2006). A link between Human Resource Management policies and the specific corporate strategy can rarely be perceived. A systematic use of 'modern' Human Resource Management activities – such as HR Information System (HRIS), job description, HR planning, job rotation, career development, Performance Management System (PMS), 360-degree appraisals, work/life balance, and Quality of Work Life (QWL), etc. – are hardly existent in most local enterprises (Quang, 2006: 243). The working conditions in these enterprises have not changed much over time, mainly because of the complacency of SOEs and the relatively small size of PEs in the early years after their establishment, despite the extensive changes in the business landscape.

In recent years, PEs have emerged as the engines of growth and, in many respects, have surpassed the position of SOEs as the backbone of the economy in terms of output, investment and employment. In total, the non-state sector contributed approximately 50 per cent to GDP, generated more than 35 per cent in investment value, and employed up to 90 per cent of the total workforce in 2007 (GSO, 2009). Nevertheless, the country's real potential for wealth creation is still largely under-developed as a result of HR constraints. To become more competitive, many private enterprises have actively started to apply basic Human Resource Management techniques, such as T&D, linking employee compensation to company performance and pay by performance (King-Kauanui *et al.*, 2006). However, in order to be recognized by the entire organization for its strategic role and contribution, the Human Resource Management function could develop into a 'centre of expertise' with relevant competencies aimed at becoming an effective and active partner, agent of change, people's champion and functional expert (Quang *et al.*, 2008). At the same time, the influx of foreign investment (in the form of FIEs) has added another dimension to the Vietnamese business landscape by introducing Western management principles in the workplace that provide local enterprises with good examples to benchmark and to follow.

Human Resource Management practices

The need for effective Human Resource Management and HRD has become more urgent after Vietnam joined the WTO in January 2007. This event exposed the inferior quality of the Vietnamese workforce and its products in globalized markets. An analysis of 'external challenges/internal response' dynamics helps to highlight the need for Human Resource Management development, particularly for SMEs, as shown in Table 2.3.

The ability of enterprises to meet their external challenges will be analyzed in the light of four key Human Resource Management areas: acquisition, development, motivation and relations of HRs.

HR acquisition

The prevailing practices in the recruitment and selection of HRs are somewhat different from one type of enterprise to another, depending on how an enterprise considers and utilizes its human assets. For instance, one survey revealed that FIEs are more active in using 'modern' recruitment channels, such as internet advertising or professional search firms in attracting potential employees, compared to local SOEs and PEs. Typically, because Vietnamese society still highly favours personal relationships, employee referral remains the most important staffing source for many local enterprises (Thang and Quang, 2005).

As the competition for qualified labour has intensified, local companies in the software development industry (such as IT-outsourcing companies FPT and TMA (An, 2007)) are following well-established FIEs (like Unilever, Nestlé, Procter & Gamble,

Table 2.3 Challenges facing enterprises in the post-*Doi Moi* period

External (environments)	Internal (organizations)
Fast changing business conditions, especially after Vietnam joined the WTO;	SOEs slow and not motivated to change because of privileged position;
Stiffer competition as a result of globalization and trade liberalization;	Most SMEs are family-owned and used to traditional management styles;
Unemployment is high, many college graduates without a job, but not willing to work in SMEs;	Human Resource Management not linked to corporate strategy;
Serious shortage of skilled labour and high-end executives;	Recruitment often based on relationships rather than merits;
'Leading' SOEs not able to provide role model, failing in Human Resource Management;	Lack of knowledge and recognition of strategic role of Human Resource Management and benefits for managers;
Vietnamese culture unfit for 'modern' Human Resource Management practices.	Working conditions and work relations not encouraging workers to perform at best;
	Most employers and employees are 'money-oriented' with short-term profits;
	Jobs are not clearly defined;
	Performance is not properly measured.

Source: Own analysis

Johnson & Johnson and British American Tobacco) in trying to lure young and 'top-of-the-class' graduates at college campuses, particularly in marketing and IT fields (Quang *et al.*, 2008). Local subsidiaries of Unilever even set up their own assessment centres to select and develop potential managers and team leaders for its expanded business strategies. In addition, many strategic-oriented SOEs and PEs have begun to seek help from newly established HR consulting agencies – in particular, head-hunting services – to fill their need for upper-end positions, even for chief executive positions (Huy, 2007; Van, 2008). The demands for professionals and high-end executives are acute in professional sectors such as hospitality services, general management, finance, banking, IT and pharmaceuticals. Since these labour market segments are growing by 20 per cent annually, several leading recruiters no longer insist on experienced candidates (Van and Ngoc, 2007). Instead, they are more willing to invest in post-recruitment T&D in order to attract young and dynamic people.

To help firms to become more competitive in the fight for a more competitive workforce, a comprehensive online survey was jointly organized, from July 2006 to March 2007, by AC Nielson, Navigos Group, and *Thanh Nien* newspaper, involving 300 enterprises from various types of business with a total population of 400,000 workers. The survey results showed a significant discrepancy between the perceptions of employees and employers with regard to several issues of satisfaction (see Table 2.4).

In many ways, the level of employee satisfaction coincides with the type of enterprise and the degree of Human Resource Management practices, as shown earlier in Table 2.2. From the list of 50 'Best Employers', which are listed in alphabetical order, FIEs lead the club with 44 per cent of the total (among them are Atlas Industries Vietnam Ltd, Bayer Vietnam Ltd, Colgate-Palmolive Vietnam, GlaxoSmithKline, HSBC Vietnam, and Procter & Gamble Vietnam), followed by JVEs and representative offices with 10 per cent; while PEs (including JSCs) made up 26 per cent, and SOEs accounted for only 6 per cent (www.vietnambestemployers.com). Despite the limited scope of the survey, its outcomes help both job seekers and job recruiters to be more effective in the search for their 'organization of choice'. On the one hand, the results also confirm that employee perceptions should be given due consideration by employers in their efforts to recruit, motivate and retain their workforce more effectively (Ngan, 2007; Binh, 2007). In this respect, in a survey by Grant Thornton, an overwhelming 84 per cent of SMEs disclosed that they

Table 2.4 Employee vs. employer perceptions as regards issues of satisfaction (in order of importance) (N = 300)

Employees' expectations	Employers' responses
1. Compensation and benefits	1. Job satisfaction
2. Training and development	2. Relationships at work
3. Job satisfaction	3. Performance management
4. Policies and procedures	4. Internal communication
5. Performance management	5. Training and development
6. Relationships at work	6. Policies and procedures
7. Health and safety	7. Health and safety
8. Internal communication	8. Compensation and benefits

Source: Adapted from T.K. Anh (2007) and http://www.vietnambestemployers.com

were particularly concerned about recruiting and retaining talented employees. This puts Vietnam at the top of the list of countries with high HR concerns, followed only by China with 81 per cent, with Japan at the bottom of the list with a mere 1 per cent (the average score comprises 55 per cent for 53 countries) (Nam, 2008). A previous survey of 200 private SMEs in the Hanoi area also supported the hypothesis that training, performance appraisal and incentive compensation have positive effects on the performance of SMEs, with incentive compensation having the greatest impact (King-Kauanui et al., 2006).

HR development

The organizational restructuring of SOEs and the development of newly established PEs require a critical mass of skilled employees and competent managers to turn these enterprises into sustainable competitors in globalized markets. Unfortunately, not much attention has been paid to prepare and develop employees for their actual job requirements since many local enterprises still regarded T&D as mere expenditure rather than as investment for their survival and success (Dinh, 1997; Ho, 1999; Thang and Quang, 2005).

However, this trend seems to be on the reverse as local firms have become more aware of the critical role of Human Resource Management. A survey among a group of managers attending an international Executive MBA programme in Hanoi in 2006 shows that T&D is now placed second in the top-four list of the most important concerns of managers, after recruitment, and followed by motivation and retention of HRs (Quang et al., 2008). Subsequently, most private SMEs that participated in the survey mentioned above acknowledged that they provided some training to their employees. The majority of SMEs *actually used* formal training (84 per cent), while 62 per cent *only offered* formal training. However, in general, training expenditures for employees were still small, averaging VND2.85 million or US$200 per head (King-Kauanui et al., 2006).

To bridge the supply/demand gap and to increase the overall competitiveness of the workforce, it is suggested that a cooperative linkage between training institutions (vocational schools and universities), public agencies (industrial and economic zones, central and local governments), and industry (represented by VCCI) and all-sector enterprises should be established and implemented using a well-planned and well-coordinated T&D strategy. Towards this end, 37 agreements between ten universities, two professional colleges and 34 enterprises have been signed, and are aimed to ensure a sufficient supply of skilled workers to match industry's real demands (Anh, 2007).

HR motivation

With GDP of US$835 per head/per annum in 2007, Vietnam is ranked among the group of 'low income countries' world wide (World Bank, 2007; GSO, 2009). Yet, salary is still regarded as one of the most important criteria that job seekers in Vietnam take into account (Linh, 2005). Hence, remuneration is utilized as an effective and primary tool to motivate employee performance and to ensure employee loyalty. Along this line, non-state enterprises often implement employee compensation by using different payment scales, based upon the principle of pay equity. Together with FIEs, local firms have participated in salary surveys or purchase reports from HR consulting agencies, such as Navigos Group and the local branches of Mercer and Watson Wyatt, in order to be industry-competitive as regards employee compensation.

In this regard, the state sector is intentionally left behind as far as employee motivation is concerned because of its continued use of its compensation system. As a consequence of the pay system's rigidity, it can lead to a wide difference in incomes between SOE and FIE staff, ranging on average from about 35 to 200 per cent for executive positions and, in some cases, even 500 per cent (Linh, 2005). Failure to meet employee expectations as to basic needs often results in poor performance, low morale and low satisfaction, high employee turnover and 'brain drain' in local enterprises. On the other hand, when it was changed in 2006 and 2008, the fixed minimum wage that was meant to protect workers' welfare instead failed to cope with the real rising price indexes, and hence caused a wave of strikes in several labour-intensive FOEs (Diu, 2008; Hookway and Nguyen, 2008).

In most enterprises, employee compensation and advancement are primarily based on performance evaluation outcomes. These logical practices are, nevertheless, still limited in scope and size across the types of ownership. In the case of PEs, the same survey mentioned above (Thang and Quang, 2005) concluded that both job and firm performance were considered to be important when making decisions concerning employee compensation. To begin with, nearly 70 per cent of SMEs reported that at least some of their employees received formal performance appraisals, which covered only 38 per cent of the total group of employees. It was also noted that 39 per cent of the SMEs used formal feedback on job performance for their employees, while 30.6 per cent did not use this technique at all. As regards the issue of fairness, 48 per cent of SMEs used objective criteria to assess job performance, while 34 per cent worked with subjective standards. As regards the incorporation of results of performance appraisals into compensation decisions, it was found that most SMEs (91 per cent) used some form of incentive compensation and bonuses. However, a large number of SMEs only paid small bonuses to their employees, which might not be sufficient to motivate them effectively (King-Kauanui et al., 2006).

Ostensibly, a stable and satisfied workforce is the foundation for building competitiveness, especially in times of economic integration. To comply with this, many private companies have followed more 'innovative' Human Resource Management practices adopted from FIEs by linking compensation to performance, offering new forms of bonuses, increasing individual benefits and insurance, and by creating new forms of working conditions, such as flexi-time, part-time and home working. In addition, stock options and 'innovative' benefits, such as life insurance, have been introduced (for example, in the case of TMA, mentioned earlier) with the aim of developing a sense of firm ownership and commitment among employees, especially in software development centres, law firms and consultancy groups (Quang et al., 2008).

HR relations

Employee relations in Vietnam are typified by the traditional patronage or mentor system, with the ubiquitous presence of a built-in trade union branch in each business organization (Kamoche, 2001). The impact of the employee–employer relationship is essentially determined by how well they are institutionalized into daily Human Resource Management practices (Quang et al., 2008).

As a result of 'socialist' principles, HR relations in Vietnamese enterprises, especially with regard to superior-subordinate and peer relationships, seems to be relatively equitable. Generally, women are treated equally and their talents are highly used and recognized. Although disabled workers are not discriminated against, their participation in the labour market still appears to be limited, with the exception of the IT field. Local enterprises have started to apply new Human Resource Management concepts, such as QWL, as an effective source of motivating employees, albeit still on a small scale. Other organizational supports include work-life balance, flexi-time and other 'innovative' services to make working conditions and environments more ergonomic and stimulating for employees (Quang et al., 2008).

In principle, the Vietnam General Confederation of Labour (VGCL), *Tong Lien doan Lao dong Viet Nam*, is the sole national trade union and is entrusted with the task of protecting the interests of the workers. In 1994, Vietnam officially introduced mechanisms for the resolution of collective disputes under the initial Labour Law, which provides for the use of the 'strike weapon' as the last resort. However, in reality the VGCL often fails to fulfil its role as the workers' champion, especially when workers go on strike in difficult times (Clark et al., 2007; Do, 2006; Nhan 2006; Y.T., 2008). The Ministry of Labour, Invalid and Social Affairs (MOLISA) reported an average of 98 strikes a year since the instruction of the (revised) Labour Law in 2002 (Nhan, 2006). The strained HR relations came to a head when the consumer price index suddenly increased as a result of the oil price hike. There were 256 'unorganized' (or 'wild cat') strikes (because they were not allowed if not officially organized by the unions) in the first five months of 2006 alone, much higher than the total of 2004 (2.2 times) and 2005 (1.9 times) (Quang et al., 2008). These industrial conflicts were concentrated in HCMC (65 strikes) and the neighbouring 'development triangle' provinces, such as Binhduong (115 strikes) and Dongnai (64 strikes). Surprisingly, most of the strikes took place in FIEs (subcontracting) (74.8 per cent) and in non-state enterprises (24.1 per cent), with only a few in SOEs (just 1 per cent) (Duc, 2006). The industrial unrest continued: by 2008 there was a record of 117 'wild cat' strikes in the first four months in HCMC, which is about the level of the whole of 2007 (Y.T., 2008). The largest wave of strikes included 21,000 workers at the (Taiwanese-owned) Ching Luh Vietnam Co factory in the southern province of Longan, one of the ten subcontracting production sites of Nike products in the country. The employees demanded that wages match rising inflation, which had surged to 27 per cent on a year-on-year basis in July 2008 alone; the highest level in more than a decade (Hookway and Nguyen, 2008; AFP, 2008). All in all, the reasons leading to these industrial conflicts were wages, unpaid bonuses/allowances for special occasions, unfulfilled contributions to social insurance and harsh working conditions (Diu, 2008; Y.K., 2008). The complaints appear to be mostly against Asian-owned labour-intensive factories from Taiwan, South Korea and Hong Kong (Duc, 2006).

The fact that the trade unions show little inclination or ability to stand up to employers on behalf of their members can be explained by the country's ultimate intention to create a stable business environment in order to lure foreign investment. It is suggested that to fulfil its traditional task (yet in an unofficial way), the VGCL has mobilized its dynamic pro-labour press (the 'third sleeve') to play mediating roles among the involved state agencies, labour union branches and the firms' management (Tran, 2007a: 1). Labour newspapers (such as *Nguoi Lao Dong* or *The Labourer*) have become alternative forums to champion workers' rights and interests against abuses, and they empower labour unions that negotiate with state bureaucracies and management on behalf of workers. By doing so, the labour press has emerged as a *de facto* champion for workers instead of the VGCL and the socialist state. This helps the VGCL to be able to compromise for political reasons as mentioned above, but still hold on to its power to monitor and control workers' collective action (Tran, 2007a).

In order to further clarify the current situation regarding the changing face of Human Resource Management, four case studies will be discussed in the following section.

Case studies

The following are typical case studies drawing from the business reality of Vietnam. They provide more insight into the ongoing development of Human Resource Management practices at both the organizational and individual level.

Case studies of organizations

Case Study 2.1: Property Development Company (PDCo)
HR function going professional

Being an architect by profession, Mr An quit his position as an expert at the HCMC Urban Planning Institute in 1992 to join the first contingent of self-made young entrepreneurs. By that time, only a few timid private companies started as a result of the *Doi Moi* campaign. After 16 years at the wheel, Mr An (now aged 49) has led his company, PDCo, to become one of the most successful businesses in the development project industry with a total revenue of VND700 billion (US$44 million) in 2007, and a total workforce of 110 people. More than 90 per cent of its staff has a university degree, with a balance between males and females. To a large extent, its success so far has been largely attributable to Mr An's relentless attempt to adopt an 'innovative' management system with a view to put the company ahead of other competitors, with Human Resource Management as the core.

As a true believer in outsourcing, Mr An is always willing to pay premium prices for the services he needs, especially in relation to matters such as resourcing and motivating HRs. For instance, he has utilized high-profile headhunting services to find the most appropriate candidates to fill key positions in the company. He also hired Navigos, the leading HR consulting agency, to help revamp the entire HR system of PDCo, including setting up a HRIS and introducing several software packages to standardize the current HR processes. Yet, after a decade-long role as an extensive service user, Mr An concluded that all the efforts made so far still lacked clear focus and are uncoordinated to deliver sustainable benefits to the company's competitiveness and, therefore, not truly justifiable for the total high costs and efforts spent. This led Mr An to establish his own Human Resource Management department. His most logical move was to hire away a top professional from Navigos to lead this function with a full mandate and personal support from Mr An as the company's founder and CEO.

After taking on this position, the new Director of Human Resource Management (also in charge of Administration and IT) quickly made a full audit of the Human Resource Management current situation and identified the following areas for improvement:

- There is a lack of a comprehensive and integrative Human Resource Management strategy logically linked with the company's strategy in the formulation as well as in the implementation phase.
- In spite of a strong focus on managing HRs more effectively,

decisions on Human Resource Management matters are exclusively centralized at the top and very much depended on the CEO's initiatives.
- While the company has no problem in acquiring the best people ('brain gain') for the positions it needs (by willingness to offer above-industry average compensation packages), the lack of a well-planned and well-coordinated development plan to further develop employees toward the new requirements of the job and changing business conditions has altogether impeded the intended growth of the company.
- Too much focus on monetary (instead of smartly combined with other non-monetary) measures to motivate people, has, in practice, reduced the effects of balancing organizational commitment and employee loyalty for the company's long-term growth and survival.

Since PDCo is presently at the end of the growth phase and has started to face fierce competition, the need for a well-oriented and organized structure in support of a competent and motivated workforce has become the CEO's top concern. His second logical move is to give the newly acquired Human Resource Management professional the title of Director and a seat on the board of directors to show that, from now on, all Human Resource Management and HRD policies and practices will be linked with the company's long-term business development strategy.

Source: Interview with the Director of Human Resource Management Department, 31 August 2008, in HCMC. Names changed to retain anonymity.

Case Study 2.2: VinaGame Co (www.vinagame.com.vn)

'The Best Employer profile'

Only established in September 2004, VinaGame Co was quickly voted as one of the 50 'Vietnam's Best Employers' as a result of its outstanding Human Resource Management practices in a survey carried out jointly by AC Nielson, Navigos Group and *Thanh Nien* newspaper in June 2007. One important success factor was its initiative in launching the 'Internship Programme' (*'chuong trinh thuc tap sinh'*) in March 2007, which offers on-the-job training opportunities to local and foreign college students in the areas of online entertainment and internet services. In total, there are 80 open positions for a period of three to six months, depending on the type of work.

During the internship, VinaGame not only provides the apprentices with practical learning experience, but also ensures basic salaries and benefits comparable to the ones received by 'normal' employees.

Since VinaGame has developed 'aggressive' plans to diversify its activities and to enter new markets in the future, the ongoing process to acquiring the required (in number) and competent (in qualification) staff becomes of major importance for the company to make its ambitious strategy a success.

Until March 2007, the total workforce of VinaGame stood at 500 employees with an average age of 25 years, of which 8 per cent were managers. To fill the HR gap, VinaGame initially planned to recruit 150 new staff members in 2007. It now comprises a total of 850 employees (May 2008) (see company website).

In conjunction with the internship programme initiative, VinaGame has been running several programmes to upgrade the professional capabilities of its existing staff, and to improve the overall effectiveness of its Human Resource Management policies and practices. All these efforts are immediately aimed at increasing its competitiveness as 'the organization of choice' in the industry, and thereby to help VinaGame match up with the increasing opportunities and challenges faced in the integration era.

Source: Adapted from Anh, T. (2007: 10).

Case studies of individual managers

Case Study 2.3: Mrs Nguyen thi Hong-Phiet
A successful woman entrepreneur

To the outside world, Mrs Nguyen thi Hong-Phiet, the Managing Director of the Huu-Nghi 2 Garment Co Ltd (167 Le Trong Tan, Tan Phu District, HCMC) often introduces herself in a humble manner as an 'unwilling CEO', although in the eyes of her business counterparts and the community, many valuable things can be learned from her. During the course of 16 years, Mrs Hong-Phiet has succeeded in building a workforce that is highly developed, and not only professionally, but also socially responsible towards co-workers, the company and society. To do this, she has consistently practised a Human Resource Management policy that is primarily based on the interests of the workers. This human-based management policy has turned her company into an 'organization of choice', even in times of business crisis.

At Mrs Hong-Phiet's company, every worker is guaranteed an industry-competitive wage (averaging 1.5 to 2 million VND per month, and in many cases even 4 million VND per month; about US$230 in 2008), and other basic benefits, such as subsidized ('safe, hygienic and tasty') meals in the company's canteen, special bonuses for key national holidays, birthday gifts, paid leave, study allowances for children, etc. Many workers have benefited from the company's financing scheme to buy their own houses with low interest instalments.

Mrs Hong-Phiet considers herself an 'unwilling boss' because she had never intended to be a top manger, and had not been trained to manage a business (she was a teacher with 36 years of experience), especially in garments, until she was unexpectedly forced to take over the bamboo-making carpet company left by her husband in 1992. At that time, the exports of rattan-bamboo product companies were on the verge of bankruptcy because of fierce competition from China and Thailand. After long deliberation, she decided to sell the company's entire equipment and transform it into a garment factory following her new business development. To prepare herself for this new venture, she frequented vocational training centres and joined factory visits to learn about the fundamentals of the garment industry. From this experience she developed an operation management model for her new factory, describing in great detail the production process, work shifts/teams and productivity norms. At the same time, she filled her management skills gaps by reading professional books, discussions with business counterparts and by carefully listening to the company's workers.

Over a period of 15 years under her leadership, Mrs Hong-Phiet's company has gradually emerged as a well-organized and reliable company; it now has business partners in many countries, and exports bags and rucksacks to the US, Japan, Germany, the Netherlands, Belgium, Italy, Denmark, etc. However, Mrs Hong-Phiet's most praised performance trait comprises her 'corporate social responsibility' (CSR) activities. In many years the company has earned the title of 'the green-clean-beautiful environment' from the city, and continuously contributed to the welfare of the community – most notably as a regular source of blood donations and as a 'welcome' place for drug addicts after their rehabilitation period to reintegrate themselves into normal life. From 2003 onwards, the company has supplied clothes and the monthly rice needs to the children-victims of Agent Orange (a chemical that can cause cancer used by the American Army during the war) at Binh Minh Special School of Tan Phu District, and sponsored the Tan Phuoc Centre for Disabled Children of Cu Chi District. Her company also contributed more than VND40 million to the City Study Fund every year. Besides the daily managerial position as the managing director of the Huu-Nghi 2 Co

Ltd, Mrs Hong-Phiet is currently chairwoman of the Women Entrepreneur Club of HCMC and Tan Phu District, and participates in several other professional and gender organizations in the southern part of Vietnam.

Source: Adapted from Ho (2008: 12)

Case Study 2.4: Three female HR managers

HR, a 'hot' profession

The role of HR managers becomes particularly important to help handle conflicts or conflicts of interest when the working environment is growing more unstable and complex. Under these circumstances, a new generation of HR professionals is emerging of young and less experienced people. First-line managers are, on average, 25 to 28 years of age, while HR directors are usually, on average, 32 to 35 years old; 70 per cent of them are female.

According to the Institute for HRD Studies (*Vien Nghien cuu phat trien nguon nhan luc*) of HCM University of Economics, the top choice for graduates is the HR profession, although they come from different study specializations. This is a profession that offers young graduates a 'top' salary. The starting salary is about VND 3 to 5 million (US$180–300) a month, with an average of VND 7 to 10 million per month (US$ 420–600). The salary for managers varies between US$1,000 to 4,000 per month. Many enterprises state that the HR profession is highly valued these days, and this requires high responsibility from HR practitioners.

Ms Cam Tien graduated in 2005 from the University of Social Sciences and Humanities in HCMC, having specialized in foreign languages; she moved from a secretarial to a sales position, and finally settled down in the HR Department of CK Vietnam, a JVE. Ms Tien states: 'After joining the HR profession, I participated in several basic and upgraded training courses to learn about the job evaluation process, performance appraisal methods, and employee motivation. It took me two years to get used to the new environment, grasp the situation and decide on taking in this profession as my career.' In her opinion, the HR profession has been significantly 'upgraded' now, away from the passive image of the past. HR managers have to reinstate their strategic role in developing human assets, retaining talents and preparing succession plans for the organizations.

As the competition for labour has become more fierce, the 'battle' to attract rare talent becomes more intense. HR professionals therefore are constantly facing several challenges. Ms Nguyen thi Phuong (HR Director of Hoang Minh Ltd Co), who has five years' experience in the profession, observed: 'Besides the professional and managerial skills, HR managers should be able to operate under high pressure and know how to listen.'

As argued by our third HM practitioner, Ms Vo thi Thu Huong (Head of the Training Department specializing in HRs at BCC Co): 'Women are often considered as emotionally sensitive, yet very suitable for the HR profession as they can better share the feelings and approach the employees much easier, and therefore, can solve the problems and conflicts with more flexibility. An effective HR manager should take the lead of the situation, not relying only on such measures as recruiting and firing employees. He or she should have the capability to propose appropriate strategy and policy, and to coordinate and anticipate HR issues and measures.'

Source: Adapted from Bay (2008: 7)

Challenges

As Vietnam is moving forward with its ambitious goal to be an 'industrialized' country in 2020, Human Resource Management remains to be the leading issue that requires quick and comprehensive solutions at both macro and micro levels. The five most critical challenges are as follows.

First, there is the imbalanced workforce. It is argued that the more developed the economy, the more serious the shortage of skilled labour becomes (Ho, 2007). The domestic supply of skilled labour continues to be a constant challenge. One of the reasons for this is that the current educational system is not ready and is characterized by generally outdated curricula, which do not meet present working requirements (Yoong, 2007). It is officially reported that up to 60 per cent of young graduates from professional schools and colleges have to be retrained to match job requirements. Many software development companies have to send 80 to 90 per cent of their newly recruited staff to professional retraining classes before assigning them to actual tasks (Anh, 2007). There should be a concrete strategy and action plan to forge the link between training institutions, industry and employment agencies to match supply and demand of all labour categories in the short and long term.

Second, a large number of local enterprises, especially SOEs, are still not paying enough attention to developing and managing their workforce to meet with the highly competitive business conditions in the integration era. The public sector – especially the so-called big corporations (*tong cong ty*) and groups (*tap doan*) – should be further restructured without justified privileges and subsidies, so that they will also be well prepared to pass the survival test, and will become more competitive on their own capacity. At the same time, there should be an effective and consistent legal framework to create the necessary 'level playing field' for all non-state sector firms, especially in the private sector, by investing more in HRs as an important means to become competitive.

Third, the import of foreign workers and expatriates to fill the open high-end positions will further 'upset' the present labour supply/demand structure and will increase the social tension between expatriates and locals. As Vietnam develops and integrates itself further into the world economic system, the need for highly skilled labour (including such top positions as CEO and Chief Finance Officer) becomes more urgent. According to the National Employment Forum (*Dien dan viec lam quoc gia*), there are about 40,000 to 50,000 foreigners currently working in Vietnam, of which 31.8 per cent are in managerial positions and 41.2 per cent are technical experts, because the local labour market cannot meet the staffing requirements of foreign investment projects (Loan, 2007).

Fourth, the stock of highly valued overseas Vietnamese professionals (in all fields) has not been utilized to fill the urgent needs for high-level HRs and to temporarily bridge the gap that the current training system is unable to fill. Among the 2.7 million people living abroad, it is assumed that approximately 3–400,000 of them are top professionals in high technology and management (Que Huong, 2008). Similarly, for Japan, Korea, Taiwan, Thailand and China, the 'brain gain' will help to bridge the gap in the short and long term.

Fifth, the Human Resource Management function is in need of further self-development in order to become more professional and to be recognized by the employer as a strategic partner and valuable people champion. The principle 'the right person in the right place' should be strictly applied when selecting and appointing the heads of HR departments, as well as its members. The functional job description should be expanded to cover more human-related aspects, not only those related to traditional personnel management. In the meantime, the development of HR consulting services can help enterprises to fill the capacity gaps in Human Resource Management (see Table 2.5).

Conclusion

This chapter has provided an overview of Human Resource Management developments in Vietnam and analyzed Human Resource Management practices in Vietnamese enterprises in four main areas: HR acquisition, development, motivation and relationships. It has also portrayed the challenges Vietnam will face in the coming years on its growth path gearing up to full globalization

Table 2.5 The HR service market in Vietnam

Firm	Established	Nationality	Location	Main services
L&A (Le & Associates)	2001	Vietnam	HCMC	Online recruitment, headhunting, Human Resource Management consulting, administration, training
FirstAlliances	1998	Australia	HCMC	Headhunting, Human Resource Management consulting, administration, training
HRVietnam (VON)	2006	Vietnam	HCMC	Online recruitment, headhunting, administration
SmartHR	2001	Taiwan	HCMC	Headhunting, HR consulting, training
HR2B	2002	Australia	HCMC + Hanoi	Headhunting, HR consulting, administration
NetViet	2000	Vietnam	HCMC	Headhunting, HR consulting, administration
TD & D	1993	Vietnam	HCMC	Headhunting, administration, training
Pricewaterhouse Cooper (PwC)	1995	Multinational corporation	HCMC + Hanoi	Headhunting, HR consulting
B & A	1992	Vietnam	HCMC	HR consulting

Source: Author's own desk work (2007)

and sustainable development. The quest for competitiveness in the integration era in tandem with a period of double-digit inflation, depreciation of the currency, unsolved corruption and widespread abuse of power, the failing role of SOEs and the global food crisis, will certainly put more strain on the already stretched domestic resources of Vietnam, especially on its abundant, yet weakly competitive, human assets.

With half of its population of working age (48.5 million in 2008) and one million workers joining the labour market every year (an annual growth of 2.5 per cent between 2001 and 2005) (Ly, 2006; Loan, 2007), undoubtedly Vietnam will not face any substantial shortages in labour-intensive industries. However, Vietnam will find it difficult to increase the 'value-added' content of its products and services to enable it to compete in the global arena. Whether Vietnam will continue its remarkable growth trend of the last decades or will succumb to a stagnation phase in the coming years depends to a great extent on the country's capabilities to develop and manage its abundant, yet underdeveloped, human assets in terms of both quantity and quality in the context of the post-2009 global financial crisis. Needless to say, a new contingent of well trained and competitive HRs is the only means to help Vietnam overcome the current structural impediments and elevate its competitiveness for sustainable growth (Linh, 2008).

Bibliography

ADB (Asian Development Bank) (2005, November) *Strategy and Program Assessment, Vietnam: Private Sector Assessment*, Hanoi.
AFP (2008) 'Thousands of workers strike in inflation-battered Vietnam', 1 August.
An, T. (2007) 'Mua bao hiem cho nhan vien: bao ve nguon nhan luc (Buying life insurance for the staff: a way to retain human resources)', *Sai Gon Kinh te Thoi bao*, 19 April.
Anh, H. (2007) 'Lien ket dao tao nhan luc (Jointly develop human resources)', *Dau tu*, 16 November, 11.
Anh, T. (2007) 'VinaGame: Nha tuyen dung hang dau (VinaGame: The top class human resources recruiter)', *Thuong Mai* (Commerce), 3 April, 10.
Anh, T.K. (2007) 'Cuoc khao sat ve nha tuyen dung dau tien tai VN (The first survey on recruiters in Vietnam)', *Thanh Nien*, 26 March, 6.
Bay, N. (2008) 'Quan ly nhan su: nghe dang "nong" (Human resource management: a "hot" profession)', *Phu Nu*, 10 June, 7.
Binh, M. (2007) 'Best employers get awards', *Saigon Times Daily*, 29 March, 1.

Clark, S. (2006) 'The changing character of strikes in Vietnam', *Post-Communist Economies*, 18, 3, 345–61.
Clark, S., Lee, C-H., and Do, Q.C. (2007) 'From rights to interests: The challenge of industrial relations in Vietnam', *Journal of Industrial Relations*, 49, 4, 545–68.
Dinh, H. (1997) *Human Resource Management* (3rd edn), Hanoi: Education Publishing House.
Diu, H. (2008) 'Dinh cong van xay ra lien tiep (Strikes keep on happening continuously)', *VietnamNet*. Available at http://www.Vietnamnet.vn, 13 March.
Do, L. (2006) 'Chinh sach luong lac hau, dinh cong la tat yeu (Obsolete wage policy, strikes are inevitable)', *Lao Dong Newspaper Online*, 11 March.
Duc, N.V. (2006) '5 thang, ca nuoc co 287 cuoc dinh cong (5 months, 287 strikes all over the country)', *Lao Dong Online*, 6 June.
GSO (General Statistics Office of Vietnam) (2009) 'General statistics: Population and employment'. Available at http://www.gso.gov.vn (accessed 17 March 2009).
Ho, N. (2007) 'Bung no tuyen dung (Explosion of recruitment)', *Phu Nu*, 20 April, 7.
Ho, N. (2008) 'Ba "giam doc bat dac di" (The "unwilling CEO")', *Phu Nu* (Women), March 21, 12.
Ho, V.V. (1999) 'Experience of SME development in Asian Countries'. Working paper presented at Workshop of SME Support Policies in Industrialization and Modernization Process. Hanoi: Ministry of Planning and Investment.
Hookway, J. and Nguyen, A.T. (2008) 'Vietnam workers strike', *The Wall Street Journal*, 2 April, B5.
Huy, D. (2007) 'Thi truong nhan luc cao cap (The market for high-end human resources)', *Lao Dong*, 1 November, 2A.
IDA (International Development Association, World Bank) (2007, February) 'Vietnam: laying the foundation for steady growth'. Available at http://siteresources.worldbank.org/IDA/Resources/IDA-Vietnam.pdf (accessed 15 April 2008).
IMF, International Monetary Fund (2006, February) *Vietnam: Poverty Reduction Strategy Paper-Annual Progress Report*, IMF Country Report No. 06/70, Washington DC.
Ishii, Shogo (2008) 'Vietnam's new challenges amid signs of overheating', *IMF Survey Magazine: Countries & Regions*, March 8. Available at http://www.imf.org/external/pubs/ft/survey/SD/2008/CAR03708A.htm.
Kamoche, K. (2001) 'Human resource in Vietnam: The global challenge', *Thunderbird International Business Review*, 43, 5, 625–50.
King-Kauanui, S., Su, D.N. and Ashley-Cotleur, C. (2006, March) 'Impact of human resource management: SME performance in Vietnam', *Journal of Developmental Entrepreneurship*, 11, 1. Available at http://findarticles.com/p/articles/mi_qa3906/is_200603/ai_n17185145.

Linh, L.U. (2005) 'Thu hut nguoi bang luong (Attracting people by salary)', *Thoi bao Kinh te Sai Gon*, 11 August.

Linh, X. (2008) 'Nhan luc: "nut that co chai" lon nhat cua tang truong (Human resources: the biggest "bottle neck" of growth)', *VietnamNet*, Available at http://www.vietnamnet.vn, 2 August.

Loan, P. and Nhat, C. (2009) 'Viet Nam: mot trong so it nuoc A chau tang truong duong (Vietnam: Among one of the rare Asian countries with a positive growth)', *VietnamNet*. Available at http://www.vietnamnet.vn, 16 March.

Loan, T. (2007) 'Loay hoay bai toan nhan luc (The human resource vicious circle)', *Hai quan*, 2 December, 5.

Ly, H. (2006), 'Vietnam workforce in 1996–2005 revised: Survey', *Vietnam Business Forum*, 21 April. Available at http://vibforum.vcci.com.vn/news (last update 22 February 2008).

MOLISA, Ministry of Labour, Invalid and Social affairs (2006, August) 'Labour and social issues emerging from Vietnam's accession to the WTO', Paper No 18. Available at http://www.yesweb.org/2006/Publications_Papers%20_august%203_2006/Agenda%20Links/.../LabourExport_ WTO_VietnamAccession... (accessed 17 March 2009).

Nam, L. (2008) 'VN dung dau ve chinh sach tuyen dung va giu nhan vien (VN ranked first in HR recruitment and retention policies)', *Tuoi Tre Online*, 10 April.

Ngan, K. (2007) '50 nha tuyen dung hang dau VN, noi giup hang trieu LD phat trien tai nang (50 leading recruiters in Vietnam, where millions of workers can deploy their talent)', *Dai Doan Ket*, 35, 30 March, 2.

Nguyen, N.T. and Truong, Q. (2008) 'Training and development in Vietnam', *International Journal of Training and Development*, 11, 2, 139–49.

Nhan, N. (2006) 'Suc nong dinh cong tran vao quoc hoi (The heat of strikes invades the National Assembly)', *Phap Luat*, 5 May, 3.

Pieper, R. (1990) *Human Resource Management: An International Comparison*, New York: Walter de Gruyter.

Quang, T. (2006) 'Human resource management in Vietnam', in A. Nankervis, S. Chatterjee and J. Coffey (eds.), *Perspectives of Human Resource Management in the Asia Pacific*, pp 231–52. Sydney: Pearson Education Australia.

Quang, T. and Thang, L.C. (2004) 'Human Resource Management in Vietnam', in Pawan S. Budhwar (ed.), *Managing Human Resources in Asia-Pacific*, pp 173–99. London and New York: Routledge.

Quang, T., Thang, L.C. and Rowley, C. (2008) 'The changing face of human resource in Vietnam', in C. Rowley and S. Abdul-Rahman (eds.), *The Changing Face of Management in Southeast Asia*, pp 185–220. London and New York: Routledge.

Que Huong (2008) 'Cong dong nguoi Viet Nam o nuoc ngoai (The Vietnamese diaspora)'. Available at http://www.quehuong.org.vn (retrieved 19 May 2008).

Scribd (2007) 'Vietnam's poverty reduction efforts set model example'. Available at http://www.scribd.com, 20 March (accessed 8 February 2009).

Swinkels, R. and Turk, C. (2003) 'Strategic planning for poverty reduction in Vietnam: Progress and challenges for meeting the localized Millennium Development Goals', The World Bank Policy Research Working Paper series, No 2961.

Thang, L.C. and Quang, T. (2005) 'Human resource management practices in a transitional economy: A comparative study of enterprise ownership forms in Vietnam', *Asia Pacific Business Review*, 11, 1, 25–47.

Tran, A.N. (2007a) 'The third sleeve', *Labour Studies Journal*, 32, 3, 257–79.

Tran, L.T. (2007b) ' "Nut that" nguon nhan luc (The "bottleneck" of human resources)', *Tuoi Tre Online*, 12 December.

Van, H. (2008) 'Se khat nhan luc trung, cao cap (There will be a high demand for middle and high personnel)', *Tuoi Tre Online*, 8 January.

Van, H. and Ngoc, T. (2007) 'Kinh nghiem khong con dung dau (Experience is no longer the top priority)', *Tuoi Tre Online*, 12 June.

World Bank (The World Bank Group) (2007, April) 'World Development Indicators Database, Vietnam Data Profile'. Available at http://devdata.worldbank.org/external/CPProfile.asp?PTYPE=CP&CCODE=VNM (accessed 10 May 2008).

Y.T. (2008) 'Chua thay vai tro cua cong doan co so (The role of the trade union chapter is still to be seen)', *Tuoi Tre Online*, 8 May.

Yoong, Cheak King (2007) 'Pitfalls of Vietnam's economic growth', *The Star Online*, 31 December. Available at http://thestar.com.my (accessed 31 December 2007).

Zhu, Y., Collins, N., Webber, M. and Benson, J. (2008) 'New forms of ownership and human resource practices in Vietnam', *Human Resource Management*, 47, 1, 157–75.

3 The changing face of marketing management in Vietnam

Pierre Dietrichsen with contributions by Elizabeth Erasmus and Thanh Phung Phuong

- Introduction
- Key issues and new developments
- Case studies
- Challenges
- Conclusion

Introduction

Marketing management in Vietnam and, in particular, recent developments in the country must be seen against the background of the ongoing general economic liberalization in Vietnam, changes in the regulatory framework and management developments in general. The Government's *Doi Moi* policy of economic reform has been fundamental in creating business opportunities, encouraging PEs and the relative free operating of market forces. These economic and business environments increasingly shape the way in which businesses manage their marketing efforts. This chapter will discuss specific marketing aspects and selected sectors, from both the strategic and the operational perspectives.

The peculiar economic development phase in Vietnam makes many conflicting demands on management priorities. Although technically a country approaching middle-income level status in terms of UN classifications, there are still significant income disparities between poor rural areas and communities on the one hand, and city dwellers on the other. Macro-economically, Vietnam can be classified as a medium-sized emerging market, or an economy in transition, with a GDP of some US$ 94 billion, less than that of Pakistan or Bangladesh, but with a higher growth rate of around 8 per cent per annum (The Economist, 2009). Yet, Vietnam's population of 84 million, of which some 50 per cent are less than 35 years old, makes it a consumer market of tremendous potential. These characteristics impact directly on the product offering, the pricing of goods and services and the promotion of those by foreign and Vietnamese companies (Neupert, Baughn and Dao, 2005: 166).

This chapter will focus on five main areas. Key issues characterizing business generally and markets specifically will be discussed at the outset, with some focus on new and potential developments which impact on marketing by firms in Vietnam. Subsequently, the role and influence of foreign firms operating in the country will be highlighted. Their impact can also be observed in the quest for professionalism in the marketing profession, which is the next section. Case studies examining the marketing strategies and activities of IBM and Unilever in Vietnam support the discussion on professionalism and the role of foreign firms. A text box in which the current status of market research is described is also included as it is linked to both of these aspects. The following section draws attention to cultural aspects in formulating and executing marketing strategies in Vietnam, and includes the differences between HCMC and Hanoi. Buyer behaviour, linked to the cultural dimension of marketing, is an important consideration in marketing and it is discussed in another text box.

Before concluding the chapter, the final section identifies and elaborates on the challenges faced by marketing managers and business strategists in Vietnam. A key aspect inherent in the nature of the Vietnamese economy and business in general, and marketing in particular, is the continuous change taking place. Although the post-2008 global economic decline may slow down this trend, managers setting up business operations in Vietnam should be aware of the possible impact of evolving practices and policies on their business planning. This emergent nature of marketing strategy is a recurring theme in this chapter. Two prominent 'voices' in business in Vietnam – the leaders of ANZ Bank in Vietnam and FPT Corporation – positioned towards the end of the chapter also demonstrate Vietnam in transition and the changing face of management in the marketing area.

Key issues and new developments

This section will focus on three areas: first, on some important business background matters which impact on the formulation of marketing strategy and marketing operations, such as pricing and product choice, as well as how these are developing. Unlike economies with mostly free markets, Vietnam is developing towards a full market economy and this characteristic determines key structural issues in the wholesale and distribution sector. A discussion of these aspects is followed by a third part which takes a closer look at market segmentation and selected market sectors in Vietnam.

Historical context in pricing and products

Vietnamese enterprises which typically progressed from production facilities of government departments to government-owned businesses in the late 1980s and early 1990s, and then to SOEs after that, have had to make major adjustments in the way in which they approach the choice of products they manufacture and the policies of pricing those products and services. Manufacturing typically depended on the resources and capacity of a specific enterprise. Those enterprises under the control of the Ministry of Agriculture engaged in the manufacture or limited importation and distribution of pesticides and fertilizer to mostly communal farmers. Those under the Ministry of Construction developed building materials and cement factories and provided construction equipment. The Defence establishment manufactured some communications, transport, and weapons equipment, and operates its own bank.

There was no real need for marketing in an economy where the state's apparatus controlled virtually every aspect of production and delivery of consumer goods to the population. Although many SOEs were progressively semi-privatized during the 1990s in a process of equitisation, with the state a major shareholder in the new SOE and equitised firms, such enterprises operated in a tightly controlled environment in which prices were set or monitored by the government price control authorities and the choice of products offered seldom reflected true market demand. Local enterprises have, therefore, had a difficult decade in adapting to a need for a more market-driven product strategy, rather than an inward looking resource-based choice of products and services.

Pricing of goods and services has also presented a variety of challenges. Because of a generally low national cost and salary level structure, local enterprises struggle to come to grips with notions of cost accounting and break-even analysis. Since many prices are still controlled in socially sensitive areas such as pharmaceuticals, agricultural input products, basic foodstuffs and transport, enterprises in these areas have an ongoing interaction with authorities to find a sensible way to reconcile costs and prices.

Product choice is an area in which growing consumer **demand, rising** incomes and increasing sophistication have **had a significant impact** in many sectors. In the retail business, the number **and quality of** supermarkets has grown. The range of their imported and local products has expanded, including fast moving consumer goods (FMCG), but with the exception of fresh foods, which are mostly sold in traditional markets. White goods and household electronics (such as washing machines, fridges and vacuum cleaners) are increasingly sought after and new retail outlets have increased in cities and large towns. In the office machinery and stationery sectors, demand has grown steadily.

The result of this across-the-board growth in demand is that enterprises are increasingly market-driven in their choice of manufactured and imported products. Sound and predictable macroeconomic policies in the 2000s have contributed to annual economic growth of around 8 per cent, and even higher growth in demand as salaries and company profits keep rising. GDP (2007) PPP is US$ 222 billion, converting to a per capita GDP PPP of US$2580 per annum (The Economist, 2009). Vietnam is currently considered to be the fourth most attractive retail market globally, according to research by A.T. Kearney (Regoverningmarkets, 2008).

The economy of Vietnam has been quite resilient and weathered the regional crises of SARS and avian flu between 2004 and 2007 reasonably well, although the impact on the tourist industry was noticeable at the time. Inflation was low until 2007 (below 10 per cent per annum) despite wage and salary increases, and general price increases. However, inflation has increased as part of the global economic slow-down and the overheated financial and property sectors in Vietnam at the start of 2008. These factors in the general economic environment will also impact on business strategies in Vietnam and will have a related effect on marketing.

Despite this generally favourable macroeconomic situation and an exciting retail sector, there are a number of areas of concern to marketers. One such aspect is the contentious issue in Vietnam, until recently between authorities and foreign companies in the marketing of products and services, in that only some 10 per cent of the costs of business could be spent on advertising and marketing. Yet, this is an increase from 7 per cent in 1999 and only 5 per cent in earlier years (VVG-Vietnam, 2008). There have also been restrictions on the use of Vietnamese nationals in advertisements, and the publication of any printed matter, which were subject to approval by the Ministry of Culture and Information. These constraints have been relaxed in recent times.

In addition to the lingering constraints mentioned above, there are some areas in which a lack of policy clarity and the continued influence of SOEs also impact on marketing options. The following brief discussion of the wholesale and distribution sectors, followed by a focus on market sectors and segmentation, will examine important market characteristics.

Wholesale and distribution

There are three main types of wholesaler in Vietnam. The most recent type is the example of the foreign-owned Metro which opened outlets in HCMC and Hanoi and is permitted to sell household goods, foodstuffs, fresh produce, white goods, electronic equipment, motorbikes and the like to retail shop owners, hotels, restaurants and similar registered businesses and organizations. There is some degree of discretion left to the management, but the firm was fined when it became too lenient with its 'membership' card being issued to some members of the general public.

Product choice is not restricted but import permits are required for foreign products, including products such as wine, meat and electronics. Products are therefore mainly brands which are available locally, while imported products are often, but not exclusively, sourced through existing authorized importers of wine, meat, electronic equipment, etc. Metro conducted intensive marketing campaigns through promotions and advertising before and after opening each new outlet, but the current limited nature of competition in the sector favours those already in the market. New entrants are not prohibited but entry is not without problems because of supply chain constraints and infrastructure limitations. There is, paradoxically, a strong focus on relationships with suppliers to ensure consistency and quality, rather than with customers.

The second type of wholesaler is, typically, the authorized importer of foreign products not seen to be in competition with Vietnamese products. Vietnam has seen a high growth in the number of these importers which range from importers of stainless steel to wine, beef, pharmaceuticals, cars, consumer electronics, dairy products, earthmoving equipment and industrial machinery. Marketing in these sectors by the importers often focuses on brand awareness promotion and advertising, as well as the setting up of a reliable distribution network, especially for new entrants such as the recent entry by New Zealand Natural ice cream. Others, such as household electronic goods, consumer electronics (such as mobile phones and cameras) and well-known luxury cars (such as Mercedes-Benz and Lexus) pursue similar strategies of branding and promotional support to retail partners. Retail outlets for these products are often individually owned or franchised and often fit into a broader advertising programme.

More traditional wholesalers in consumer goods and industrial goods (e.g. chemicals and steel) are those who have been in operation for a long time with SOE or government ties. They rely strongly on existing networks of retail customers, or exploit current restrictions on foreign-owned enterprises operating distribution channels to service a captive market of small shops and manufacturers. Advertising and marketing activities are somewhat limited, but this is likely to change as WTO obligations result in liberalization of distribution channels in 2009 and the arrival of new foreign entrants. (Vietnam Investment Review, 2008: 11.)

Market sectors and segments in Vietnam

A challenge for marketers in Vietnam is the segmenting of markets based on consumer behaviour and characteristics in order to understand customers, to optimize the use of resources in developing that part of the market and in deciding on the positioning of the firm's products (Czinkota and Kotabe, 2001: 195). Another challenge is the shortage of reliable market intelligence on matters such as sector size and consumer spending, although the VCCI can be of some help. SOEs and local PEs do not have recognized international reporting and corporate governance obligations, for example, in the area of publishing of company information.

In a recent trend, beauty shops, cosmetic outlets and beauty salons, for example, have experienced a remarkable expansion. This is not only the result of higher disposable income among urban professional young females, but also because of the cultural phenomenon of household decision-making in collectivist societies (Hofstede, 1980). In Vietnam (as in Japan) household budgets are largely controlled by females. As these matriarchs become more emancipated in their spending and lifestyle priorities, they are more inclined to spend money not only on household necessities and children's education, but also on their own happiness (Peterlik, 2007). Marketing of products (e.g. cosmetics) and services (e.g. beauty salons and holiday resorts) should carefully consider these two categories of decision-maker: middle-aged middle-income females and young high-income professional females (see Text Box 3.1 on buyer behaviour).

The possession of family cars is an increasing status symbol in Vietnam and small cars have been positioned as one step up on the ladder from imported Italian or Japanese high-end motorcycles. Such a car purchase represents a significant expense since most cars are expensive because of a 100 per cent or more 'super import tax'. Also, the culture of financing for large purchases, such as cars, is still unknown and most large purchases still entail an extended savings period to purchase in cash. Car loans and leasing arrangements are not easy to obtain in Vietnam, which means the decision to buy a car is not likely to be that of one individual, or to be based on individual choice, but rather to be that of the family. To a lesser extent, but still true, the purchase of household white goods and electronic appliances are similarly decided in the family where typically three generations form the household. The extended family is, therefore, a far more important segment than in individualist societies such as the UK, US or Australia. Marketers must keep this in mind; too often, advertising will focus on the individual, rather than on the group making the decision (De Mooij, 2005).

The disparity between rural communities and city dwellers, and the gap in income between the growing city middle income (or, perhaps, middle class) and the higher income group can be observed in the choice of products based on price (e.g. local brand shampoo versus foreign brand locally made) as well as the distribution (small corner shop with low margin versus new luxury department store selling essentially the same product at a higher mark-up). The promotion of products in this sector of the retail business and building brand awareness require careful analysis of the sector, especially for new entrants into the market. A careful analysis using Porter's five forces industry analytical tool would be useful for firms becoming active in the Vietnamese market (Porter, 1985).

Other segments that do not differ from overseas markets are possibly university students, computer owners, the young music MP3/iPod fraternity, travelling business people, high-income bank customers and foreigners living in Vietnam. This similarity could be seen as part of the growing internationalization of consumer identity and the role of the internet in shaping consumer behaviour (Czinkota and Kotabe, 2001: 201).

Segmenting of the market is also affected by a number of other factors which should be kept in mind. Land ownership does not exist, only long leasehold. This relates not only to the housing market itself, but also to the fact that expensive housing and scarce land force two or three generations of a family to live together. Space is therefore scarce and the quantity of household goods, clothing, white goods, furniture, etc. that can be bought is restricted. Relatively small numbers of families use deep freezers or large fridges. Fresh food is bought daily at the local market and consumed quickly.
These practical factors influence buying decisions and, therefore, the way firms can effectively promote their products. While more families are moving to larger high-rise apartments, they are the minority in cities such as HCMC (population 6 million) and Hanoi (population 4 million), and an even smaller minority in other cities. Buying

decisions are often influenced by a simple practical matter such as the maximum size of an item that can be delivered on the back of a motorcycle via narrow city lanes. This reality impacts on the selection of available products and the marketing plans of companies should reflect this.

The influence of foreign companies

Vietnam has successfully promoted itself as a profitable destination for FDI (and easier than China) and annually receives substantial amounts in realized foreign investment. The Ministry of Planning and Investment (MPI) is expecting some US$30 billion of the US$65 billion FDI approved in 2008 to be realized (MPI.gov.vn). This is evident in the growing number of industrial parks and special economic zones near cities such as Hanoi, Hai Phong, Danang and HCMC, not to mention many coastal and inland provinces. Such FDI is also visible in the presence of many such manufacturing and processing facilities in areas of electronics (e.g. Panasonic, Canon, LG), cars (e.g. Ford, Toyota), steel (e.g. Midway Metals, Blue Scope Steel, Zamil Steel), household consumer items (e.g. Unilever, Kao Corporation, Procter & Gamble, Johnson & Johnson), cement, food processing (e.g. Nestlé), furniture, shoes (e.g. Nike, Bata, Adidas) and many others that may focus predominantly on manufacture for export to developed markets (e.g. Intel and Maxport). Firms in services such as hotels (e.g. Hilton, Sheraton, and Intercontinental), banks (e.g. HSBC, ANZ, Citi, Standard Chartered), insurance, tourism operators, IT (e.g. IBM, Microsoft), logistics (e.g. UPS, FEDEX, DHL) and auditing/consulting firms have also become household names. The case of ANZ Bank in Vietnam and its General Manager, Ms Thuy Dam is an example of the influence an international company can have on a specific sector in Vietnam (see Case Study 3.4).

Unilever is another foreign company playing a significant role in shaping the marketing function in Vietnam. It is reported to be the biggest spender in advertising (US$35 million) compared to the largest local spender, Vietnam Post & Telecom (US$8 million). The Vietnam Advertising Association estimates that some 80 per cent of advertising spending is still done by foreign firms. Local firms are said to be learning, but still are lagging behind in know-how in areas of public relations and advertisement conceptualization and design (Yin, 2007). There is growing awareness in Vietnam of the importance of CSR and in this area several prominent foreign firms, including IBM and Unilever, are setting an excellent example (see Case Studies 3.1 and 3.3).

Apart from the positive impact that foreign firms have on levels of brand awareness and the sales of their products, they have all had a more significant impact on Vietnam's business community. This is also true in the area of developing the marketing function in Vietnam. Traditionally, with SOEs and government enterprises having a low awareness of the customer as a factor in their strategies, marketing was fragmented within companies and even received a low priority. However, Vietnam's accession to the WTO, the arrival of foreign competition and the examples of foreign firms are contributing towards change. Vietnamese firms are responding positively and are not only changing general management practices but specifically their marketing practices and their attitudes towards consumers in general and their customers in particular. This trend is becoming clear from meetings with marketing managers who are progressively following best practice. An example of this is FPT Corporation. As importer and distributor of computers and mobile phones, an internet service provider/telecommunications operator, a financial services/brokerage firm and provider of IT training, the firm appointed a foreign director of marketing to focus on building the brand, positioning FPT and expanding its market as a pioneer in the electronics business.

On the negative side, there are incidents and situations where foreign best practices are in conflict with local perceptions about marketing and distribution, especially where ethics and employee conduct are concerned (Neupert, Baughn and Dao, 2005: 170). This matter forms part of the broader topic of good corporate governance, but which is not the focus of this chapter. Nevertheless, it is a challenge that marketing managers face, both in the planning of a realistic marketing strategy and the managing of marketing activities. The case of IBM's marketing in Vietnam demonstrates both international best practice and localization (i.e. adaptation of strategies to suit local conditions).

The quest for professionalism in marketing

This section will focus on the HR dimensions of professionalism, followed by a discussion on the current state of, and developments in, events management and promotions, as well as branding and public relations as part of the marketing profession. The challenges of creating an awareness of the importance of promoting a good 'made in Vietnam' image follows. A brief case study of events involving Nestlé and Dutch Lady also focuses on some of these aspects.

Marketing is becoming popular as a profession in Vietnam. In common with developing economies elsewhere, however, there is still considerable confusion in the minds of company officials, educators and entrepreneurs about marketing as a function of the firm. In the minds of many, marketing is no more than advertising and promotion. Frequently the marketing function is no more than sales promotion. It is not uncommon to find in a business three managers independently responsible for sales, distribution and marketing, the latter frequently doing no more than public relations. This structure can result in fragmented management and incoherent strategies. As a result, there is a tactical focus on sales and logistics, rather than an integrated strategic marketing mix focus. In a survey conducted by Neupert, Baughn and Dao (2005: 171), local managers cited several problems in marketing, such as a lack of professionalism, lack of experience, divided loyalty and the difficulty of finding suitable distribution partners.

The focus on sales and short term profits – rather than systematic strategic marketing with a coherent price, promotion and distribution mix of products and services desired by customers – remains one of the apparent shortcomings in marketing management in Vietnam. Local firms struggle to establish brands, partly as a result of a shortage of branding experience and professionals, but also because of the transient nature of many businesses. Businesses have often only existed for a few years since the opening of the economy and there is a lack of a sense of permanence and the importance of brands. Companies, especially SMEs, frequently change names, logos and locations. Shareholders and managers, especially in newly equitised firms, try to impose their own identity on products and brands. In some cases this is an intentional tactic associated with poor or dangerous products, infringement of intellectual property rights, or other unprofessional business conduct.

Good branding trends and marketing practices seem to develop in upmarket garment design, manufacture and retail firms, especially those that are vertically integrated, such as KhaiSilk, IpaNima, Dome and Marie Linh. Some of these have foreign partners. Limited brand recognition of small local supermarket chains is developing but is not adequately pursued. Local pharmaceuticals focus on generic products and little branding takes place, although a quality problem would suggest that more would be required to restore their credibility with retail pharmacists. Construction firms have a higher profile and use their construction sites and finished buildings in branding efforts. Local banks are under financial pressure, partly as a result of increasing local and foreign competition. They use their expansion of retail branches as part of their branding efforts.

After Vietnam's experience with an overheated stock market from late 2007, and the subsequent crisis, it is clear that companies have started paying more attention to relations with shareholders and good communication practices. Another positive trend is towards an increase in customer relations management (CRM) with managers being appointed to focus on this aspect as part of the broader marketing focus. It is possibly too soon to speak of the good use of customer databases to enhance marketing, but there is evidence that some firms are starting this, such as banks, insurance firms, tourism operators and airlines (Kotler, 2003: 53). The practice of appointing a business development manager to focus on developing new CRM, opening new markets, and building customer loyalty would appear to be an aspect that supports the developing of the marketing function, assuming that these managers are acting in collaboration with marketing managers, not in isolation. The involvement of such managers in the activities of chambers of commerce (e.g. AMCHAM, EUROCHAM) would seem to lend anecdotal support that this may be a positive trend.

According to a statement by the MPI, FDI into Vietnam in 2008 increased by some 57 per cent from 2007, the previous highest, a final amount of more than US$65 billion (Vietnam News, 2008b). Foreign firms and JVEs will increase their large share of the production of goods and the provision of services. By implication, marketing management will continue to be influenced by foreign firms for the foreseeable future, rather than becoming localized. The exception may be in the area of FMCG in which key operators, such as Unilever, follow more of a customized local strategy in branding specifically and marketing in general.

HR dilemmas and issues in marketing professionalism

The business press and employment websites, such as Vietnamworks, frequently highlight the shortage of skilled employees. Although the country has a high student population, access to tertiary education is somewhat limited with an enrolment ratio of 16 per cent. The shortage is made especially more acute by a relative lack of business experience among lecturers and inadequate university education, resulting in shortages of IT professionals, marketing staff, management and finance staff (Deutsche Bank Research, 2007: 7; Trinh, 2007).

In addition, staff members are now more frequently inclined to move to new employment for a higher salary or better conditions. Traditionally, staff in the management category tended to remain in the employ of one firm for several years and looked towards promotions, visits abroad and further T&D as ways of meeting personal aspirations. The increasing openness of the job market has changed that. Competent people remain in a job for shorter periods and have little hesitation in moving from company to company every 18 months or two years. Typically, until 2008 foreign firms, such as those in auditing and banking, had to advertise several times before a competent and experienced marketing manager could be found, just to be faced by excessive salary demands – perhaps arising from a perception that they are in a seller's market. The post-2008 economic slow-down may temper this phenomenon.

Indications are that university graduates are less willing to become involved in sales than they were before. Although the VCCI and others offer sales T&D courses, SMEs are not inclined to release working staff to attend courses, while non-employed individuals are not financially able to afford training before seeking employment. On the other hand, well run firms, such as FPT and Vietnam Airlines, offer regular in-house sales and CRM T&D courses.

Staff shortages, and the costs of giving staff in-house or external T&D when there is a risk that they may resign soon, are factors in the overall competence of marketing staff. This is not unlike the shortages of IT professionals and any management level staff (Vietnam News, 2007a, 2007b, 2008a). Businesses also typically complain that university educated students have little practical training or experience, thus lacking a good understanding of business. Companies are said to be partly at fault for not offering internships and entry-level posts to students (Thanh Nien News, 2008).

According to the VCCI (2007) and Nguyen and Neelakantan (2006) 96 per cent of all registered firms in Vietnam are technically SMEs generating 25 per cent of GDP. The size of these firms implies that marketing, while an important function for the survival of the firm, is often a shared function with finance, general management or production. The other significant sector is the SOE sector, with large numbers of employees and sometimes ill-defined strategies or fragmented marketing/sales/customer relations functions. Many are in stages of equitisation, meaning that core competences are being redefined (e.g. military industries and agrifood businesses) and the marketing function is not well understood. Similarly, there are Human Resource Management and HRD challenges. A third important sector is the FDI or FIEs where the core business is clear, the marketing function is understood and being developed, but with a shortage of competent marketing staff. Foreign firms are responsible for more than 50 per cent of Vietnam's exports (CIEM, 2008).

Events management and promotions

Vietnam is no different from China, Japan and Korea when it comes to its love of festivals and ceremonies. Government, company and household events are often elaborate celebrations with substantial ceremony, music, noise and decoration. The opening of new buildings and shops often takes place on dates and times carefully chosen for being auspicious. There is tremendous attention to detail, and flowers and elaborate symbolic actions by people in authority are essential.

For a company launching new products, opening new branches or factories, merging with former opponents or being new arrivals in Vietnam, there is no shortage of events management firms to use for such promotional events. Careful selection based on a track record is recommended. On the negative side, this trend also strengthens the existing perception among local firms that marketing consists of sales and promotion. Although recently it has become common to see the grand opening of new multi-storey electronic shopping centres and department stores, it is also common to observe a passive approach in subsequent weeks and months, the assumption being that an auspicious opening, a good location and being new and modern is enough to compete against traditional family-owned shops, small firms and outlets of famous international brand names. An all too common trend is for expensively appointed new restaurants, consumer electronics, upmarket garment and fashion shops to close in less than a year after launch because of insufficient turnover to cover growing rentals.

It could be argued that many firms are not adequately in touch with their customers, both in communicating about their products and services as well as in receiving feedback from customers. Customer service can be improved substantially in many areas, not only as a matter of good marketing but also as an ongoing practice in learning about customer concerns and preferences. The link between good communications and sound marketing practices was tested during the 'Chinese melamine scandal' of 2008, which is discussed in the Dutch Lady and Nestlé study (see Case Study 3.2).

Branding and public relations: creating a 'made in Vietnam' image

Reference has been made to the absence of a 'made in Vietnam' association with quality, style, value, experience or any other generic marketing or competitive advantage. Coffee and silk garments are possibly ideal products for such an awareness campaign. Vietnamese government ministers have complained that there are no famous Vietnamese brands abroad, and only a few locally. The 'made in Vietnam' issue goes even further. Vietnam has been a member of WTO since 2007 with more reductions of tariffs and other barriers. Therefore, foreign firms will be able to operate more freely, including in currently restricted areas such as food retailing and distribution logistics. Telecommunications and energy are two areas in which foreign firms could only participate as strategic partners, not operating as independent firms. Similarly, Vietnamese firms will have greater access to foreign markets, as long as they are not guilty of dumping their products at below-cost prices. Competing with foreign firms will require new thinking in marketing.

One of the difficulties with the branding of Vietnamese products is that local marketers adopt a wait-and-see attitude to see what and how foreign brands are promoted, in the process losing time and market share (Matthaes of TNS, quoted by Yin, 2007). Recent experience shows that the careful use of Vietnam's heritage is a good way to promote products. Unilever used it in their Omo advertising, and commercials for milk powder by Nuti IQ (Yin, 2007). With an optimistic, literate and highly IT-aware young population, marketing with a distinctive Vietnamese character stressing the uniqueness of Vietnam, or the product, and using the right medium, advertising and public relations will increasingly play a role in marketing to create a 'Vietnam awareness'. Surveys by Consumer Insights Express and TNS indicate that 86 per cent of people learn about new products and trends in magazines and 70 per cent from TV advertisements (Yin, 2007).

Despite the concerns about a lack of recognizable brands, FPT Corporation has been a visible exception and has managed to build a good reputation and brand recognition in the industries where it operates. Its success can partly be attributed to dynamic leadership and partly to its productive working relationship with firms such as IBM (see Case Study 3.1).

HCMC and Hanoi: the differences

This section will explore the cultural differences between the north and the south of the country, using Hanoi and HCMC as examples, as well as the impact of cultural issues on buyer behaviour and marketing in Vietnam. In a general sense, Hanoi, HCMC, Danang, Hai Phong port city and Hue, the main cities in Vietnam, are quite similar. Vietnamese cities and provinces have few federal powers, the same laws are applicable, the same language is used for official documents, and the same business practices are generally in place. However, this superficial similarity should not obscure the underlying differences. HCMC and provinces in the south had a longer exposure to French, and later US, business in the pre-war days of the last century. Although those generations have largely disappeared or may find themselves abroad as migrants, their descendants in Vietnam have keenly integrated themselves into the market economy and private enterprise in the last 20 years. It is the general experience that southerners are more entrepreneurial and business-minded. They are also more aggressive in their pursuit of a 'deal' and their understanding of the 'bottom line', and are less concerned with formality than the northerners. Business people in Hanoi focus strongly on relationship building, formality, observing the 'rules of the game', and having official support for initiatives. This somewhat more bureaucratic approach does not mean that business is less well understood or supported. Authorities in Hanoi actively encourage FDI in the Hanoi area. Although there is also an expectation that managers in the north would be more collective in their decision-making and management styles, with the south being more individualistic, research by Ralston, Nguyen and Napier (1999: 11–12) has shown that Hanoians have become more assertive, being close to the seat of power, while HCMC southerners are more adaptable and inclined to 'play the game' of the collectivist to achieve their objectives. Recent research carried out by TNS Global supports this, indicating that Hanoi consumer trends lag behind those of HCMC by about six months (Matthaes, 2008).

Hanoi consumers are 'face-driven'. They see the products they use as a measure of success in life. Until recently it was not acceptable to show your high income or flaunt wealth – that was the specialty of the 'cool kids' of HCMC. Yet, northern consumers are now more likely to show off their designer clothing and famous brand-name jewellery or accessories despite the presence of the taxman around the corner (Stocking, 2007: 1–3).

Do you launch your new product in Hanoi or HCMC first? This is a debate among marketers which has no definitive answer. Hanoi consumers are more cautious about new products and look at issues such as its status, its place in the market indicated by price, how it is launched, its content/components or origin, and its inherent value. There is a high curiosity level. HCMC buyers are more enterprising and adventurous, they spend more generously, are more likely to buy for fun, and do look at value-for-money (see Text Box 3.1 on buyer behaviour).

Cultural issues in marketing

A very positive aspect of culture in marketing in Vietnam is the high literacy rate and curiosity of the Vietnamese consumer. Consumers want to be informed and read product information. They are interested in new brands, new products and new services, especially the urban consumer. The poor road infrastructure outside major urban areas is a major challenge in building consumer awareness, product distribution and market expansion. These factors impact on marketing planning, brand awareness and promotion. New products reach rural areas and small communities far from cities last, as seen in Text Box 3.1.

Text Box 3.1: Buyer behaviour in Vietnam and its impact on marketing

The study of buyer behaviour or consumer psychology in Vietnam is relatively new. Following the decision to 'renovate' the economy in 1986 and to move away from the centrally-planned socialist model where consumers were considered equal in terms of their needs, wants and forms of consumption, Vietnam now has a more 'open' economy, allowing business to exist according to open market principles and consumers to choose what, where and how they spend their money.

Cross-cultural models to understand Vietnamese cultural considerations

Cross-cultural models have been used to classify the cultural and value differences between cultures and nations. These classification systems are also applied to Vietnam, often through comparison with China, although little research has been done locally to prove these conclusions. Although different countries, there are many commonalities between Vietnamese and Chinese culture – the Chinese influence dating back to when for a millennium Vietnam formed part of a greater China.

A dominant factor in Vietnamese culture is collectivism (as opposed to individualism); there is a strong sense of belonging to a group and people consider the interest, values and acceptance of the group as a significant influence on their consumer decisions. The Vietnamese family unit is the main point of consideration in every decision, ranging from basic consumption items such as soap, to the choice of husband or wife for a son or daughter. According to the World Values Survey (2001) 83 per cent of Vietnamese rank their family as very important in their lives, by far more important than friends, work, leisure pursuits, politics or service to others. The influence and importance of the family unit extends that of a typical household per definition (Neal et al., 2005).

The Vietnamese consumer is risk averse and consumers are sceptical and careful in their purchase decisions (De Mooij, 2005). The impact on consumption results in a slow uptake of new products and innovations for most segments. National differences indicate that consumers in the southern metropolitan area of HCMC are generally more adventurous and willing to try new things, rather than their more conservative cousins in Hanoi, who prefer word-of-mouth recommendations from family, friends and colleagues before investing time and money in new products and innovations.

Despite being grouped with other South and South East Asian countries in the World Values Survey (2001), Vietnam belongs to the East Asian grouping of Confucian, high-context cultures, where communication is very subtle, indirect and nuanced. The communication aspects of advertising and promotion campaigns reinforce the importance of long-term relationships and politically correct communication through TV and radio, as well as showing consideration for utilitarian appeals rather than aesthetic appeals (De Burca et al., 2004). Further evidence of collectivism indicates that consumer responses to communication messages were more often influenced by their desire to conform than by behaving individualistically (De Burca et al., 2004).

The consumer

Vietnamese households typically consist of five or more people (Euromonitor, 2008a) ranging over three or possibly four generations, rather than the average three or four people over two generations in the typical Western household. The average household may also have more than two earners, boosting purchasing power and consumption by more than 75 per cent between 2000 and 2007 (Regoverningmarkets, 2007).

In 2008 Vietnam overtook India as the most attractive emerging retail market (Global Retail Development Index TM, 2008). Despite a much smaller comparative population than India, the Vietnamese economy has shown a consistently high annual growth rate since 2001 and there are still only a few players in this lucrative market.

The Vietnamese are generally optimistic about their economic situation, future and income and believe that today's children will be better off as adults than they as parents are now (Pew Global, 2002). Unlike most other consumers surveyed in the June 2008 A.C. Nielsen consumer report (A.C. Nielsen, 2008), the Vietnamese spend their money on communication and IT-related products and save a little after covering essential living expenses, but not on holidays, vacations and new clothes.

Some 63 per cent of Vietnamese put money away in some form of savings, to prevent the famine and poverty that today's middle-aged Vietnamese endured and, very importantly, to secure money for education. Confucian ethics still prevail in modern day Vietnam and education is highly valued, regardless of its usefulness. It is not unusual to find a normal office secretary with a master's degree from a Vietnamese university. Education at government institutions is highly subsidized but, for middle class Vietnamese, school does not provide the necessary knowledge and training required to succeed in life and any child whose parents can afford it attends extra classes every day of the week. The Ministry of Education announced (Baothanhhoa, 2008) that it would become obligatory for primary school children to learn English at school, a step that would greatly assist in preparing young Vietnamese for a career in the growing services sector.

Typically, the Vietnamese do not want to spend money on health insurance or visiting doctors; they prefer to self-medicate and can do so as there are no pharmaceutical regulatory frameworks and pharmacies sell prescription medicines over the counter. Until very recently, medical services were provided through the government – each ministry and department had its own clinic and workers were encouraged, through subsidization, to use these for all kinds of treatments ranging from vitamin supplements to contraceptives.

Culturally, the strongest influence on Vietnam has always been China – the good (economic prowess), the bad (dangerous chemicals in consumer goods) and the ugly (cheap fake goods). Considering that 84 per cent obtain their news from TV (Pew Global, 2002) it is no surprise that Korean 'soaps' have a huge following and have paved the way for a wide range of Korean cosmetic and toiletry products (many under the umbrella of LG).

Japan has led the way as one of the top three investors into Vietnam, contributing to the building of the Vietnamese economy through FDI and ODA. Japanese firms have been able to take advantage of the excellent brand awareness of Japanese products to be the market leader in many fields; the Honda Dream was the first high quality motorbike of choice to be locally assembled and later manufactured. Names like Komatsu, Panasonic, Toyota, Kikoman, Toshiba, Sony, Shiseido,

> Kanebo, Suzuki and Yamaha are automatically positioned in a higher quality price bracket than comparative products and immediately create confidence and trust in the mind of the Vietnamese consumer.
>
> How can a person earning around US$800 per month afford to buy a luxury car worth around US$40,000, pay US$16,000 per year in annual school fees at an international school in Vietnam, and own more than one house, worth at least US$50,000? How long and how much do you have to save to afford any single one of these large capital items? The answer is multifaceted. Many middle and upper class Vietnamese families have more than one stream of income with the middle class often keeping more than one job: an officially declared job at a government or semi-state organization, and the other streams of revenue that occur by virtue of a network of business and/or political connections. The personal income taxation system, a fact of life in most countries, is still relatively new in Vietnam and consumers have many creative ways of avoiding tax. This provides more cash in hand for spending, explaining the common trend of spending more per month than what is officially earned and declared. Additionally, the comparatively low cost of living creates many opportunities for consumers to enjoy the new economic freedom available to them in Vietnam.
>
> The typical Vietnamese consumer is sceptical, careful and thrifty, concerned about their health and that of their children, wary of unknown brands and products yet curious, has endured a difficult life growing up and is now enjoying the fruits of prosperity in a peaceful, prosperous country, living for the short and medium term. Parents and grandparents dote on their children and grandchildren (maybe because they are still allowed to have only two) and will give children whatever they want while they are young, but expect a lot from them when they grow up: they should work hard, be responsible, and show respect and tolerance for others (World Values Survey, 2001). Parents rarely hesitate to spend money on their children's education, entertainment and pleasure. These trends are clearly visible in the growing popularity of franchised fast-food outlets such as KFC (from five restaurants in 2002 to 34 in 2007 and targeted for 100 in 2010) (Ven, 2008) and the concurrent increasing children's obesity in a nation that has traditionally held the record for very low average weight and size among adults.
>
> Research and text by Elizabeth Erasmus

The shortage of market intelligence in some sectors, the changing nature of Vietnamese consumers, the increasing presence of foreign firms in Vietnam in terms of its WTO commitments and ongoing increases in disposable income for spending on consumer goods make the Vietnamese market more complex than it seems. Market research is therefore an essential part of new product planning and obtaining feedback about consumer preferences. The current state of market research in Vietnam is briefly discussed in Text Box 3.2.

Text Box 3.2: Market research in Vietnam

The emerging market research industry in Vietnam is estimated to be a US$23 million industry. Currently there are about 12 firms with revenues above US$200,000, but the market is concentrated with the three biggest players accounting for nearly 70 per cent of the total market share.

The earliest international syndicated market research companies in Vietnam were A.C. Nielsen (1993) and TNS (since 1996). There were other smaller companies such as Indochina Research (1995) or GfK (1996) (Amchamvietnam, 2008; TNSPS, 2008). In terms of tiers of revenues, it could be seen that the first tier companies are the two market leaders TNS and Nielsen with more than US$5 million of annual revenue. The second tier companies have annual revenues between US$1 million and US$5 million. This second tier includes Cimigo, ICR (Indochina Research), CBI (Customer Behaviours and Insights, a member of ESOMAR), FTA (a member of ESOMAR), IMS (Meridian Research), and GfK.

In terms of rates, average costs for a Nielsen research project is US$15,000, with projects ranging from US$5,000 to US$150,000 (Openshare, 2008; Doanhnhansaigontieubieu, 2008). An average Brand Tracking Project is 6–12 months long and costs about US$42,000 to US$50,000 each. Usage and Attitude (U&A) studies are shorter, about two to three months at a cost of between US$15,000 and US$25,000 each for a sample size of around 1,000 to 1,500 units (Massogroup, 2008). Local companies tend to charge at lower rates.

The current size of the industry is said to be relatively small compared to South East Asian neighbours. Data from 2005 indicated that Vietnam spending on market research per capita was US$0.12 per year, while average Vietnamese spending on advertising was US$2.40 per year, Malaysians spent US$1.25 per year per person; Thailand and the Philippines spent US$0.6 and US$0.38 per year per person respectively (VNTrades, 2008).

It is estimated that the industry is currently growing at the rate of approximately 15 to 20 per cent per year, and will continue to grow in the future when Vietnamese companies and other organizations realize that they need to find more effective ways of spending their marketing dollars by understanding more of their consumers' behaviour. It is expected that the industry would reach a total revenue of US$50 million by 2012. It is predicted that the market place would become more crowded with more local firms and international agencies.

Currently, at least one well known international market researcher, Euromonitor, is providing basic market research reports on Vietnam from abroad, carried out by freelancers, usually MBA graduates, who work on a project basis. As the industry grows, it could be expected that companies like Euromonitor might have enough interest in this market to establish branches in Vietnam. An office of MS Trade Finance LLC, a company specializing in stock market and financial information, was opened in Vietnam in August 2008. This type of firm needs to be licensed by the State Securities Commission of Vietnam (ATP Vietnam, 2008).

Local boutique firms render a valuable service to smaller clients who are more cost-conscious and have relatively smaller budgets, compared to international companies. As the global trends indicate that clients tend to use the same market research firm to ensure consistent methods, and that clients are moving toward more syndicated research methodology, international market research firms enjoy a competitive advantage over their small local competitors. On the other hand, as the market is becoming more sophisticated, more specialized research firms and local companies will try to develop their competitiveness in this area.

Research and text by Thanh Phung Phuong

Case studies

In this section a number of case studies will serve to illustrate characteristics of the market in Vietnam and local marketing practices and issues. The cases of Unilever and IBM relate to the influence of foreign firms in Vietnam, the quest for professionalism and the use of marketing tools, such as advertising and CSR. Unilever in Vietnam, for example, is a major FMCG manufacturer and distributor which has been a trendsetter in marketing and advertising, CRM, CSR and constructive partnerships with local firms since the 1990s. The brief discussion of the Nestlé and Dutch Lady experience, with consumer awareness and food safety issues, also illustrates a growing use of public relations and integrated marketing communication (IMC) in direct customer education and 'damage control' activities. The subsequent discussion of managers also aims to promote understanding of marketing developments and challenges in Vietnam.

Case studies of organizations

Case Study 3.1: IBM

IBM established a representative office in Vietnam in 1994 and in 1996 was given a licence to operate as a wholly FOE, IBM Vietnam, the first IT company permitted to do so. It is the largest IT services and consulting firm in Vietnam, forming part of IBM's 386,000 employees worldwide with revenue of US$98 billion and net profits of US$10.4 billion in 2007. It has operational partnerships with local firms and is known for its proactive role in CSR educational activities at school and tertiary level. IBM Vietnam reports strategically to the IBM ASEAN regional office in Singapore.

The marketing strategy of IBM in Vietnam reveals a number of key elements. Broad branding promotion and advertising activities to promote brand awareness are mostly done on a regional basis. One is more likely to see an advertisement for IBM consultancy and customer network and other solutions on Bloomberg, CNN, and on Korean and Chinese international TV services, than on local Vietnamese TV. The thinking is that high-level decision makers are watching these TV services, rather than local TV, and regional branding enhances consistency of message and is corporate Head Office-controlled. The focus of marketing within Vietnam is on CRM in the areas of likely customers such as banks, SOEs, government ministries (i.e. the Ministry of Finance), international companies and SMEs. The latter is a key customer segment in HCMC especially. This is quite different from the earlier days when IBM was also targeting users of desktop and laptop computers.

IBM is positioning itself to be a comprehensive service provider in its core business area and also to differentiate itself from competitors such as PWC, Accenture, Oracle, Microsoft and Dell. To achieve this, a number of carefully planned marketing tactics are typically used, such as workshops with local CEOs to brief them on trends, innovation and technology developments, seminars with insurance and bank executives to discuss systems solutions (e.g. for ATMs), and information sessions presented in collaboration with the VCCI. Customer education is an underlying philosophy. Local or foreign-based IBM executives may lead these sessions. While the CRM focus in Hanoi is often on smaller customer groups, or segment-specific, HCMC marketers are more comfortable to attend 'mass' marketing events. To a large extent it could be said that marketing activities are aimed at converting strategies into sales. Regular feedback from customers by sales teams, surveys and sales results are key elements in formulating marketing strategy. Other marketing activities focus on corporate affairs and community relations, handled by a special division located in Hanoi.

The IBM marketing strategy is noticeably different from companies opting for localization, such as Pepsi and Unilever. The latter's focus is heavily on building awareness of their locally available brands, informing and persuading local consumers and retail shop owners, and on community affairs, including well-publicized community projects in areas such as health and education. The IBM strategy serves as an example of careful analysis of the profiles of their likely and existing customers, deliberate market segmentation and consistent focus on customer relations, including relations with stakeholders such as government regulators and chambers of commerce. Following an early (1995) collaboration between IBM Vietnam and FPT, the latter appears to model some of its consultancy and customer solution services on IBM in Vietnam.

Marketing strategy is naturally evolving and in the post-2008 global economic conditions. IBM is developing its 'smarter planet' strategy aimed at energy saving technologies and systems. According to the marketing manager of IBM in Vietnam, marketing strategy is dynamic and many developments are also likely to have an impact on its marketing plans in Vietnam. Current approaches may well be quickly outdated.

Sources: IBM (2008); IBM Marketing Manager and discussions with managers in the IT sector (2008–09).

Case Study 3.2: Dutch Lady and Nestlé

Nestlé Vietnam has been operating as a fully foreign-owned firm since 1995 and is a major producer and distributor of dairy and other foodstuffs, especially coffee and tea produced locally. Dutch Lady

Vietnam, linked to Frieslands MNE, first exported milk to Vietnam in 1924 but has been operating in Vietnam since 1993. It has achieved recognition as one of the top ten most recognized brands in Vietnam (after Coca Cola and Nike).

As two significant players in the dairy consumer business in Vietnam, together with Vinamilk, these two MNEs have been quietly changing consumer habits and the dairy industry itself during the last five years by creating a new awareness of dairy products as a daily food. Yoghurt, cheese and fresh milk are now more widely consumed and generally available than before. Instead of finding 'long life' Australian and New Zealand milk on shop and supermarket shelves, consumers can now buy locally produced fresh milk which needs refrigeration. Advertising and promotional activities played a key role in creating this growing market. This growing consumer awareness and spending have incidentally resulted in the growth of associated markets for household fridges.

The production of baby-milk formula and powdered milk has been an important part of their business for some time and has always been a key focus of advertising and other marketing activities. Because of the relatively small capacity of Vietnam's herd, a significant volume of milk powder has traditionally been imported from China and other Asia-Pacific sources. In September 2008 it became known, through international news reports, that Chinese dairy products had been contaminated with the industrial chemical melamine. Following the deaths of infants and sickness of many more, Singapore and several other Asian countries banned the import of Chinese dairy products. In Vietnam, the origin of consumer products is not always stated on the packaging. However, it is known that dairy products are imported from China and the news of the contamination, or rumoured deliberate adding of melamine, resulted in a sudden drop in the sales of dairy products in Vietnam. Uncertainty among consumers and a growing awareness of food safety issues in Vietnam landed dairy companies with a dilemma. Their rapid response was full-page advertising in several newspapers and public relations activities to reassure consumers that their products had not been imported from China and were not contaminated with melamine. This is a useful case study for companies, and a reminder, especially for those in the food and pharmaceutical industries, that Vietnamese consumers are becoming more discerning, well informed and aware of safety issues. Marketers in Vietnam would do well to keep this in mind.

Sources: Nestlé (2008); Dutch Lady (2008); company media statements.

The case study of IBM illustrates the role that multinational enterprises operating in Vietnam as FIEs play in areas such as professional marketing practices and marketing strategy. In the case of IBM there is a strong element of 'think global and regional, and act local'. Branding has a strong global corporate focus. Unilever has a strong local branding and marketing focus for a broad variety of FMCG. Both firms are prominent leaders in the area of CSR and responsible marketing. Nestlé and Dutch Lady have also been strong in branding their food products locally, but the brief case in this chapter serves to demonstrate recent experience and developments in the area of food safety and communications with customers through public relations activities to restore consumer confidence in their products after suspected food contamination scandals. Increasing consumer awareness and buyer education are issues that marketing managers must consider in their IMC and CRM.

Text Box 3.3: Household and personal consumer goods – Unilever and others

Unilever is the leading FMCG manufacturer and distributor in Vietnam. It operates a network of its own and licensed local manufacturers of household cleaning, foodstuffs and personal care goods. As part of Unilever globally (turnover €40.5 billion in 2008 and 174,000 employees), it is one of the largest foreign firms operating in Vietnam.

The supermarket business in Vietnam is still developing and there are several smallish groups and a vast number of family-operated stores that are not quite yet convenience stores in the Seven Eleven category, but meet similar demands. Only the French Casino group operates 'hypermarkets', or large supermarkets, under the name BIG-C in Hanoi, Hai Phong and HCMC. While growing in popularity, they only serve the more sophisticated and higher income consumer. FMCG are therefore found anywhere from tiny kiosks to BIG-C. Fresh vegetables, fruits, rice and meats are still purchased daily by households at open wet markets. Fresh food markets are omnipresent in cities and towns. There is effectively no marketing of these products and the rare promotions and advertising of such products come from small and medium supermarkets trying to increase their share of fresh produce. Fresh dairy products are not consumed much in Vietnam, partly because of a lack of such a custom and partly because there is such a low production of milk in Vietnam. Dairy products are often imported from Australia, New Zealand, Malaysia and China. Supermarkets aim their promotion at foreigners and upper-income 'Westernized' Vietnamese (see the Dutch Lady and Nestlé case, Case Study 3.2).

Very tough competition exists among the MNEs and a few locals involved in household cleaning, beauty and personal products. Unilever, Proctor & Gamble and, to a lesser extent, Kao Corporation of Japan are the major players. However, because this is an area where changing consumer habits manifest early, new players are arriving and changing the 'rules of the game'.

There are some new players in the market. LG Household & Health Care Ltd has been promoting its range of shampoos and personal care products actively by sponsoring TV quiz shows under their brand name 'Double Rich' in collaboration with a local partner. UNZA International of Singapore has partnered with a local company to produce similar products under the 'Romano' brand. However, they are still small and their marketing is limited compared to the bigger MNCs.

Unilever ('from soaps to soups') includes CSR and respect for the environment as key parts of its marketing message. It equates its presence in Vietnam with a desire to make a contribution to Vietnamese society. Focus areas are community involvement through health and hygiene, child development and empowerment of women, linked to consumer education and training. As mentioned earlier, Unilever is said to be the biggest spender on advertising in Vietnam. Unilever brands such as P/S toothpaste and Omo washing powder have been the focus of aggressive advertising and a general marketing campaign since 2003, following Unilever's initial struggle against P&G's Tide brand. The result is that Unilever products are now better known than local brands in brand equity and sales performance.

Procter & Gamble has a JVE with Vinachem (Vietnam National Chemical Corporation). Vinachem is a conglomerate with at least another ten similar JVEs and partnerships in the chemical, rubber and other industries. Marketing focuses on brand awareness of its known consumer goods such as Pantene shampoo. It would appear as if marketing, and particularly advertising, have been less aggressive and less successful than those of competitors.

Kao is a latecomer to Vietnam and is principally known through its Kanebo cosmetics brand (a late acquisition in Japan) and efforts to popularize a brand such as Sofina. It is in direct competition with Shiseido of Japan which has a brand awareness advantage.

Sources: Unilever (2008); Unilever Foundation Report; Yin

(2007); Unilever Vietnam (2008); Vinachem (2008); author's analysis of media reports and interaction with company managers.

The case studies dealt with the IT sector and FMCG, especially personal care, household goods and foodstuffs. These sectors were chosen because they are some of the sectors which have shown remarkable growth and development in terms of product choice, consumer education levels and company leadership in their industries. The marketing strategies and practices of these Vietnamese subsidiaries of MNEs, and their social awareness, serve as valuable benchmarks for local firms.

Case studies of individual managers

The managers introduced in this section represent two divergent examples of successful strategists and marketers. One is a female Vietnamese financial specialist leading the local subsidiary of a foreign bank through a period of successful change and growth. The other is a male mathematics professor taking the lead in establishing an IT company, now one of the most widely recognized Vietnamese brands and the most important local IT service provider. They have both proved the value of vision, insight and perseverance.

Case Study 3.3: Ms Thuy Dam, Country Head, ANZ Bank Vietnam

Thuy Dam has been the Australia New Zealand Banking Group's General Manager for Vietnam since 2005. She came from a banking background with ANZ in Singapore (1996) and as co-founder of an investment consultancy firm in Vietnam. The appointment of a Vietnamese female as General Manager and Thuy's highly visible leadership have broken the trend of foreign and local banks being led by men and the notion that women are destined to take a back seat in the corporate world in Vietnam.

Soon after her appointment, she set out to increase the profile of ANZ

Vietnam and to market it as a bank of choice for businesses and individuals, especially for international banking. While ANZ was already known as a reliable and user-friendly bank among foreigners and some Vietnamese banking at their branches in Hanoi and HCMC, Thuy wanted to expand that role to more Vietnamese businesses and locals. ANZ has won The Asian Banker's award as 'The Best Retail Bank in Vietnam' and the 'Best Service Bank in Vietnam', voted by Saigon Tiep Thi newspaper readers, among others.

ANZ, under her leadership, has sponsored the Annual Golden Dragon Award for the best foreign businesses in different categories and it pursues an active advertising and general marketing strategy. Thuy has also led ANZ as the first foreign bank to obtain permission from the SBV for off-site ATMs at prominent sites in cities. In the process she multiplied ANZ's visual presence and its prominence in Vietnam. This was followed by the opening of highly visible foreign currency booths at airports and the launch of Mobile Bankers services in Hanoi and HCMC. She has also played a key role in the consultation with Vietnamese authorities to allow foreign banks to establish fully foreign-owned local banks, giving them the same business opportunities as local banks, and ANZ was one of the first to be granted the 100 per cent local incorporated licence in late 2008. New branches and transaction offices will now be opened outside the previously allowed Hanoi and HCMC venues. Although still known as a business-friendly corporate bank, under Thuy's leadership ANZ is now challenging local banks in the retail sector. 'Competition is healthy as it benefits the customers with better services', she recently said. A major concern for banks now is the difficulty of finding suitably trained staff. In this area she has also showed leadership by recruiting and training significant numbers of staff at an early stage in anticipation of expansion and of ANZ's higher profile. Her leadership has significantly enhanced ANZ's brand recognition.

As a result of her drive and 'quiet' confidence, she is a member of several chambers of commerce and other business committees, advising and interacting with ministries and the central bank on the banking and financial sectors. She has not only transformed the quaint ANZ head office building in Hanoi to a modern bank, but also played a key role in shaping the modernizing of banking in Vietnam.

Source: ANZ (2008); conversations with Thuy Dam

Case Study 3.4: Dr Truong Gia Binh, Chairman and CEO, FPT Corporation

FPT was established in 1988 based on the concept of 'the promotion of finance and technology'. Truong Gia Binh, then recently graduated with a PhD in mathematics from Lomonosov University (former Soviet Union) and Dean of Hanoi School of Business, was a founding member of FPT. It survived the 'dotcom bubble' and the 1997 Asian financial crisis to develop into a key driver of Vietnam's information and related technologies emancipation.

Currently, FPT is one of the largest private corporations in Vietnam with revenue of over US$1,000 million in 2008 and 9,000 employees. FPT group consists of more than 14 subsidiaries, or branch companies, covering telecommunications, software distribution and development, hardware and mobile telephone distribution, entertainment, media, technical education and investment activities. Its own shares have been trading consistently among the top performers in Vietnam for several years.

Although still surrounded by energetic, competent young managers who were his initial founding partners, Binh is considered to be the key driving force of the team. A creative thinker who is constantly devising new ways to use technology to improve the quality of life, Binh is also one of the most influential forerunners in the new brand of Vietnamese leaders. He has not only made the jump from 'central economic planning thinking' to 'market economy thinking'; he is effectively one of the leaders and drivers in Vietnam's silent revolution.

FPT describes its vision as 'striving to be a company guided by technology innovations, committing to the highest level of customer and shareholder satisfaction, contributing at best to the society, and having the most favourable working environment for all employees that enables them to explore their maximum potential in their professional career as well as spiritual life'.

Under Binh's leadership, FPT's strategy is to be a leading infrastructure development force providing e-services to the community. IT and telecommunications play an essential role in the digital age to provide the most convenient products and services for 'e-citizens'. By providing effective competition to Vietnam's state-owned telecommunications organization, FPT is leading the drive for modernization in this sector.

The strategy is based on the perception that the internet has made profound changes to the world and has become an opportunity for

Vietnam on its integration path into the world (after also joining the WTO). With the rapid growth and widespread use of the internet, e-services are seen as key tools that not only support organizations to compete effectively, but also to bring about convenient and innovative improvements in daily life.

Binh has taken FPT to become a key distribution partner with software giants such as Microsoft, Cisco, Oracle and IBM, and also as a major distributor of Nokia and other hardware products. Yet, Binh says his dream is for Vietnam to become a key software developer and exporter. His vision was also clear when FPT decided to convert its in-house training capacity into 'FPT University' to ensure a steady supply of qualified technicians and engineers for FPT's expansion. Binh has not only managed to lead FPT but also to establish a clear recognizable FPT brand and corporate identity by using one of the most effective marketing tools available to business: consistent success. This happy course of events for FPT is in large measure attributable to Truong Gia Binh.

Sources: FPT (2008); news media and informal conversations with Dr Binh

Challenges

It can be expected that the marketing function in Vietnam will be faced with a number of challenges in the coming years. On the one hand, there will be the challenges resulting from good economic growth and continuous changes in the business and regulatory environments. On the other hand, the post-2008 global economic downturn will bring challenges of a different kind. First, managers need to develop an integrated marketing approach, not only in regard to management coherence in sales, promotion and distribution, but also to the strategic integration of product choice, pricing policy, promotional activities and the developing of consistent and reliable distribution channels. This integrated approach must be supported by an integrated marketing communication strategy (IMC) as a form of adding value to marketing efforts. The design of such plans to maximize the marketing message and develop strategic advantage through professional marketing is a key challenge (Kotler, 2003: 583).

Secondly, in addition to an integrated management approach, firms must endeavour to reduce reliance on sales promotion as their main marketing activity *inter alia* by developing more rounded staff. Pharmaceutical firms, for example, are legally obliged to hire only qualified medical doctors and pharmacists as marketing and sales staff. This situation of unsuitable but highly educated staff causes a shortage of these people in their professions, but does not enhance professional marketing. Engineering graduates seeking jobs have no business, financial or marketing training, which makes them inadequately trained to deal with marketing their company's services, negotiating contracts, project management or evaluating feasibility of projects.

Thirdly, Vietnamese firms must develop the capacity to market abroad to be able to compete successfully. Vietnam is increasingly dependent on exports to sustain economic growth, and to generate foreign currency reserves. Along with the challenge of developing Vietnamese brands, marketers need to develop competitive skills to market their products abroad successfully and to build good customer relations with foreign partners. This aspect is also linked to the need to develop more indigenous Vietnamese brands able to be exported. Vietnam is a leader in the production of fine silk garments, many of which are exported to fashion houses and upmarket department stores and boutiques in Europe and the US. However, hardly any of these are recognizable brands domestically and none are recognized abroad. Coffee, nuts, rice, rubber, wood, furniture, ceramics, crude oil and seafood are also important Vietnamese exports with no recognizable brand awareness abroad. Vietnam Airlines, FPT and Vinashin shipbuilding may be the exceptions.

Fourthly, brand awareness, brand reputation and brand management can be developed more aggressively and coherently in the domestic market. Firms such as Vinamilk, Vinaphone, FPT and some of the banks are making progress in this area. As Vietnamese consumer habits change, their traditional loyalties to local brands decline and consumers have no hesitation in switching to foreign products on the basis of perceptions of quality, safety and reliability. Prime examples of these are preferences for known foreign brand pharmaceutical and cosmetic products. High-end luxury goods, such as Piaggio motorcycles and Japanese-manufactured expensive Honda scooters, enjoy better reputations than locally produced models, although the latter compete well as cost leaders.

Vietnamese firms should focus on developing a longer-term perspective in CRM. The short-term focus on quick profits harms relations with actual and potential customers and there is a need for sensible and sustained CRM. This fifth challenge is also linked to the issue of IMC discussed above. Press and public relations are high priorities of firms in developed markets, not only in times of crisis, but also for new product launches, to publicize important company news and to enhance brand awareness (Czinkota and Kotake, 2001: 430). In Vietnam this is a complex issue. Essentially newspapers and magazines are tightly controlled by authorities, while local TV stations are in the hands of government. Journalists have little discretion in the printing of news items or writing opinion columns. These are controlled by editors from a 'politically acceptable' perspective and, where this is not the criterion, financial incentive is the rule rather than the exception. Building good relations with trade journals and journalists still needs to be supplemented with further measures to ensure company 'publicity'. Advertisements are also scrutinized for 'correctness' and to ensure that public morals are not corrupted. This is part of a wider issue of low salaries and wages, cost structure and ethics, which will not be elaborated on here but which impacts on the planning of integrated marketing communications.

Sixthly, managers also need to develop sales tools such as direct marketing, the internet, public relations and other buying incentives (Kotler, 2003: 609). The balance between the cost of advertising, promotion, sales activities, and public relations is evolving and a challenge for firms in retail marketing is to 'rise above the clutter' that Kotler refers to, to be able to differentiate themselves from the many others with similar colourful posters, brochures and advertising. The cost of mass marketing tools has thus far outweighed the perceived benefit and more focus has been given to people-intensive sales techniques (Meyer *et al.*, 2006) while the alignment of these costs with regional averages would greatly benefit local industry and consumers as well (Mindshare, 2007).

Socially responsible marketing is only at an early stage, although some examples of CSR activities are evident. Generally, there appears to be a high awareness among reputable Vietnamese and foreign firms of the need to have ethical and responsible advertising and other promotions. In the real estate market CBRE and Savills, for example, have set the trend with professional conduct, but this is still an area where unscrupulous smaller operators exist and where a proliferation of sales websites and advertising channels have added to consumer headaches. The introduction of ADSL and broadband to Vietnam has increased the number of internet users and the number of commercial websites 30-fold or more since 2003. While control is still an everyday phenomenon in parts of business life in Vietnam, this is largely an unregulated area where suspicious innovation and creativity are found. This seventh challenge will come under the spotlight as WTO commitments and greater awareness of responsible corporate governance evolve.

Management development and business training need more focus. Neupert, Baughn and Dao (2005: 173) found that local managers most often identified the 'need for professional development' as the most important aspect for managers to be successful in international business, followed by issues such as interpersonal skills, problem solving skills, business knowledge and marketing skills. Foreign managers in Vietnam, on the other hand, identified challenges as Human Resource Management (shortages, communications, T&D), product knowledge and local business practice, ethics and corruption, and cultural differences. Not only foreign investors in Vietnam, but also local firms need to focus on employee and manager development to ensure success in business, including the multi-dimensional marketing function. Considering that there are some two million household enterprises and 120,000 private companies in Vietnam, not counting the large SOE sector, the development need is significant (Vietnam Economic News, 2008).

Finally, the ninth challenge relates also to foreign firms in Vietnam (i.e. the need to promote the transfer of marketing management competence). While foreign partners in joint venture marketing companies (still a government requirement to operate in this sector) are often seen as the source of both knowledge and capital, the transfer of knowledge to Vietnamese marketing professionals is usually limited to those within the JVEs. There is little horizontal transfer between private JVEs and SOEs. SOEs offer limited career mobility, restricting benefits such as status, career advancement opportunities and connections to those willing to work for many uninterrupted years in the same SOEs (Speece *et al.*, 2003). Government contracts therefore favour local SOEs, continuing the cycle of unprofessional, uncompetitive marketing practice. The future of a JVE partnership in Vietnam depends not only on the commitment of the foreign partner but, to a great extent, on the ability of both the foreign and local partners to establish a relationship of trust, effectively manage conflict and transfer knowledge and skills (Tsang *et al.*, 2004). This underscores the importance of 'soft skills' and relationship building as a critical business and management skill for Vietnam.

Marketing managers and staff in Vietnam are faced with the challenge of developing marketing practices suited to business conditions and the characteristics of their customers. This means neither copying best practices in developed economies blindly nor continuing with outdated practices and habits learned at a time of a centrally planned economy. The solution is to develop professionalism among marketing staff, and marketing practices which are effective and at the same time aligned with the level of 'consumer maturity' in particular sectors. Studying the experience of forward-thinking enterprises would assist in that quest for professionalism.

Conclusion

Marketing in Vietnam is undergoing changes in step with broad economic change and developments in business management. International firms operating in Vietnam set the trend by applying known marketing best-practice in their operations, and well-managed Vietnamese firms are increasingly following these practices. At the marketing management level, among local firms, key developments are in the organizational place and status of marketing management, as well as in the involvement of marketing managers in strategic decision making about products, prices and distribution. In cases where marketing managers are not enjoying the same status as production or financial managers, firms increase the risks of strategies being too inside-out, based on resources, with little consideration to market intelligence and market characteristics – the outside-in approach to strategy. The former was traditionally the case in Vietnam. Companies in different markets for particular products and services need to reflect carefully on the impact the wrong focus could have on their positioning and core competences.

In the area of marketing professionalism, there are still mixed practices in Vietnam. Sales, promotions, public relations, corporate communications, customer and community relations are a few of the functional business areas associated or equated with marketing. Among SMEs in Vietnam it may be some time before those in the medium-sized category can overcome this mindset and confusion about the true role and place of marketing as a key integrating management function. Among small and micro enterprises, there is still, generally speaking, a long way to go. SOEs are still enjoying a privileged place in the economy as a result of government support, but this will inevitably become more difficult to sustain fiscally. These organizations will have to develop more professional marketing practices to be able to compete and survive. Universities are in a position to improve marketing management education and training. The government can play a role by lifting the remaining restrictions on foreign firms establishing operations in advertising and branding, and by equitising the SOEs operating in advertising and promotion.

Buyer behaviour is changing rapidly in Vietnam and it is quite possible that consumers are ahead of producers and local marketers in their grasp of the dynamics of the market place. A 'young' population profile is shaping the future of business in Vietnam. Suppliers in all spheres are being challenged to understand and keep up with the nature and quantity of demand. Market research is rapidly adapting to play its role in understanding the needs, product/service usage and attitudes of increasingly sophisticated consumers. The current relatively small size of the consumer market, because of traditional economic limitations, is a constraint but the potential for rapid growth cannot be over-estimated. Marketing managers and their associated business colleagues in sales, promotion, and other areas of customer interface will have to make a concerted effort to develop more professional practices.

Finally, marketing management in Vietnam should build on its steady progress to develop towards the concept of more strategic marketing performance, moving beyond merely managing the marketing function well. Marketing performance requires marketing managers to assume a leadership role in the enterprise to develop the strategic core competence of their businesses. This would bring Vietnamese businesses closer towards best practices in other Asian countries such as Korea, Singapore and Japan. Global economic conditions became significantly more turbulent post-2008 and this unpredictability will also challenge Vietnamese marketing managers. Variable consumer confidence, the shortening of product life cycles (especially those imported from abroad), and the tight financial situation in firms highlight the risk that business leaders may think primarily about short-term survival rather than long-term prosperity.

The SBV estimated that Vietnamese banks are less exposed to the global financial crisis than banks abroad, but the crisis would inevitably impact on Vietnam's export markets and therefore their level of exports, while domestically firms and individuals would find it more difficult to obtain access to credit. Reduced growth may lead to reduced consumer confidence and reduced consumer spending in Vietnam. This, in turn, would impact on company revenues and spending on advertising and other marketing tools. Nevertheless, Vietnam is relatively well positioned to weather the storms of the post-2008 global economic downturn and this should assist firms to maintain wise marketing strategies aimed at long-term survival and prosperity.

In conclusion, this chapter examined the state of marketing management in Vietnam, the ongoing changes managers face and the future challenges they will have to cope with. Widely divergent practices, ranging from outdated marketing practices to professionally accepted best practices in strategic marketing and marketing management make Vietnam a complex marketing environment. External threats in the form of post-2008 global economic conditions and foreign competition following accession to the WTO also bring opportunities for local firms which have trained marketing staff and comply with international standards of business practices. Domestic weaknesses in the areas of poor marketing training and fragmented marketing practices can be overcome while better branding activities and marketing communications with a long term orientation could make a significant contribution to more effective marketing. Fundamentally, Vietnam is an economy in transition with strengths such as intelligent consumers, focused leaders and innovative business people. Marketers will be challenged to harness the dynamism of the continuously changing business environment towards building the marketing profession and implementing effective marketing strategies and practices. This is the dynamism of the changing face of marketing management in Vietnam.

Bibliography

A.C. Nielsen (2008) Available at http://vn.nielsen.com/site/index.shtml (accessed October 2008).

Amchamvietnam (2008) Available at http://www.amchamvietnam.com (accessed October 2008).

ANZ (2008) Available at http://www.anz.com/Vietnam (accessed October 2008).

ATP Vietnam (2008) (ATP news service). Available at http://www.ATPVietnam.com (accessed September/October 2008).

Baothanhhoa (2008) Available at http://www.baothanhhoa.com.vn/news/32416.bth (accessed 11 October 2008).

CIEM (2008) (Central Institute for Economic Management) Available at http://www.ciem.org.vn (accessed October 2008).

Czinkota, M.R. and Kotabe, M. (2001) *Marketing Management*. (2nd edn), Australia: South-Western, Thomson Learning.

De Burca, S., Fletcher, R. and Brown, L. (2004) *International Marketing: An SME Perspective*. Harlow, England: Pearson Education Limited.

De Mooij, M. (2005) *Global Marketing and Advertising, Understanding cultural paradoxes*. (2nd edn), California: Sage Publications.

Deutsche Bank Research (2007), 26 July 2007, ISSN Print 1612–314X. Available at http://www.dbresearch.com (accessed October 2008).

Doanhnhansaigontieubieu (2008) 'Chris Morley, former Managing Director of A.C. Nielsen'. Available at http://www.doanhnhansaigontieubieu.com.vn (accessed October 2008).

Dutch Lady (2008) 'Double confirmation: Dutch Lady Vietnam products free from melamine', 10 October 2008. Available at http://www.dutchlady.com.vn (accessed October 2008 and 17 March 2009).

Economist, The (2009) 'The World in 2009', January 2009. Available at http://www.economist.com/countries/Vietnam.

Euromonitor (2008a) Available at http://www.euromonitor.com (accessed 3 October 2008).

Eurominotor (2008b) Available at http://www.portal.euromonitor.com.ezproxy.lib.rmit.edu.au/passport/DocumentView.aspx, source for Euromonitor consumer research reports (accessed 3 October 2008).

Euromonitor (2008c) Available at http://www.euromonitor.com/Consumer_Foodservice_in_Vietnam (accessed 11 October 2008).

Farley, J., Hoenig, S., Lehmann, D.R. and Hoang, T. N. (2008), 'Marketing metrics use in a transition economy: The case of Vietnam', *Journal of Global Marketing*, 21(3), 179–90.

FPT (2008) Available at http://www.fpt.com.vn (accessed October 2008).

Global Retail Development Index TM (2008) Available at http://www.atkearney.com/index.php/Publications/at-kearneys-global-retail-development-index.html (accessed October 2008).

Hicks, R. (2008). 'Gough to lead newly-formed Red in Vietnam', *Asia's Media & Marketing Newspaper*, 26 March 2008, 9.

Hicks, R. (2008) 'Vietnam: the truth about the "new China" ', *Media, Asia's Media & Marketing Newspaper*, 10 January 2008, 18–9.

Hoa, V. (2007) 'Teenage market hard to please', *The Saigon Times Weekly*, 31 March 2007, 14, 22–3.

Hofstede, G. (1991) *Cultures and Organizations*. New York: McGraw-Hill.

Hofstede, G. (1980) *Culture's Consequences*. California: Sage Publications.

IBM (2008) Available at http://www.ibm.com/vn/ (accessed October 2008 and 15 March 2009).

IconGroup International, Inc. (2000). 'Marketing & Distribution in Vietnam, Executive Report on Strategies in Vietnam'. Available at http://www.icongroupedition.com.

Kluckholn, C. and Androdtbeck, F. (1961) *Variations in Value Orientations*. Evanston, Ill: Row, Peterson.

Kotler, P. (2003) *Marketing Management*. (11th edn), New Jersey: Prentice Hall.

Massogroup (2008) 7 April, 2004. Available at http://www.massogroup.com (accessed October 2008).

Matthaes, R. (2006) 'The middle class has landed', *Vietnam Investment Review*, 20 November. Available at http://www.vir.com.vn (accessed October 2008).

Matthaes, R. (2008) Presentation to British Business Group in Vietnam (BBGV) in Vietnam, 3 November 2008. Available at http://www.TNS-Global.com.

Meyer, K.E., Tran, Y.T.T. and Nguyen, H.V. (2006). 'Doing business in Vietnam', *Thunderbird International Business Review*, 28(2), 263–90.

Mindshare (2007) 'Who says $1000 doesn't buy you much in Asia?' 18 June 2007. Available at http://mindshare.mindshareworld.com/output/page1818.asp.

Neal, C., Quester, P. and Hawkins, D. (2005) *Consumer Behaviour: Implications for Marketing Strategy*. (4th edn), Australia: McGraw-Hill.

Nestlé (2008) News statement dated 30 September 2008. Available at http://www.Nestlé.com.vn (accessed October 2008 and 17 March 2009).

Neupert, K.E., Baughn, C.C. and Dao, T.T.L. (2005) 'International management skills for success in Asia: A needs-based determination of skills for foreign managers and local managers', *Journal of European Industrial Training*, 29(2/3), 165–81.

Nguyen, T.D.K. and Neelakantan, R. (2006) 'Capital structure in small and mediun-sized enterprises: The case of Vietnam'. ASEAN Economic Bulletin, 8 January 2006 (Copyright 2006 Institute of South East Asian Studies (ISEAS)). Available at http://www.accessmylibrary.com/comsite5/bin/comsite.pl?page=document_print&item (accessed 27 July 2007).

Nguyen, T.T.M., Jung, K., Lantz, G. and Loeb, S.G. (2003). 'An exploratory investigation into impulse buying behavior in a transitional economy:

A study of urban consumers in Vietnam', *Journal of International Marketing*, 11(2), 13–35.

Nguyen, T.T.M, Nguyen, T.D. and Barrett, N. J. (2007) 'Hedonic shopping motivations, supermarket attributes, and shopper loyalty in transitional markets: Evidence from Vietnam', *Asia Pacific Journal of Marketing and Logistics*, 19(3), 227–39.

Nguyen, V.B. (2008) Deputy Governor, State Bank of Vietnam; EUROCHAM Vietnam briefing, Hanoi, 24 October 2008 (Nguyen Van Binh briefing attended by author).

Openshare (2008) Available at http://www.openshare.com.vn (accessed October 2008).

Peterlik, R-U. (2007) Unpublished doctoral dissertation on buyer behaviour in Vietnam. University of Vienna, Unit for Economic Psychology, 2007–08.

Pew Global (2002) Available at http://pewglobal.org (accessed 3 October 2008).

Porter, M.E. (1985) *Competitive Advantage: Creating and sustaining superior performance*. New York: The Free Press.

Ralston, D.A., Nguyen, V.T. and Napier, N.K. (1999) 'A comparative study of the work values of North and South Vietnamese managers', *Journal of International Business Studies*. 4th quarter, 30(4) Online. 00472506.

Regoverningmarkets (2007) Available at http://www.regoverningmarkets.org (accessed 3 October 2008).

Schwartz, S.H. (1994) 'Beyond individualism/collectivism: New cultural dimensions of values', in U. Kim, H. Triandis, C. Kagitcibasi, S.C. Choi, and G. Yoon (eds.), *Individualism and Collectivism: Theory, Methods, and Applications*. Thousand Oaks, CA: Sage.

Speece, M., Quang, T. and To, N.H. (2003). 'Foreign firms and advertising knowledge transfer in Vietnam', *Marketing Intelligence and Planning*, 21, 3, 173–82.

Stocking, B. (2007) 'Cultural divide splits Vietnam', *Seattle Times, Nation & World*, 26 February. Available at http://seattletimes.nwsource.com/html (accessed 13 June 2008).

Thanh Nien News (2008) 'Local IT training just not worth it: meeting', 2 October. Available at http://www.thanhniennews.com/education/?catid=48&newsid=42480 (accessed 5 Novemebr 2008).

TNSPS (2008) Available at http://www.tnsps.com (accessed October 2008).

Trompenaars, F. and Hampden-Turner, C. (1998) *Riding the Waves of Culture*. (2nd edn), New York: McGraw-Hill.

Trin, T. (2007) 'Understanding Vietnam – A look beyond the figures'. Deutsche Bank Report. Frankfurt.

Trung, T. (2007) 'Competition seen stronger in marketing services', *The Saigon Times Daily*, 16 January, no 2862. Available at http://www.saigontimes.com.vn (accessed October 2008).

Tsang, E.W.K., Nguyen, D.T. and Erramilli, M.K. (2004) 'Knowledge acquisition and performance of international joint ventures in the transition economy of Vietnam', *Journal of International Marketing*, 12, 2, 82–103.

Unilever (2008) Available at http://www.unilevervn.com (accessed 4 September 2008, October 2008 and 16 March 2009).

Unilever Vietnam (2008) Available at http://www.unilever.com.vn/ourcompany/newsmedia/default.asp (accessed October 2008).

Unilever Foundation Report (2008) Available at http://www.unilevervn.com (accessed 16 March 2009).

Van, T. and Trung, T. (2008) 'Portrait of the consumer', *The Saigon Times*, 30 August 2008, 36, 26–27.

VCCI (Vietnam Chamber of Commerce and Industry) (2008). *Vietnam Business Annual Report 2007*. Hanoi: National Political Publishing House.

Ven (2008) Available at http://www.ven.org.vn/business-law/kfc-vietnam-a-ten-year-story (accessed 11 October 2008).

Vietnam Economic News (2008) xviii (6162), 15, 21 October 2008.

Vietnam News, 19 October 2007. 'How to improve corporate governance', 17. Available at http://www.vietnamnews.com.vn.

Vietnam News (2007a) 'Finance industry faces skills shortage', 1 August. Available at http://vietnamnews.vnagency.com.vn/showarticle.php.01LAB010807.

Vietnam News (2007b) 'Real estate workers badly needed', 22 October. Available at http://english.vietnamnet.vn/social/2007/10/7508361.

Vietnam News (2008a), 'Training and foreign consultants needed to meet demands for CEOs', 10 March 2008, xviii (5940), 3.

Vietnam News (2008b), 29 October 2008, xviii (6170), 1–2.

Vietnam Investment Review (2008), No 888, 1–13, 22 October.

Vinachem (2008) Available at http://www.vinachem.com.vn (accessed 4 September 2008).

VNTrades (2008) (VNTrades news service) Available at http://www.vntrades.com (accessed September/October 2008).

Vu Quoc Thai (2007) 'Real estate workers badly needed', *Vietnamnet*, 22 October 2007. Available at http://english.vietnamnet.vn/social/2007/10/7508361 (accessed October 2008).

VVG-Vietnam (2008) Available at http://www.vvg-vietnam.com (accessed 4 September 2008).

World Values Survey (2001) Available at http:://www.worldvaluessurvey.org (accessed October 2008).

Yin, S. (2007) 'Brands at the starting gate' *Media: Asia's Media & Marketing Newspaper*, 23 February 2007, pp.20–21. Available at http://web.ebscohost.com.ezproxy.lib.rmit.edu.au/ehost/delivery.

Other websites

http://atpvietnam.com/vn/doanhnghiepvoicodong/10266/index.aspx (accessed October 2008).
http://www.esomar.org (accessed October 2008).
http://www.marketingvietnam.org (accessed 16 March 2009).
http://www.mpi.gov.vn (Ministry of Planning and Investment).
www.vinamilk.com.vn (accessed October 2008).

4 The changing face of financial market management in Vietnam

Oliver Massmann and Chris Rowley

- Introduction
- Key issues and new developments
- Case studies
- Challenges
- Conclusion

Introduction

Vietnam is one of the most dynamic markets in the Asian region. Since financial institutions and authorities are part of the overall economic system, they are not only heavily involved in changes but firmer financial foundations would benefit the country's competitiveness. The financial sector in Vietnam has been undergoing substantial and structural changes at tremendous speed. These changes entail major challenges for financial managers – for example, pressure on the currency with regard to its exchange rate and inflation, and stock market fluctuations between huge daily gains and losses. At the same time, the debt market remains underdeveloped and, as a consequence, requires attention by both the authorities and managers to enhance the system and to cope with new developments. The main challenges consist of transforming the state-owned banking sector and establishing a sub-national debt system.

This chapter first outlines Vietnam's financial environment and the key issues and developments in the area. Organizational cases are provided to allow comparison between banks of different origins which are starting to compete in the financial market in Vietnam. Case studies of individual managers are also provided to add extra 'voice' to developments in this area. Finally, some of the challenges and the tasks still waiting to be addressed in the changing face of financial market management in the future are outlined.

Key issues and new developments

In the next section we outline the key issues and developments in the area of financial management. These include those revolving around:

- currency and monetary policy;
- the banking system;
- sub-national debt;
- the stock exchange.

Currency and monetary policy

Monetary policy – and the currency policy that is part of it – is a key influence of the financial system of a country, affecting the pace and direction of overall economic activity. Therefore, the currency system and monetary policy, an outline of its recent history, together with implications for managers, are provided.

The Vietnamese currency can be characterized as a typical emerging market currency, with all its advantages and drawbacks for companies and managers working with it. On the plus side there is the competitive advantage caused by the relatively low value of the VND compared to other currencies in the developed world. This has been one of the key factors contributing to overall low production costs. One effect of this is seen in companies transferring their production to Vietnam, not only away from developed countries but also increasingly from China or Malaysia, two of the more developed emerging markets (Jung and Wagner, 2008).

With regards to the currency, the public foreign exchange control, currently governed by the OFE adopted in 2005, is the main responsible authority. As depicted in Figure 4.1, the currency is strongly connected to the US dollar; the OFE endeavours to keep the exchange rate at a certain high level and reacts quickly to global economic changes to keep the rate at a relatively consistent value.

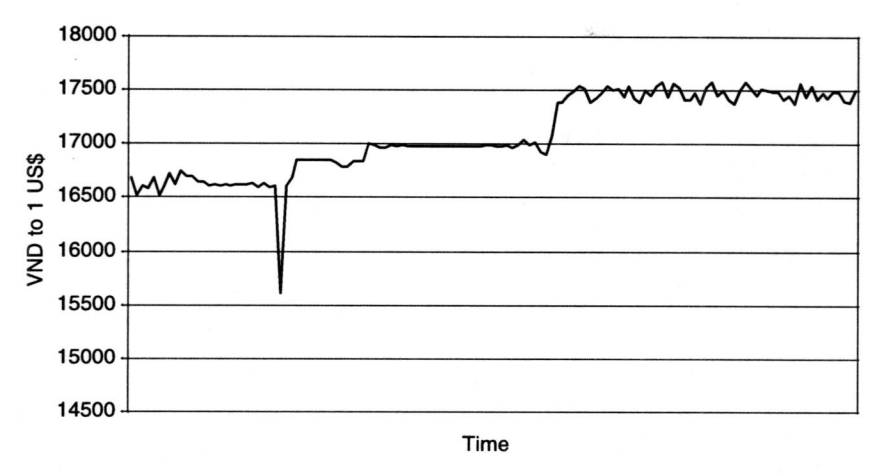

[Figure: line chart with y-axis "VND to 1 US$" ranging 14500–18000 and x-axis "Time"]

Figure 4.1 US$ versus VND exchange rate, 1 September 2008 to 1 July 2009.

Source: Self-made

Vietnam used to have a double exchange rate system: one officially determined and fixed rate for official and certain business affairs (e.g. banking); the other a free exchange rate formed by all the other market participants (see Canler, 2008). This dichotomy was replaced with a single rate that reflected market forces. Nevertheless, exchange rates are still subject to certain state controls to prevent exchange rate shocks. As a consequence, the exchange rate of the VND is, in practice, pegged to the US dollar, although as a managed exchange rate within a determined corridor. This pegging is the main reason for the relatively low value of the VND and it is aimed at boosting the competitiveness of the export industry, one of the most important areas of the economy.

The breakouts from the narrow rate corridors meticulously created by the OFE occurred only with the devaluation of the US dollar against all other currencies with the post-2008 global financial crisis (as shown in Figure 4.1). The government tried to maintain a value of the VND that enabled the country to remain an important and expanding production- and export-based economy. Managers and companies doing business in Vietnam can rely on the government for actions to comply with this goal for two reasons. First, the economy is still not sufficiently developed to assimilate a shift from the production of low technology goods because there are not enough skilled workers for high tech production (see Chapters 1, 2 and 9 of this book).

Therefore, it is important to be competitive on costs. Second, the huge demand for imported goods requires considerable exports for a balanced trade account. Hence, a finance manager working for a company in Vietnam, despite its characteristics as an emerging market, can also rely on currency stability. On the other hand, the economy is still small in absolute figures and more sensitive to turmoil on the financial markets.

The main drawback of an emerging market currency in the world economy, and a monetary policy primarily aimed at growth, is the higher exposure to inflationary risks, as will be discussed later. This exposure limits the possibilities to boost growth by means of monetary policy if inflation takes off. The government had managed to keep inflation at sustainable levels until 2007 given the annual GDP growth of approximately 7.5 per cent since 2000. Figure 4.2 provides an overview of recent growth rates. This changed from late 2007 when inflation increased as a result of the depreciation of the US dollar against most other currencies, the widening money supply in Vietnam and the surge in food and energy prices (Morgan Stanley, 2008).

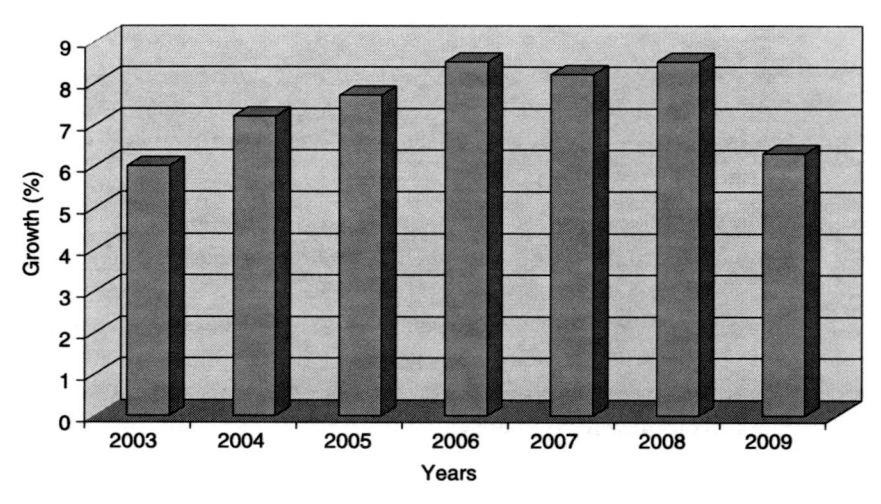

Figure 4.2 Year-on-year GDP growth.

Source: Self-made

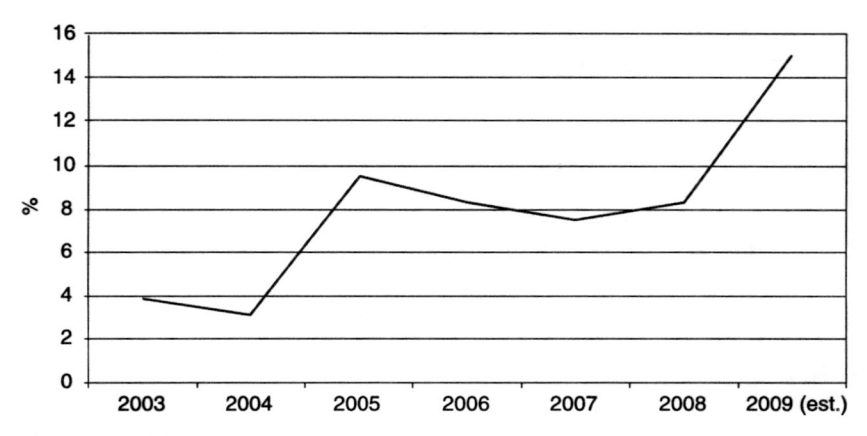

Figure 4.3 Year-on-year inflation (%).
Source: Self-made

Figure 4.3 shows the average year-on-year inflation rates. Inflation poses a serious threat to the ability of Vietnam to meet its growth targets, and it even jeopardizes any real growth in the short term (Qiao, 2008). Furthermore, as Vietnam's own past shows, the general experience is that even the potential threat of inflation is enough to disrupt normal production and consumption practices and depress investment, thus lowering growth. This situation is likely to worsen as a result of the post-2008 global financial crisis. On the other hand, the declines in commodity prices, triggered by lower growth expectations, could ease inflationary pressures and thus benefit the overheated economy.

Independently of the post-2008 global financial crisis, inflation is taken seriously by the government and the SBV. As a reaction to post-2007 inflation the authorities implemented anti-inflationary measures, such as increasing interest rates by 850 basis points (discount and refinancing rate) and 575 basis points (base rate), reducing public expenditure by 10 per cent (excluding salaries) and issuing a cap on credit growth at 30 per cent (Lee, 2008).

On the other hand, managers need to be aware that, in the long run, currency pegging to the US dollar contributes to the VND being undervalued because the economy is steadily growing at a faster pace than the economies of the developed world. This trend triggers pressure on the VND to appreciate against currencies like the dollar, yen and euro, which in turn would have a negative effect on the export competitiveness of Vietnam. This issue will be examined in later sections.

Nevertheless, the VND, by emerging market standards, is a stable currency. Monetary policy basically targets growth, but at the same time is gradually shifting towards the control of inflation so that the monetary environment can be regarded as sufficiently reliable for companies to work in it.

The banking system

The banking system was reorganized in 1990, separating the central bank, the SBV from commercial banks and paving the way for the entry of the private sector. The restructuring and strengthening of the SBV continued with a view to transforming it into a modern and independent central bank charged with executing monetary policy and supervising the banking system. According to the orientation given by the banking reform roadmap in 2006, the SBV is to be relieved from the responsibility of exercising the ownership rights of the SOCBs, by 2010, since this conflicts with its role as supervisor of the same banks. These rights and duties will then lie with the new shareholders – either the state or private investors – after the equitisation process.

As a result of the reforms, the banking and finance sector now has more participants, is more diversified and offers an expanded variety of financing activities. There are four main types of credit institution: commercial banks, policy lending institutions, credit funds (operating mainly in the countryside), and financial companies. Commercial banks include three SOCBs, 37 domestic private JSBs, 37 branches and sub-branches of foreign banks, and five JVE banks established with foreign and Vietnamese capital and 100 per cent foreign-owned banks (VTO, 2008). There are also 45 ROs and foreign financial and credit organizations in Vietnam, more than 20 leasing companies and nearly 1,000 people's credit funds.

The SOCBs are all owned by the SBV, which is heavily involved in their day-to-day management and controls the appointment of board members and senior management. The banking sector in Vietnam is still dominated by the SOCBs, which account for 70 per cent of total assets in the banking system as well as 70 per cent of total bank loans. Some 37 JSBs, which serve mainly SMEs, account for about 15 per cent of total credit and 20 per cent of the total chartered capital in the banking system. Banks with foreign capital, whose clients are mainly FIEs, account for about 10 per cent of bank loans (VTO, 2008).

State-owned banks

The six SOCBs are set to decrease. The equitisation (privatization) of SOCBs is under way and is scheduled to be completed before 2010, except for the Bank for Agriculture and Rural Development (Agribank, *Ngan hang nong nghiep va phat trien nong thon*), whose equitisation is expected to be completed later. According to the government's roadmap, the state's shareholding in equitised banks will be gradually reduced to 51 per cent by 2010. A single institutional investor will be allowed to hold a maximum of 10 per cent and the total foreign holding of shares will be limited to 30 per cent. It is also planned to convert the Development Assistance Fund (one of the two existing policy lending institutions) into a development bank – one of its functions will be to serve as an export–import bank providing financial services to exporters and importers.

The process of equitisation of Vietcombank, one of the 'big four' SOCBs that dominated the banking sector, started with an initial public offering in late 2007. The government sold about 97.5 million shares, which represented a 6.5 per cent stake in the bank, raising VND 10.5 trillion. The three remaining wholly SOCBs – Vietinbank (formerly Incombank), BIDV and Agribank – are set to follow a similar route. However, the process is already behind schedule.

Joint stock banks

Whereas each SOCB specializes in one area of finance – for example external trade, industrial development or infrastructure projects – the private or semi-private JSBs generally operate in major urban areas and specialize in providing credit to smaller companies or in retail finance. The JSBs are quicker to adopt new technologies and are considered better managed and more profitable, since they depend on their cost efficiency and profit ratios.

Foreign banks

Foreign banks, branches, fully foreign-invested subsidiaries or JVE banks, account for the smallest part of the banking market. These banks are subject to different treatment, depending on their country of origin. The most favourable treatment is enjoyed by US and EU banks since bilateral trade agreements have been signed and ratified with those countries.

As a consequence of WTO membership, it also became possible in 2007 for international banks to establish fully foreign-owned subsidiaries under Vietnamese law. These subsidiary banks are in principle entitled to 'national treatment', which means that they are to be treated on an equal level with locally owned banks. They are, for example, allowed to take unlimited local currency deposits from corporate borrowers and issue credit cards.

In general, the banking sector has come a long way since 2000. The number of financial institutions has increased, people's confidence in the banking system has improved and more private funds have been attracted. The rapid development of banks and credit organizations has been directly attributed to the attractiveness of the Vietnamese monetary sector as it has a much higher profitable ratio and ownership capital than other economic sectors. Yet, the banking sector remains underdeveloped and it still has a long way to go to fulfil its function of efficiently allocating financial resources. Also, there are large troubled loan portfolios as a consequence of the absence of systematic accounting practices, a weak legal framework governing the banking sector, poor financial disclosure, a lack of skilled HR in the credit area, pressure from local and central authorities on banks to lend to SOEs, and also corruption.

Sub-national debt

Another important area regarding the financial system is the development of an additional, private level of finance. Sub-national debt describes a state-independent lending system which helps to form a broader basis for the finance sector and is common in developed countries. The needs and requirements for such a development, and considerations concerning a sub-national debt system, have been noted (De Angelis *et al.*, 2008), and include the following. The government has recognized the urgency of improving the physical infrastructure because of its importance in social and economic development of the country. Infrastructure is considered one of the critical bottlenecks that is seriously eroding competitiveness and constraining the economy.

Various factors have combined to create a major financial constraint to creating the required improved infrastructure as Vietnam has developed. These include the following:

1. limited reliance on official development aid loans, especially as Vietnam will no longer have subsidized credit from international financial institutions as a key source of financing;
2. reliance on central government budgets to finance infrastructure that cannot sustain the capital investment requirements; and
3. banking system's practice of mobilizing short-term deposits to finance long-term investments that raises the cost of capital and creates burdens on the financial system.

These issues underscore the need to develop alternative sources of long-term financial resources for infrastructure development. The availability of long-term financial resources for financing infrastructure investments is essential for enhancing economic development, attracting FDI and domestic investment and enabling authorities to cope with globalization.

The pressure on the government to expand borrowing options for the regional administrative bodies (sub-nationals) has increased, intensified by the trends towards decentralization, privatization and globalization of financial markets, resulting from *Doi Moi* and WTO reforms. A widened and free debt market offers the promise of increased access to capital and lower borrowing costs provided by competing companies.

Another desirable result could be more efficient allocation of capital. Thus, the existing dichotomy of disposable capital with HCMC in the South and Hanoi in the North could be displaced by a more comprehensive system of capital allocation. Also, the implementation of local projects (e.g. expanding infrastructure) could be realized more easily and in a shorter time because of fewer bureaucratic obstacles connected to the current centralism.

Many policy, institutional and legal changes are needed to improve results on the ground in infrastructure financing. These include capacity development at the sub-national level and an improved legal and regulatory framework for sub-national financing in conjunction with the development of sub-national capital markets. The absence of a comprehensive and consistent legal framework leaves major risks from contingent liabilities to the national treasury from irresponsible local borrowing (as happened in Brazil in the 1990s and Argentina in 1999–2002).

A legal and regulatory framework of rules and regulations would stimulate demand because investors would gain familiarity and confidence with tradable securities, investment choices and information regarding risks. Clear and binding regulations on borrowing for sub-national bodies would mitigate moral hazard and encourage hard budget constraints. Additionally, the utilization of sub-national state bonds, whether general obligation or revenue backed or a combination thereof, could help to develop capital markets just by adding additional asset classes to the market of tradable securities.

The new Law on Securities (2007) means that there is now an understanding that a comparable level of effort is needed to thoroughly examine the legal and policy framework for the financing of sub-national investments. This includes revenue backed bonds for infrastructure such as ports, bridges and roads.

At the request of the Ministry of Finance and Ministry of Planning and Investment to help Vietnam to develop a strategy for financing and developing infrastructure, the VCCI conducted an assessment of the need for a comprehensive framework for sub-national project/infrastructure finance in Vietnam. It outlined a Work Plan that identified the steps necessary to establish a legal and regulatory framework for sub-national financing activities and recommended the development of a comprehensive sub-national debt framework.

However, the promotion of sub-national debt is clearly *not* an end in itself (De Angelis *et al.*, 2008). It is important for financial managers to be aware that longer term sub-national debt to finance current account deficits only increases the stock of debt obligations that must be paid from future revenues without increasing productivity and means of repayment. Premature borrowing, before a sub-national entity has established its creditworthiness or identified clear investment priorities, is likely to drain local budget resources and add risk to the fiscal system. The underlying purpose of sub-national credit market development is to increase the volume of local capital investment in support of essential sub-national services. Prudent borrowing can augment investment capacity. Well-designed investment and borrowing plans can finance the construction of needed infrastructure facilities and repay debt incurred from the future earnings of the facilities themselves through user charges or cost savings in service operations.

Also, general obligation, revenue-based financing or combinations thereof, rather than the use of physical collateral, is likely to be the source of sustained growth in the volume of private sector sub-national lending (De Angelis *et al.*, 2008). If debt repayment is predicated on revenues or cost savings to be generated from the project, both the sub-national borrower and the lender tend to focus with more discipline on the economic costs and benefits of the proposed undertaking.

The stock exchange

Important steps in economic development were the opening of the HCMC and Hanoi securities trading centres and the Vietnamese stock exchanges in HCMC (2000) and Hanoi (2005). Establishing a functional stock exchange market supports the policy of global integration, economic renewal and establishing a market economy with 'socialist characteristics'. On a comparative basis, the HCMC stock market price index (VN Index) is a more reliable indicator of long-term trends in Vietnam's financial market than the Hanoi stock exchange price index (HASTC). While the Hanoi stock exchange accounts for about one-third of Vietnam's total stock market capitalization, it was very small until 2006 when a large number of new listings increased its importance (IMF, 2007).

The inflow of foreign currency and FDI is supported by the establishment of a modern stock exchange market. Many incentives can be found in the securities trading system. Tax incentives for securities trading came into effect in 2000 and a precept for more transparency to protect against expropriation was passed. These tax incentives apply also to companies with activity in the funds management sector and similar listed commercial papers for emitters. Finally, private investors can benefit from an income tax exemption for profits from dividends, bonds and trading with commercial papers.

At the same time as these developments, Vietnam is anxious to keep the currencies of foreign investors in the country. All stocks and funds at the HCMC stock exchange have to be listed and traded in VND. As of 2008, 156 stocks and 391 bonds are listed on the HCMC stock exchange, as shown in Table 4.1.

At the start of the stock market's existence, some initial problems had to be overcome. The first official trade was delayed several times because of technical difficulties; trade was only conducted on Monday, Wednesday and Friday for two hours; and initially, only two companies were listed for trading (Jeffries, 2001: 417 *et seq.*) Initial growth by the number of companies and market capitalization was rather slow. At the end of 2000, just five JSBs were listed, which were joined by five more listings in 2001 and another ten listings in 2002 (Truong, 2006: 138).

The real emergence of the stock market occurred in late 2006. At the end of 2005 the market – including the HCMC and Hanoi securities trading centres – still consisted of only 41 listed companies, with a market capitalization of less than US$1 billion. This number had risen to 193 listed companies by April 2007, representing a market capitalization of about US$20 billion (World Bank, 2007; Vuong, 2008). Also, nearly 400 former SOEs were privatized and transformed

Table 4.1 Vietnam's Stock Exchange, 2008

	All	Stocks	IFCs	Bonds
Total listed shares (1 share)	551.00	156.00	4.00	391.00
Per cent (%)	100.00	28.31	0.73	70.96
Listed volume (1,000 shares)	4,917,019,00	4,490,393,22	252,508,99	174,116,80
Per cent (%)	100.00	91.32	5.14	3.54
Listed value (VND mil.)	64,954,517,47	44,903,932,21	2,520,555,76	17,530,029,50
Per cent (%)	100.00	69.13	3.88	26.99

Source: Adapted from HCMC Stock Exchange (July 2008).

into JSCs. Those firms will come into consideration as investment targets for domestic as well as foreign investors in the future. Further SOEs are also to be first equitised and then privatized. Nevertheless, in the first instance, a majority stake is to be held by the government as it wants to retain control in the sensitive sectors.

The required permission of the SSC (*Uy ban Chung khoan nha nuoc*) is a bottleneck for new applicants who want to enter the stock market. A company's economic data has to comply with a number of strict requirements before it is allowed to emit its shares onto the stock market. According to Article 12 of the Securities Law (No 70/2006/QH11, 2007) applicants have to hold at least VND 10 billion as ordinary capital. In addition, in accordance with later decrees, applicants must also have realized profits during the previous two years, at least 20 per cent of the shares have to be sold to more than 100 different investors and the emitting companies have to undergo separate auditing (Decree 14/2007/ND-CP of the Government dated 19 January 2007, Setting Forth Detailed Regulations for Implementing a Number of Articles of the Securities Law).

The government's concern to tackle these difficulties has led to the passing of a number of rulings. The SSC and the STC want to adhere strictly to the guidelines given by the government and the CPV. The SSC and STC aim to enter into a close cooperation with the competent ministries and organizations to improve the legal framework step by step. The education of HR will be improved by international cooperation. In addition, public attention will be directed to the stock exchange and the securities market. The stipulated fees for business enterprises and companies that are involved in trade with commercial papers may not exceed the legal limits. The LFI already contained a plan for the admission of FDI companies to listing on the stock exchange. Despite the willingness to implement foreign know-how regarding trade in commercial papers, foreign investors were only allowed to buy the shares of Vietnamese companies to a limited extent to avoid a foreign majority and retain a degree of independence. Foreign investors are allowed to buy up to 49 per cent of the shares of listed companies and up to 100 per cent of unlisted companies, except in some specific sensitive sectors like telecommunications, energy and oil exploration. Consequently, limitations on foreign investors who want to conduct business on the Vietnamese stock market, remain.

The stock market, together with the inward remittances, has increased the availability of capital to ensure stability in the national balance of payments. However, many organizations, including a number of SOEs, have fallen into the temptation of easy money making in stocks. By late 2007, SOEs had invested 37 per cent of their capital in securities, banking and real estate rather than focusing on their core business activities and 'this had negative effects on their solvency and, in some cases, even threatened their economic viability' (EU Counsellors, 2008: 12).

As can be seen in Figure 4.4, the VN Index has been in turmoil since 2005. However, despite this, the stock exchange plays an invaluable role in channelling investments to listed companies concentrated in construction, industrial goods and services and the exploitation of

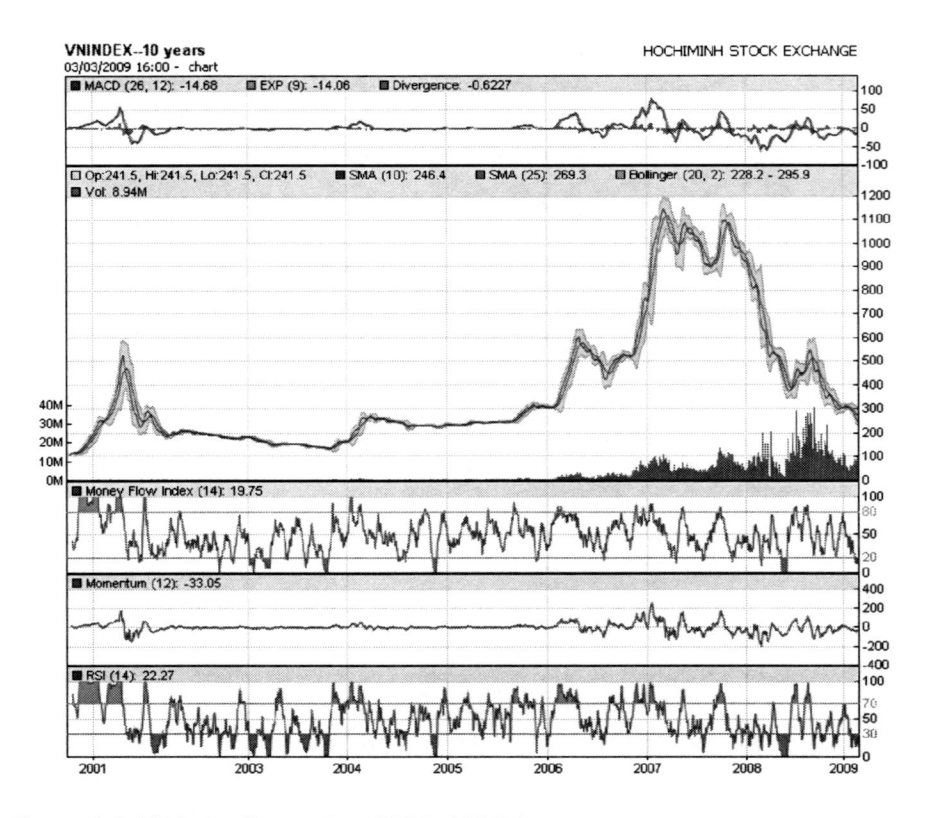

Figure 4.4 VN Index fluctuation, 2000–2007.

Source: HCMSE (2009)

natural resources (EU Counsellors, 2008). Similarly, the IMF, in its country report, suggests a further tightening of prudential controls on the banks' stock market-related and foreign exchange rate risks, proactively dealing with banks whose soundness may be threatened by exposure to such risks and further strengthening the enforcement of securities market regulations (IMF, 2007).

The management of the HCMC stock exchange is aware of the problems ahead and has passed an agenda to further improve trading conditions. These include:

1. creating better conditions for JSCs to list their stocks on the exchange;
2. developing information systems in order to publicize information fully, timely and accurately;
3. improving software to follow and detect insider and corner trading;
4. upgrading IT systems to meet the market's requirements and international standards, continuing to apply and complete the 'remote terminals' project, and move to non-floor trading methods;
5. proposing sensible policies for a strong securities market;
6. continuing to sign more memoranda of understanding with other stock exchanges and together hold the cross-listing on the exchange floors.

These points may appear to be rather general and vague, but they are at least evidence of the awareness of, and understanding for, the needs of companies, shareholders and investors.

Case studies

The following section of case studies add detail and 'voice' to developments in the changing face of this area of management in Vietnam. The organizational cases of a public SOCB and a private JSB are quite alike regarding the amounts of assets, income and deposits. In this comparison we sum up the cornerstones of both banks, compare them and set them in the context of state and private ownership. This comparison helps to show whether the different positions of the banking houses within the Vietnamese system (with regard to the founders, owners and controlling systems) is mirrored in their balance sheets or business plans. These are followed by case studies of individual managers in this area, again adding the all-too-often missing real life 'voice' to developments in management.

Case studies of organizations

> **Case Study 4.1: Southeast Asia Commercial Bank (SeABank)**
>
> Founded in 1994, the SeABank was one of the first Vietnamese commercial JSBs. Its long-term aim is to be among the leading commercial JSBs in Vietnam. The SBV rated SeABank with 'A' for four consecutive years. The head office is located in Hanoi. By the end of 2007, the total number of SeABank branches and sub-branches in Vietnam was 50. It planned to open 37 more in 2008 in the provinces of Vietnam. In 2009, an additional 39 branches and sub-branches in both existing locations and new provinces, will be established.
>
> SeABank is striving to become a banking–financing group (SeABank Group) with brand reputation and asset quality in the Vietnamese market and gradually in regional markets. The bank aims to offer a wide range of products, from conventional commercial banking to investment banking and financial services to targeted customer segments. SeABank provides loans, products for accumulated interest saving, flexible original deposit withdrawals, as well as funds for manufacture, commerce and import–export. Medium-term finance borrowing, mortgage of valuable papers, discount from vouchers and local and international remittance services, are also available. The bank serves enterprises in various economic sectors operating in the production and trading fields.
>
> In August 2008, Société Générale announced the acquisition of 15 per cent of SeABank to gain access to the Vietnamese market via a reference bank. The SBV has approved the transaction.
>
> Source: SeABank (2008)

Case Study 4.2: The Housing Bank of Mekong Delta (MHB)

MHB, a SOCB, was founded as a financial institution in 1997 and is headquartered in HCMC. MHB has 160 branches and sub-branches spread over 32 provinces and cities in Vietnam and maintains relationships with approximately 300 foreign banks in 50 nations worldwide. The bank house wants to establish 30 more sub-branches to adequately serve the growing banking service and credit needs of the country's emerging SMEs and to respond to the demand for housing and infrastructure construction, particularly in the Mekong Delta.

Among the SOCBs, MHB is the youngest and fastest growing, ranked seventh in total assets, with nearly VND30 trillion. MHB provides loans and investments for housing development and socio-economic infrastructure development. The company also acts as a so-called 'bank of foreign affairs', which means that it gives bank guarantees to foreign affiliates of domestic companies. This is common practice in industrial countries to encourage foreign companies to have business connections with domestic entities.

MHB's core business includes the granting of loans to SMEs, as well as to individuals and households. In particular, MHB provides asset-secured loans for construction companies to develop infrastructure for residential areas, especially in the Mekong Delta region, mobilizing the capital of individuals, domestic and foreign organizations.

Loans and investments have grown from VND1,206 billion in 2001 to VND14,453 billion in 2006, representing a twelve-fold increase. The loan portfolio includes mainly credit to finance housing and infrastructure constructions and repairs, trade and services and agricultural production.

In early 2008 the government approved the partial privatization of MHB. The bank will be allowed to sell up to 31.9 per cent of its shares: 15 per cent to strategic investors, 13.11 per cent to the public, 1.79 per cent to employees and 2 per cent to its trade union. The remaining 68.1 per cent will be held by the state. MHB has hired Deutsche Bank AG Singapore to draft a privatization plan and advise on the initial public offer.

Sources: MHB (2008); Reuters (2008)

Although different in their ownership structure, in both cases the banks are competing for the same type of customer, mostly private individuals. By comparing the balance sheets and profit gains we can analyze whether these different structures have any effect regarding the efficiency and rentability of the banks. As can be seen from Table 4.2, the banks are nearly equal regarding their total assets. This is also true for their planned growth. Both banks want to raise their total assets to approximately VND40 trillion. SeABank, nevertheless, seems to have grown more quickly – for instance, its total 'owner's equity' has increased threefold, where MHB's only grew by approximately 10 per cent.

Table 4.2 Comparison of balance sheets of SeABank and MHB (VND million)

	SeABank 2006	SeABank 2007	MHB 2006	MHB 2007
Total assets	10,200,417	26,241,087	18,734,297	27,531,552
Fixed assets	32,655	65,056	171,969	232,397
Long-term investment	27,500	44,900	36,000	–
Trading securities	263,488	759,110	–	550,601
Loans to customers	3,353,998	10,994,812	9,976,585	13,756,662
Balances with the SBV	214,771	511,669	261,926	402,160
Total liabilities	9,144,881	22,874,629	17,805,270	26,436,061
Borrowings from SBV	–	–	941,965	447,494
Deposits from customers	3,511,683	10,744,177	5,005,864	9,939,911
Total owner's equity	1,055,536	3,366,458	929,027	1,069,197
Chartered capital	500,000	3,000,000	774,200	810,191

Source: Adapted from MHB (2009); SeABank (2009).

Concerning loans to customers, MHB was able to increase the level from VND9,976,585 million in 2006 to VND13,756,662 million in 2007, a remarkable growth of 30 per cent. At the same time, however, SeABank managed to increase its levels from VND3,353,998 million to 10,994,812 million, a 300 per cent growth. This achievement may result from the more independent position of SeABank. MHB, as a SOCB, has a planned and more or less fixed scope of business and is meant to operate mainly within that. While this is also true for SeABank, it can also choose more where to specialize and on what to focus. SeABank is more flexible and can adapt faster, hence is able to respond to customers' needs more precisely (see Table 4.3).

While the gap between the total incomes of the banks is becoming smaller, SeABank seems to have better control over expenses and,

Table 4.3 Comparison of income statements of SeABank and MHB (VND million)

	SeABank 2006	SeABank 2007	MHB 2006	MHB 2007
Net profit	98,551	298,847	74,092	138,025
Net interest income	176,146	469,014	428,742	593,858
Net gain from fees and commissions	8,236	6,692	2,293	10,026
Net gain from dealing in foreign currencies	−12,985	1,421	1,910	17,411
Net gain from dealing in trading securities	24,442	27,523	–	7,875
Net gain from dealing in investment securities	–	–	–	10,313
Total operating income	195,845	552,330	436,457	645,821
Total operating expenses	52,126	103,920	283,048	417,073

Source: Adapted from MHB (2009); SeABank (2009).

therefore, claims higher profits. With regard to the specific sources of income, there are major differences between the banks. While SeABank relies more on trading securities, at MHB a larger share of income originates from dealing in foreign currencies.

At a HR level, MHB remains larger, while SeABank is growing more quickly. While MHB increased the number of its staff from 2,338 in 2006 to 2,580 in 2007, SeABank nearly doubled its workforce, increasing the number from 498 in 2006 to 831 in 2007. As far as staff education is concerned, in both banks about 70 per cent of employees hold a university degree.

Another similarity between the banks is the ability to attract more private customers. Both banks are continually trying to offer attractive services concerning loans as well as availability and access to banking services. This is, for example, by establishing more branches and sub-branches, issuing as many cash and ATM cards as possible and getting connected to other electronic banking systems. So, their customer base is not at all as different as one might expect. This is confirmed by the rapidly increasing number of ATMs being installed. The banks are trying to increase the access to, and availability of, their services to the public, especially private individuals. For these, a higher number of ATMs can be the important criterion when choosing a bank.

In summary, the SOCB and JSB have more similarities than one would expect given the difference in their positions within the banking system and their origins. Even though one is a state and the other a private entity, there are no major differences in annual balances with the SBV; both are growing and positive. Yet, there is a considerable difference in the amount of borrowings from the SBV. While SeABank did not need such borrowings at all, MHB did. This shows the inability of SOCBs to act as independent market participants, especially in respect to acting as 'banks of foreign affairs', where decisions are made in political terms and not in economic ones and certain losses are in the nature of things. A SOCB also has to expand and develop a business plan in order to be able to compete for customers.

The equality in almost all of the benchmark data certainly can be seen as a harbinger of a process in Vietnam's banking sector, adjusting the state and the private banks to a certain level of equal competition. In the long run, *Doi Moi* and WTO obligations will lead to a more consistent way of banking in Vietnam, and one which is more similar to world standards. This competition-driven environment, together with the necessity for sensible management and planning, is one of the key factors in the way to the establishment of an independent banking system serving as a sub-national debt system.

Case studies of individual managers

Case Study 4.3: Mr Sandy Flockhart, CEO, HSBC Asia Pacific

Mr Flockhart was appointed CEO in 2007. He gave his views on HSBC's development in Vietnam: 'It is common knowledge among global investors that Vietnam has one of the fastest growing economies in the region, with GDP averaging 7 per cent plus over the past few years, and continued robust FDI growth – a record $20.3 billion in 2007. However, what is more exiting to us are facts such as GDP per capita doubling over the last 10 years, 50 per cent of Vietnam's 87 million people being under the age of 30 and only 9 per cent of the population having a bank account. These factors point to a very compelling growth story, particularly in the financial services sector.' Mr Flockhart thinks that Vietnam's financial and banking industry is still in its infancy, but that competition is likely to increase, as the government has sharpened its focus on financial sector reform over the last few years by gradually easing banking restrictions and creating a level playing field for foreign banks. Thus, the CEO notes: 'Yes, competition will increase as a result but we believe this is a good thing as it will foster industry development and encourage competitive pricing and service improvements to the benefit of banking consumers.'

Outlining HSBC's strategy for growth in Vietnam, Mr Flockhart refers to a two-pronged approach: 'This comprises both strategic investments and organic growth. Our investment in Techcombank and Bao Veit give us greater participation in the growth of Vietnam through our partners' large customer reach and established businesses. Local incorporation will give us balance in developing our own operations organically. This will allow us to operate on a larger scale and expand our service and product range.'

With regard to the comparative strengths and weaknesses of foreign and local banks, Mr Flockhart outlines the limitation on branch networks for foreign banks as a clear disadvantage for foreign banks. For example: 'As you can see, although we have a long history in Vietnam we only have one branch in Ho Chi Minh City and another in Hanoi, together with a representative office in Can Tho. The new decree allowing foreign banks to incorporate locally will put foreign players on a level playing field with local banks, and it will allow us – as a foreign player – to expand our network nationwide and bring in products and services that we have successfully offered in other parts of the world to the local market in Vietnam. Local banks on the other hand have a good understanding of the local market, including the spending behaviour of local consumers. But the local players are also fast learners, with many large local banks quick to realize the benefits of partnering with foreign institutions. Our alliance with Techcombank, Vietnam's fifth largest, is testament to that.'

However, HSBC's growth strategy is also faced with the general problem of finding, and keeping, qualified staff, which HSBC has to address. So, the CEO asserts: 'We, as well as the other foreign banks in Vietnam, are facing a scarcity of banking talent. It takes a lot of time to recruit, train and develop a professional banker, so the topmost priority for us is how we ensure staff retention.' With regard to this, Mr Flockhart outlines the long-term vision to build HSBC into the 'best place to work'. HSBC has also been cooperating with some of the top universities in organizing workshops and seminars and, in 2007, launched its own training centres in Vietnam.

Source: Vietnam Economic Times (2008a)

Case Study 4.4: Mr Ashok Sud, Chief Executive, Standard Chartered Vietnam (SCV), Laos, Cambodia

Mr Sud is, *inter alia*, responsible for SCV's franchise and strategic development in Vietnam. Standard Chartered was, together with HSBC, the first international bank to receive the in-principle approval to establish local incorporations as a consequence of Vietnam's WTO commitments. The approval was announced during a visit of Vietnam's Prime Minister Nguyen Tan Dung to the UK in 2008. Mr Sud said this announcement reflected two things: 'First, the strong desire for Vietnam to further strengthen its banking sector by allowing a select few, large international players to play a bigger role in the sector. Second, it is a strong statement on Vietnam meeting its WTO commitments both in spirit as well as process.'

SCV intends to open between 20 and 30 branches throughout Vietnam over the next three to five years. Mr Sud thinks that local banks will continue to dominate, at least numerically. For instance: 'So, by opening the sector up there will be a 'qualitative' rather than a 'quantitative' change in banking services, with local Vietnamese banks continuing to dominate the sector by retaining a more than 90 per cent share in the foreseeable future of say five to ten years.'

With regard to the future development of the banking sector, Mr Sud believes that the SBV should try to ensure 'that the banks are well capitalized given their risk profile and the turbulent international environment. Additionally, whilst there is clearly a need to have more banking services given that less than 10 per cent of Vietnam's population have bank accounts, the SBV, I am sure, are ensuring that licences to open new banks are given to those who have a strong track record in the financial sector, as experience has clearly shown in other developing countries that only such banks survive in the long run'.

In light of the post-2008 global turmoil in the financial markets, Mr Sud describes SCV's strategy for sustained competitiveness as being based on four key pillars – the first two being strong capitalization and the ability to create appropriate products and services for local consumers. As a third pillar, he lists SBV's ability to lead its corporate customers into the international debt markets to raise funding as 'in the near future it would be critical for large corporates in Vietnam to tap into these international markets for debt on a continuous basis. Standard Chartered will assist our client base in Vietnam to enter these markets with relatively smaller amounts in the early stages but

> gradually increasing to very sizeable raisings in the future. This has been our experience in most developing Asian markets'. As a fourth pillar Mr Sud stresses the importance of the bank's employees: 'Last but not least, competitive advantage, especially in the service industry, will come from the quality and attitude of its human resources.'
>
> Source: Vietnam Economic Times (2008b)

Challenges

The financial environment in Vietnam entails difficult challenges for the government as well as for financial managers in private companies. Some of the most important issues are highlighted in the following section.

Currency and monetary policy

The main challenge regarding the currency system is to preserve its stability both in terms of price and exchange rate. While the latter has been the main objective of monetary policy, inflation pressures after 2008 became so strong that a shift towards a policy targeting inflation became more important. Given the fixed exchange rate, the authorities are limited to the policy measures to fight inflation, as outlined in Text Box 4.1.

> **Text Box 4.1: Vietnam's monetary policy measures and exchange rate regime**
>
> **Interest rates**
>
> After the liberalization of deposit and lending interest rates, the SBV only intervenes through the prime rate, rediscount rate and refinance rate. However, as a result of market expectations on VND appreciation, the central bank is constrained on further interest rate hikes for fear they may attract more hot money inflows and exacerbate the liquidity problem.

Open market operations and reserve requirement ratio

The SBV has the right to use repo/reverse repo, central bank bond issuance/retirement and reserve requirement ratio adjustment to absorb or inject liquidity into the banking system. In addition, in late 2007, the central bank enacted a suspension of foreign exchange activities in non-current account transactions to prevent further liquidity injection through capital inflows. Other non-conventional sterilization measures include issuance of short-term deposit certificates (in late 2007) and involuntary issuance of promissory notes to commercial banks (in early 2008).

Credit control

The monetary authority has no direct control over commercial banks' loan extensions (except through regulations on loans in specific categories such as equities).

Exchange rate regime

The SBV officially maintains a managed floating exchange rate, but this regime is classified by the IMF as a conventional *de facto* fixed peg, based on the fact that the VND has depreciated against the US dollar at a less than −2 per cent per year pace since 2003, with a daily trading band capped at +/−1 per cent.

Source: Qiao (2008)

According to the World Bank (2008), Vietnam's money stock grew by 47 per cent in 2007, posing a severe threat to price stability. The reasons for this were the sharp increase in lending mentioned earlier in the chapter, together with the steady inflow of FDI and indirect investment caused by a policy of free capital flow. Usually a currency would become more expensive under these circumstances. However, with the exchange rate pegged to the US dollar and the authorities determined to maintain its low value, this was not an option. As a consequence, the widened money supply (caused by the government buying US dollar-denominated assets to hinder an appreciation of the VND) resulted in inflation (World Bank, 2008).

This situation above constitutes the core problem of monetary policy in Vietnam – the conflict with the hypothesis of the so-called

'Impossible Trinity' with its three elements: (1) free capital movement, (2) fixed or quasi fixed exchange rate, and (3) independent interest rate policy. According to some, a combination of these three elements is not possible. Vietnam has opted for a fixed exchange rate and free capital movement. This is similar to Hong Kong but it accepts the fact that it is subject to interest rates that are (albeit set by the Hong Kong Monetary Authority) determined mainly by the US Federal Reserve Bank and thus not appropriate to the economic phase in Hong Kong; this is not an option for Vietnam because it has a much younger, less developed and more diverse, economy.

Vietnam sets its own interest rates and separates the domestic markets from the US-led Western financial markets. Yet, in doing this, the government has to keep in mind that high interest rates make foreign capital more attractive to investors. This would put the VND under pressure because its value towards other currencies could then quickly fall, resulting in inflation. To increase the money supply subsequently – for example, by lowering interest rates – would only boost inflation because there would only be limited confidence in the stability of the VND. Thus, the SBV is not as independent in its interest rate policy as it might seem at first glance.

The challenge is to allow the VND to moderately appreciate against the US dollar, which would ease inflationary pressure to some degree. Furthermore, the authorities could think about limiting capital inflows (as China did). Finally, capital gains tax and a moderate property tax could be introduced. In the long term these measures would enhance price stability and outweigh the short-term negative effects on export competitiveness. Also, inflation at sustained high levels can have the same effect as an appreciation of the currency.

In the longer term, as the whole economy develops, Vietnam could have the objective of introducing a fully independent central bank by substantially amending the Central Bank Law. The SBV executes the policies of the Ministry of Finance and the Ministry of Planning and Investment, but this could be changed by such a move.

The monetary situation entails a challenge for financial managers in Vietnam to react to potential changes. China is a good example of showing that a gradual appreciation of the currency does not necessarily pose insurmountable problems for the companies affected.

Moreover, Vietnam still has a price level significantly lower than China's, particularly owing to its shorter economic growth period. Therefore, Vietnam will be able to preserve its competitive advantage in costs for some time. Depending on the size and business of the company, a hedging strategy covering the risk of appreciation of the VND in the medium term can help to minimize the exposure to exchange rate changes.

Banking system

Vietnam's banking sector risk was rated at CCC (Economist Intelligence Unit, 2008). This was mainly as a result of the excessive credit growth post-2008 mentioned earlier in the chapter, which adds to the risk that the non-performing loan (NPL) ratio will increase and surging inflation will erode the real value of the banks' receivables. Also, despite making remarkable improvements in banking services, other new services – such as property and capital management, securities trading, financial consultancy, insurance and investment – have not yet been developed fully. Meanwhile, the workforces at SOCBs are regarded as abundant in terms of quantity, but these banks suffer a shortage of qualified HR (see also Chapter 2). In addition, SOCBs are dominated and controlled by state management agencies and are facing difficulties, such as poor property quality, financial reporting and profitable possibility, and high management costs and rates of bad debts (Vietnam Business Finance, 2008).

The government is working to dispose of the banks' large portfolio of NPLs, tightening loan classification standards, ensuring appropriate provisioning against loan losses and increasing capital requirements to meet internationally accepted minima. The latter has been introduced in an attempt to promote the establishment of a small number of strong banks in contrast to a large number of weak banks. During the period 2001 to 2005 the government invested VND 10 trillion to recapitalize the banks and encourage them to establish their own asset management companies to facilitate NPL disposal. Market analysts have been sceptical, however, about the officially reported NPL levels, suggesting that the true ratios in the SOCBs range from 15 to 30 per cent, well above the reported ratios of 1 to 3 per cent in 2006. Moreover, rapid growth in retail and real estate lending, as well as direct and indirect credit for stock purchases, still suggest a possible build up of NPLs.

Some see an inherent conflict of interest in combining both the ownership and supervision of SOCBs in one agency – namely, the SBV – with negative implications for a strong supervisory regime. Importantly, management of the SOCBs will pass at some point from the SBV to the State Capital Investment Corporation (Vietnam's holding company for equitised entities), which will remove the SBV from the daily control of banks. In addition, the government is drafting legislation to make the SBV more independent, including the reorganization of banking supervisory responsibilities. In the meantime, the Vietnamese authorities continue to focus on further strengthening supervision and improving the efforts of the banks to comply with regulations (Mayeda, 2008).

Sub-national debt

The challenges a sub-national debt system will face include the following (De Angelis *et al.*, 2008). To begin with, Vietnam's laws and regulations do not adequately allow for the development of a viable sub-national debt market or the utilization of modern financing techniques, such as project revenue bonds and securitizations. Therefore, stabilizing the legal and fiscal framework in a manner that clarifies legal rights and supports predictable sources of revenue for sub-national entities, while giving them clear policy control over part of their finances, is required. Potential participants in a sub-national credit market – borrowers, banks and other interested parties – are a natural and important constituency for these reforms. Recommendations as to the elements of a legal framework to assist the development of sub-national borrowing have been suggested (see De Angelis *et al.*, 2008).

A successful sub-national credit market should be built in two directions: from the top down, in terms of a legal and policy framework that will support efficient credit market operations; and from the bottom up, in terms of practical experience for banks and other lenders in making loans and investors in securities, and for sub-national entities in borrowing to finance high priority investments and making timely debt service payments. Both tracks – building a supportive legal and policy framework and accumulating practical experience in sub-national lending – could move forward simultaneously. In several countries, where sub-national credit markets have developed the utilization of pilot projects, this has turned out to be effective in creating templates for final implementation. Commencing pilot projects is also very useful in identifying possible issues that need to be addressed to further the development of the credit market.

As in many developing countries, Vietnam's regional administrative bodies are faced with the challenge of under-investment and under-maintenance in basic infrastructure and building stock, and addressing stricter pollution control requirements. Properly regulating sub-national access to the capital market can increase efficiency on sub-national expenditures and present alternative financing sources to badly needed local infrastructure investment, while being consistent macro-economically. Such borrowing regulations would help to bring local budgets explicitly into compliance with the standard national budgetary system consistently, which is a critical step in the institutional reform process.

Vietnam has a window of opportunity to establish a well-conceived legal framework for sub-national credit markets that can help preclude the emergence of problems that other transitional countries had to address retrospectively. Low sub-national creditworthiness and capital market failures are not inducing much municipal borrowing. Such modest current sub-national borrowing may also be viewed as an advantage. Many other countries have found themselves confronted with the reality of large-scale sub-national borrowing, and then have been obliged to try to construct *ex post facto* a legal framework that will accommodate the healthy borrowing that occurred while curbing the excesses.

Vietnam is in a position to develop the legal and policy framework first, and to do so at a reasonable pace, in anticipation of future market development. Vietnam also can learn from risks that have become clear in other countries. Excessive borrowing by sub-national entities or debt issuance in the absence of an adequate legal framework (one that clarifies critical issues like the status of guarantees or remedies available to lenders in the event of a sub-national entity's non-payment) has exacerbated national economic crises in several countries. The promises of soundly based sub-national borrowing are large, but the risks involved in badly prepared borrowing are also high. Poor experiences in sub-national borrowing at the initial stages of market development can substantially stall credit market development. For example, after a US$25 million default in 1998 by Odessa in Ukraine on a poorly conceived and structured municipal bond issue, more than 10 years passed before investors were willing to extend credit to sub-national entities without a central government guarantee.

All parties (sub-national entities, national government, banks and potential investors in sub-national debt) share an interest that the policy issues surrounding credit market development be well understood. Also, an appropriate legal framework needs to be in place before the market springs into action and substantial lending occurs.

A sub-national credit market, in short, fits within a public finance system that assigns significant decision-making power and financing responsibility to sub-national entities. A sound system of inter-governmental finance is an important precondition for the development of a sub-national debt market. Particularly important are efforts to make the revenue stream to sub-national entities more predictable through improved incentives to raise local revenues and user charges and by creating a clear and transparent system of transfers.

Experience has shown that once certain essential elements of a comprehensive legal framework are put into place and the key stakeholders and institutions are prepared, the development of a sub-national credit market can develop very quickly. This can be seen in the following case examples in Text Boxes 4.2 and 4.3.

Text Box 4.2: The Credit Market in Romania

The law on local public finance was adopted in 1999. The first two issues of municipal bonds were issued in 2001 with short maturities (two years) and high interest rates (37 per cent). These issues were 'pilot projects' and created both procedural and documentation templates that were then followed by other issuers. Within three years the annual volume of municipal credit had increased and represented 14 per cent of all domestic debt; maturities were extended to 20 years, and interest rates were in single digits. Interest rates are between that of the Treasury debt and commercial loans. Several hundred bond issues and bank loans were issued (although many have been paid and are no longer outstanding because of the initial short maturities) and there has not been any reported default.

The legal and regulatory framework sets a permissive, but prudent guide for bank loans and bond issues. Most of the borrowing has been for water supply, sewage, roads and housing. Issuers are mostly larger cities, but these are also smaller cities that have good economic potential, for example, tourism or strong industry.

Source: Qiao (2008)

Text Box 4.3: The Credit Market in the Philippines and Mexico

The legal frameworks of these countries established the right of the local authority to pledge certain elements of the internal revenue allocation that it received from the central government and to have such funds deposited on behalf of creditors. Once the legal basis for the pledge of these funds was established, local authorities were immediately able to access the capital markets utilizing the pledge of such funds and additionally to have their debt guaranteed by third party financial institutions. This structure did not expand the central government's financial liability and created investor confidence.

Source: Author's research

Stock exchange issues

The price-to-earnings (PTE) ratio of a stock is a measure of the price paid for a share relative to the annual net income or profit earned by the firm per share. It is a financial ratio used for valuation: a higher PTE means investors are paying more for each unit of net income, so the stock is more expensive compared to one with a lower PTE ratio. The PTE ratio has units of years which can be interpreted as 'number of years of earnings to pay back purchase price', ignoring the time value of money. PTE ratios show that current investor demand for a company share in many of the largest listed companies was out of line with reasonable assessments of these firms' projected earnings and growth potential. A risk results from the lack of clear and present control systems. A number of observers claimed that the equity market was overvalued, noting PTE ratios.

The nascent stock market is used by two groups of investor: the large foreign investor with huge amounts of capital backing it and the inexperienced domestic investor with mostly limited capital stocks. Both groups are very sensitive to trends that could move downwards. Such trends can lead to 'pack behavior', seen in markets all over the world: if one or two major players in the market sell big packages, the rest will follow on a proportional process. The authorities are particularly concerned that a rapid reversal of the post-2008 portfolio inflows could lead to severe losses for domestic investors and threaten financial and social stability. These concerns led to the introduction of a number of measures, mentioned earlier in the chapter. The possibility of introducing some controls on capital inflow was also considered.

The IMF acknowledges that the Vietnamese authorities have taken the following five early measures in order to tighten stock market regulation and supervision, and limit the fall-out on the banking system from a possible stock market crash (IMF, 2007).

The first of these measures are the SBV's new regulations (Decision 03/2007 issued in January 2007) on the adequacy of bank capital, liquidity ratios and lending and investment limits, which have restricted the scope for new bank lending for the purchase of stocks. In particular, credit institutions are not allowed to extend credit to their securities company affiliates or grant unsecured loans financing investment or trade in securities. Additionally, the risk weight of securities-related loans was raised from 100 per cent to 150 per cent. Credit institutions were given one year in which to conform fully to the new restrictions.

Second, and at the same time, various implementing regulations of the securities law were issued to strengthen the supervision of stock market-related activities. These regulations relate to disclosure requirements, stiffer penalties for violations and requirements for improved corporate governance, including the organizational structure of securities companies and fund management companies.

Third, the SSC (also in January 2007) issued a number of official letters to securities companies and investment fund managers requesting information on their recent operations in the stock market and requiring representative offices of foreign investment funds to re-register with the SSC, as provided for in the securities law. In addition, the SSC tightened the enforcement of regulations regarding market transparency and asked listed companies to improve their provision of accurate and timely information to the public.

Fourth, the Prime Minister (in a letter issued 29 January 2007) instructed the Ministry of Finance, the SSC and the SBV to improve their monitoring of stock market-related activities of foreign investors and commercial banks, tighten the enforcement of existing market regulations and improve the dissemination of information to the public regarding the risks of investing in the stock market. In addition, the SBV was instructed to consider possible amendments to the forthcoming implementing regulations of the foreign exchange control ordinance for the purposes of tightening controls on capital inflows and/or the repatriation of capital by foreign investors.

Fifth, the SBV issued Directive 3 (in May 2007) which, among other provisions, limited the total securities-related credit exposures of banks to less than 3 per cent of their total loan portfolio. Thus, banks are required to submit reports to the SBV indicating their total outstanding securities-related credit exposures, as well as the measures taken or planned to comply with the 3 per cent cap. Reports have to be submitted monthly. The SBV's supervision department will exercise strict monitoring over any bank with total securities-related exposures exceeding 10 per cent of total loans.

Another challenge for Vietnam is the inflation rate. Along with the rising inflation rate was the descent of the VN Index in early 2009. Profits and dividends increase by roughly the same amount as inflation. Yet, the yield return cannot catch up with the inflation rate, even if they correlate quite closely (Clariden Leu, 2007). So, shares cannot offer complete protection from inflation, which reduces their attractiveness at times of high inflation. As a consequence, fighting inflation is a major task to keep the young stock exchange market attractive.

Conclusion

This chapter has indicated the opportunities and challenges of the financial market in Vietnam and the specific developments that managers have to carefully consider in view of the immature nature of the financial environment. Owing to the phenomenon of the 'the Impossible Trinity', it is critical for management to stay informed about forthcoming changes with regard to monetary policy. Vietnam's banking sector will change considerably as the government proceeds with the equitisation of the SOCBs. WTO commitments will also play an important role since foreign banks are allowed to participate in the Vietnamese market with many new freedoms and permissions.

Since the stock price boom was fuelled in large part by bank-financed retail and institutional domestic investors, well-targeted prudential measures were appropriate as a first policy response. The SBV's post-2008 steps to tighten monetary conditions have also shown some effect. While other countries have resorted to capital controls to stem inflows, the effectiveness and benefits of such measures need to be weighed carefully against their likely costs.

The stock market has gone through a phase of consolidation since early 2007, but this is still prima facie evidence of the over-valuation of some stocks. The authorities have made policy responses. Conditions, of course, changed dramatically with the unfolding of the 2008 global financial crisis. As a consequence, the risk that stock market volatility could have spill-over effects on the rest of the financial system and the real economy is more serious than ever.

In sum, the 'face' of financial market management in Vietnam has changed and has approached world standards step by step. The decision makers in the Vietnamese authorities and PEs are still in a tough learning process, although the efforts and developments show that Vietnam is able and willing to abolish established structures and try to find its own ways of transiting the socialistic economy to a competitive free economy with respect to its own history, culture and traditions. The way that the Vietnamese react to the post-2008 global financial crisis and other recent obstacles reveals that the necessities and tools of banking and financing are recognized and used.

Bibliography

Canler, Ed (2008) 'Pesos, poverty and perversions: What's wrong with Cuba's money and how to fix it'. Online. Available at http://lanic.utexas.edu/project/asce/pdfs/volume11/canler.pdf (accessed 17 March 2008).

Clariden Leu Investment Research (2007) 'Perspektiven'. Online. Available at http://www.claridenleu.com/pdf/news/home_allg/perspektiven_2007_q2_de.pdf (accessed 18 February 2009).

De Angelis, M., Winkler, J., Hoang Anh Do and Uyen Tran (2008) *A Strategy for Financing and Developing Infrastructure in Vietnam*, USAID Vietnam Competitiveness Initiative.

Economist Intelligence Unit (August 2008) *Country Risk Service Vietnam*. Online. Available at http://store.eiu.com/product/60000206VN.html

EU Counsellors (2008) European Union Economic and Commercial Counsellors, '2008 Commercial Counsellors Report on Vietnam'. Available at http://www.delvnm.ec.europa.eu/eu_vn_relations/trade_economic/Greenbook_08.pdf (accessed 18 February 2009).

HCMSE (2009) Ho Chi Minh City Stock Exchange. Available at http://www.hsx.vn (accessed 18 February 2009).

IMF (2007) International Monetary Fund, 'Vietnam: Selected issues', *IMF Country Report No.07/385*. Online. Available at http://www.imf.org/external/pubs/ft/scr/2007/cr07385.pdf (accessed 18 February 2009).

Jeffries, Ian (2001) *Economies in Transition: A guide to China, Cuba, Mongolia, North Korea and Vietnam at the Turn of the Twenty-First Century*. London: Routledge.

Jung, Alexander and Wagner, Wieland (2008) 'Vietnam is the new China: Part II – The caravan moves on', at Spiegel Online, issued 15 April 2008. Available at http://www.spiegel.de/international/business/0,1518,553301,00.html

Lee, J. (2008) 'Vietnam trip notes', *Asia Economics Special*, Deutsche Bank Global Markets Research, 25 July 2008. Available at http://www.stox.vn/stox/download.asp?id=343

Mayeda, A. (2008) 'Vietnam's banking sector', *Asia Focus*, February 2008, Country Analysis Unit, Federal Reserve Bank of San Francisco. Online. Available at http://www.frbsf.org/publications/banking/asiafocus/2008/Asia_Focus_Feb_08.pdf (accessed 18 February 2009).

MHB (2008) Available at http://www.mhb.com.vn (accessed 17 August 2008).

MHB (2009) *Annual Report 2006/2007*. Available at http://www.mhb.com.vn/en/?p=bctn.asp (accessed 18 February 2009).

Morgan Stanley (2008) *Public Information Book*. Online. Available at http://www.morganstanley.com/about/ir/shareholder/morganstanley_co_inc_may2008.pdf

Qiao, H. (2008, April) 'Vietnam: The next tiger in the making', Goldman Sachs, Global Economics Paper No 165. Online. Available at http://

www2.goldmansachs.com/ideas/global-growth/vietnam-next-asian-tiger.pdf

Reuters (2008) Online. Available at http://in.reuters.com/article/asiaCompanyAndMarkets/idINHAN25879320080325 (accessed 18 February 2009).

SeABank (2008) Available at http://www.seabank.com.vn (accessed 17 August 2008).

SeABank (2009) *Annual Report 2006/2007*. Available at http://www.seabank.com.vn/en/index.php?option=com_content&task=view&id=250&Itemid=552 (accessed 18 February 2009).

Truong, Dong Loc (2006) *Equitisation and Stock-Market Development, The Case of Vietnam*. Groningen: Centre for Development Studies (accessed 18 February 2009).

Vietnam Business Finance (2008) 'State-owned commercial banks: Opportunities and challenges', 16 February. Available at http://www.vnbusinessnews.com/2008/02/state-owned-commercial-banks.html (accessed 18 February 2009).

Vietnam Economic Times (2008a) 'Strategic and organic CEO Guest: Mr Sandy Flockhart from HSBC', issued March 2008.

Vietnam Economic Times (2008b) 'Four Pillars: Interview with Ashok Sud', issued April 2008.

VTO (2008) Vietnam Trade Office in the United States of America, 'Banking system and foreign currency regulation'. Online. Available at http://www.vietnam-ustrade.org/index.php?f=news&do=detail&id=31&lang=english (accessed 18 February 2009).

Vuong, Minh Giang (2008) 'Vietnam's emerging stock market: Profitability and growth in a statistical view'. Online. Available at http://www.ssrn.com (accessed 18 February 2009).

World Bank (2007) 'Taking stock: An update on Vietnam's economic developments'. Online. Available at http://www.worldbank.org (accessed 18 February 2009).

World Bank (2008) 'East Asia and Pacific Update: Testing times ahead'. Online. Available via http://www.worldbank.org (accessed 18 February 2009).

5 The changing face of strategy management in Vietnam

Quang Truong and Thiem Ton That Nguyen

- **Introduction**
- **Key issues and new developments**
- **Case studies**
- **Challenges**
- **Conclusion**

Introduction

Advice is judged by results, not by intentions.

Cicero

To survive in the global arena of today, any country and enterprise should have the ability to revise its strategy on a regular basis since the pace and scope of change can be surprisingly far more drastic than is usually expected. Since the introduction of the *Doi Moi* policy in late 1986, Vietnam has reaped significant economic achievement. There was a high growth in terms of GDP of almost 10 per cent annually between 1990 and 1997 (Quang, 1997; Kamoche, 2001). Even during the 1997 Asian financial crisis, Vietnam managed a considerable GDP growth rate of between 5 and 7 per cent per year on average until 2000 (CIEM, 2002). The period thereafter boasted one of the most stable and outstanding growths, which put Vietnam among the top performers in Asia, after only China (see Table 5.1).

To sustain this high growth level, the country placed emphasis on enticing FDI, overhauling the SOEs, developing HRs and unleashing the private sector. There was a new challenge to face when Vietnam decided to join the world economic mainstream. In order to narrow the existing gaps with other countries, Vietnam needs to focus more on strategy development and implementation at both

Table 5.1 Economic growth in Vietnam, 1986–2010

3rd Five-Year Plan 1986–1990		4th Five-Year Plan 1991–1995		5th Five-Year Plan 1996–2000		6th Five-Year Plan 2001–2005		7th Five-Year Plan 2006–2010	
1986:	6.5	1991:	6.0	1996:	9.3	2001:	7.1	2006:	8.2
1987:	3.4	1992:	8.6	1997:	8.2	2002:	7.0	2007:	8.5
1988:	4.6	1993:	8.1	1998:	5.8	2003:	7.0	2008:	6.2
1989:	2.7	1994:	9.0	1999:	4.8	2004:	7.5	2009:	5.0f
1990:	2.3	1995:	9.5	2000:	6.8	2005:	8.4	2010:	5.3f
Average:	3.9%	Average:	8.2%	Average:	7.0%	Average:	7.4%	Average:	6.5%

Sources: Aggregated data from Tuoi Tre (27 June 1996); TBKTSG, (16 January 2003); Quang (2006); EIU (2008);

Notes: f = forecast.

national and enterprise levels to enhance its overall competitiveness in global markets.

Generally, Vietnam's competitiveness is still low by many standards, particularly when benchmarked against many other countries in the region (see Table 5.2). This disadvantage shows the complexity and difficulty of expediting the country's socio-economic development in the new phase (CIEM, 2002). Some improvement has been made in the quality of growth and the efficiency of resource allocation, in

Table 5.2 Vietnam's overall competitiveness ranking (socio-economic indexes)

Organization	Survey	Ranking	Year
The Heritage Foundation/the Wall Street Journal	Index of Economic Freedom (1)	135 out of 162 countries	2008
The Economist	Worldwide Quality of Life Index (2)	61 out of 111 countries	2005
Reporters Without Borders	Worldwide Press Freedom Index (3)	168 out of 173 countries	2008
Transparency International (TI)	Corruption Index (CPI) (4)	121 out of 180 countries	2008
United Nations Development Programme (UNDP)	Human Development Index (HDI) (5)	105 out of 177 countries	2007
World Economic Forum (WEF)	Global Competitiveness Index (GCI) (6)	70 out of 134 countries	2008

Sources: Compiled data from (1) www.heritage.org, (2) www.economist.com; (3) www.rsf.org; (4) www.transparency.org, (5) www.hdrstats.undp.org, (6) www.weforum.org; accessed on 11 November 2008.

particular with regard to the newly emerging private sector. Nevertheless, it remains to be seen how the country will handle the complex issue of surviving the multi-sourced and mostly superior competition as an immediate result of full global integration as a new member of WTO.

Vietnam is facing a strategic choice in the post-WTO period: (a) will it be able to sustain the pace and methods of development that have been attributed to the economic and political stability of the country in the 2000s, and (b) should it continue to adapt itself to the changing conditions in the quest for further development and integration into the world's economy. Against this backdrop this chapter will first identify several prevailing problem areas that the government and business community should tackle in the face of globalization and integration. It will also discuss the country's continued efforts to adjust its strategies in response to new challenges. Case studies are presented which advocate the benefits of matching a firm's business strategies with external conditions. Finally, future challenges will be anticipated and suggested solutions provided with a view to enhancing Vietnam's competitiveness and sustainability.

Key issues and new developments

The advent of Doi Moi

Prior to *Doi Moi*, virtually everything in Vietnam was centrally organized following the operational dogmas of a communist system. However, since 1986, the economy has been in transition, moving away from a centrally planned system towards a socialist-oriented, 'multi-component' or mixed system. Although the country attained independence in 1945, it underwent 30 years of division and resistance wars before reunification and economic integration between north and south. A programme of socialist development was implemented, with collectivization of agriculture within the framework of strong centralized control and the state sector as the engine of growth. The adverse effects of the centrally planned socialist programme were heavily felt between 1975 and 1985 when the economy stagnated and there were huge budget deficits, rising public debts, rice shortage and high inflation (Tri, 1990).

In response to the poor performance of the economy and the low growth rates achieved in the mid-1980's, the CPV in its Sixth National Congress introduced the comprehensive economic programme known as *Doi Moi* (renovation) to end the subsidy-based, centrally planned command and controlled economy and replace it with a socialist-oriented, multi-sector market economy under state control. Agricultural output increased as a result of the new land reforms, along with de-collectivization of agriculture and improved private property rights, price liberalization and the opening up of the agricultural sector to market forces. The effects of the *Doi Moi* policy on the agricultural sector were tremendous as it transformed Vietnam, which faced chronic food shortages, from a net food importer to the world's second largest exporter of rice, coffee and pepper. The focus of *Doi Moi* was also to shift resources away from import-substituting heavy industry to the production of food, consumer goods and exports, reduce state intervention in business and encourage domestic and FDI by improving the business climate (Tri, 1990).

Although the CPV was still protective of SOEs, it did pass legislation aimed at creating a more favourable business climate to encourage both domestic investment and FDI so as to develop a vibrant private sector. This new series of legislation included the Commercial Law, the Law on State Bank, the Law on Credit Organizations, the Law on Import and Export Tariffs, the Law on Value Added Tax, the Law on the Encouragement of Domestic Investment, the Enterprise Law, the Land Law, the Law on Bankruptcy, the Labour Code, the Law on Encouragement of Domestic Investment, the Law of Enterprise, and the Law on FDI, which was considered to be one of the most liberal in the region.

The collapse of the Soviet Union in 1989 and other communist countries in Eastern Europe ended decades of military and economic aid. This prompted the government to reintegrate itself regionally and multilaterally to replace the loss of a major trading partner. The government initiated reforms to replace the Soviet capital flows by FDI and foreign aid. The first FDI Law passed by the NA in 1987 was revised several times and was replaced by a more comprehensive law in 1996. The new legislation was amended again in May 2000 to create an even more favourable business environment to attract FDI. The inflow of FDI peaked in the mid-1990s before it began to decline even before the onset of the Asian financial crisis in 1997 (Quang, 2000).

Economic structure

In spite of remarkable achievements as a result of the reforms, Vietnam remains very much an agricultural-based economy, with an unbalanced structure. In this economy the state-controlled sector is still considered to be the backbone of the economy and a 'level playing field' is yet to be created for the emerging private sector to operate at its full potential (see Table 5.3).

The state-owned sector

As part of the economic reform, the government put considerable effort in unravelling the state-owned sector to make it more effective and efficient. The restructuring of SOEs was considered to be a *sine qua non* condition to improve the quality of the country's economic growth. SOEs accounted for more than 38 per cent of GDP and nearly half of the bank credit in 2000 (GSO, 2009). Nevertheless, it is estimated that 60 per cent of them were loss makers or marginally profitable by 1997, notably as a result of management inefficiency, overstaffing and outdated technology (World Bank *et al.*, 2000). Until the 1990s the government still provided about 2.2 per cent of GDP annually in supplementary

Table 5.3 Vietnam's economic structure, 1995–2007

Indicators	1995	2000	2005	2007*
1. Economic structure (% GDP)	100	100	100	100
Agriculture, forestry and fishery	27.2	24.5	21.0	20.3
Industry and construction	28.8	36.7	41.0	41.6
Services	44.0	38.8	38.0	38.1
2. Sector structure (% GDP)				
State sector	40.4	38.5	38.4	36.5
Non-state sector	53.5	48.2	45.6	45.9
Foreign-invested sector	6.10	13.3	16.0	17.6
3. Labour structure (%)				
Agriculture, forestry and fishery	71.1	65.2	57.2	53.8
Industry and construction	11.4	23.4	29.9	31.9
Services	17.5	11.4	12.9	14.3

Sources: Aggregated data from MPI (2006); GSO (2009); US Department of State (2009).
Note: * Preliminary statistics

capital, subsidies, tax exemptions, debt write-offs and preferential credits to help these SOEs survive competition (World Bank *et al.*, 2000). The total debt of SOEs was estimated at VND126 billion (equivalent to US$9 billion or 32 per cent of GDP) at the end of 1999 (World Bank *et al.*, 2000); a large part of this was in the form of non-performing debts, thus further requiring more radical restructuring of the sector.

In the future, reform of SOEs will emphasize the following programmes for improving competitiveness:

- diversifying ownership through equitisation (i.e. the sale of state shares) and divestiture of loss-making SOEs, outright sale or free transfer of an entire SOE;
- liquidating SOEs that are classified as non-viable;
- restructuring the large SOEs that remain in government hands;
- establishing an adequate and effective social safety net for displaced SOE workers, estimated to be around 400,000, over five years (World Bank *et al.*, 2000: 30).

The non-state sector

The non-state sector consists of household enterprises, the domestic private sector and the FIE (wholly-owned and JVE) sector. In 1990 a new set of laws (e.g., the Enterprise Law, the Law on Domestic Private Investment, and so on) allowed household and private sector ownership to join the national economy for the first time. The growing contribution of this emerging sector will have a large impact on the country's overall economic growth in the future, both in qualitative and quantitative terms.

To meet the 7–8 per cent annual growth target for the first decade of the 2000s, total domestic private investment will need to rise to 11–13 per cent of total GDP (World Bank *et al.*, 2000: 25). This requires a more 'level playing field' for all parties involved and especially official recognition of the essential role of the domestic private sector (as in China).

As a move towards unleashing domestic economic potential, the Enterprise Law of 1999 substantially simplified the business start-up procedure. As a result, more than 10,000 different domestic firms were registered in the first five months of 2000 – an average of 2,000 new businesses per month (Saigon Times Weekly, 2002). Within only two years, by the end of 2002, there were 93,000 private enterprises and 2 million household workshops in operation, contributing up to 40 per cent of the country's total GDP. With this quick pace of development, the private sector has become a *de facto* leading economic driver, with a growth rate of 13.9 per cent annually compared to 14.7 per cent of the FIE sector and 11.9 per cent of the SOE sector (Saigon Times Weekly, 2002).

It is clear that the private sector, especially household enterprises, has had an important role in manufacturing, especially in producing goods for export (e.g. handicraft, agricultural products, etc.). According to one estimate, there were around 600,000 micro household enterprises in manufacturing, a quarter of which contributed 28 per cent of manufacturing value-added and 5,600 private SMEs in manufacturing accounting for 10 per cent of GDP (World Bank *et al.*, 2000: 26). As they are mostly stand-alone businesses having no international experience, state support to help them to improve their competitiveness in the world market is of paramount importance. In more concrete terms, comprehensive measures need to be taken by the government to allow more expansion and diversification of domestic private activities in parallel with the sluggish SOEs and advanced FIE sector.

The foreign-invested sector

FDI has contributed substantially to modernizing the Vietnamese economy since the 1990s (see Chapters 1 and 6). After a slow start, FDI inflows reached their peak between 1995 and 1997, during which time around US$2 billion per year was disbursed (GSO, 2009), making Vietnam one of the most attractive destinations among the ASEAN nations. This trend slowed down dramatically as a result of the Asian financial crisis in 1997, with investment falling from US$8.3billion in 1996 to about US$1.6 billion in 1999 (GSO, 2009). To help reverse this trend, the government moved to slowly implement a series of structural reforms and improve the investment climate needed to revitalize the economy and produce more competitive and export-driven industries (see Table 5.4).

By the end of 2007, Vietnam had attracted 9,810 FDI projects, with a total registered capital of US$99.6 billion from more than

Table 5.4 Investment structure in Vietnam, 1995–2007

	1995	2000	2005	2007*
Total investments (in VND billion) of which (%):	72,447	151,183	343,135	521,700
State sector	42.0	59.1	47.1	39.9
Non-state sector	27.6	22.9	38.0	35.3
Foreign-invested sector	30.4	18.0	14.9	24.8

Source: Aggregated data from GSO (2009).

Note: * Preliminary statistics

69 countries and territories. In total, FIEs provide 1.5 million jobs and contribute 17.7 per cent to the GDP of Vietnam (GSO, 2009).

In practice, FDI is mostly focused on quick 'return on investment' and urban-concentrated projects such as manufacturing, hotel and housing development and services. Many of the (low-tech) manufacturing projects with promising invested capital but low value-added content have, in practice, helped to relieve the pressure of growing unemployment; yet, at the same time, this form of FDI posed potential risks to the environment and social unrest. Only a minuscule number of projects are devoted to rural areas (VVG, 2008).

Export-orientation

The economy is largely export driven. After two years of recession following the Asian financial crisis, the economy began to show signs of picking up thanks to increasing exports and domestic consumption. In 2000, exports were equivalent to 44 per cent of GDP, compared to an average of 27 per cent for developing countries (World Bank et al., 2000: 19).

Most of Vietnam's trade revenue comes from exports to Asian countries, which account for 58.4 per cent of the total export value in 2001 (Ministry of Trade, 2002; Saigon Times Weekly, 2002). Significant increases in exports are found in products like fruits (up 54 per cent) and seafood (up 25 per cent) in 2001. The conclusion of the Vietnam–US Bilateral Trade Agreement (VNUSBTA) in 2000 quickly made the US a promising import customer of Vietnam, especially for the top export items, as listed in Table 5.5.

Table 5.5 Vietnam's top export items in value, 2005

	Value US$ billion	% growth vs. 2004	Key destinations
Total export value	32.45	+22.5	
o/w 7-top export items	22.30		
Rice	1.40	+47.3	Asia Pacific, Africa and Middle East
Crude oil	7.39	+30.3	China, Singapore, Japan, USA, UK
Garments and textiles	4.81	+ 9.6	USA, EU, Japan
Footwear	3.00	+11.7	Japan, USA, Africa, EU
Seafood	2.74	+14.2	EU, USA, Japan, China
Electronic goods	1.44	+34.1	Japan, South East Asia
Wooden products	1.52	+32.2	EU, USA, Japan, Taiwan

Sources: Combined data from EIU (2008) and Runckel and Associates (2005).

However, the reliance on these top export items (Runckel and Associates, 2005) makes Vietnam's trade volatile in the face of economic recession, as has the sudden fall in the world price of many agricultural commodities (such as rice, coffee, nuts, etc.) and crude oil. Such potential threats and volatility limit considerably Vietnam's ability to increase its export revenue and mitigates the sustainability of its economy. Thus, the growth of exports seen since the early 2000s is not stable. One of the most critical challenges is that the country relies heavily on agricultural products, which are highly sensitive to both climatic conditions and fluctuation in world market prices. For instance, in 2000 the turnover of five agricultural export items (rice, coffee, cashew nuts, tea, and groundnuts) fell by about US$517 million as a result of the sudden drop in the international prices (EIU, 2008). Moreover, a large part of non-oil industrial products for export have low local or value-added content, further reducing export income. An illustrative example is that the export of garments and footwear – the two pillars of Vietnam's exports – rose: in 2000 those products actually earned US$1.2 billion, which increased to US$4.81 billion in 2002 as a result of being accessible to new markets, especially the US. The rest of the export earnings were spent on importing raw materials, which usually accounts for up to 65 per cent of the finished product. Statistics from the Ministry of Trade in 2002 showed that Vietnam's imports in 2001 grew by 2.3 per cent with an import turnover of about US$17.7 billion, which caused a trade deficit of 5.7 per cent of export revenue (see Table 5.6). The gap

Table 5.6 Balance of trade, 1990–2010 (US$ billion)

	1990	2000	2005	2007*	2008*	2009**	2010**
Exports	2.40	5.45	14.49	48.56	61.98	49.26	55.19
Imports	2.75	8.16	15.64	58.92	76.59	58.02	61.56
Balance	−0.35	−2.71	−1.15	−10.36	−14.61	−8.76	−6.37

Sources: Adapted from EIU (2008) and GSO (2009).

* actual; ** forecast

became even wider, setting a record, with an estimated deficit of US$14.6 billion in 2008 (EIU, 2008).

The implementation of the VNUSBTA in 2002, the effects of the AFTA agreement from 2003, and WTO membership in 2007 all are critical events for the Vietnamese economy. This requires a new strategic approach to enhance the country's overall competitiveness.

The quest for competitiveness

In general, the overall competitiveness of the economy remains low, reflecting an underdeveloped system. Quality improvement has become an imperative for balancing the competitiveness of Vietnamese products against other substitutes in global markets. This strategy involves promoting higher productivity levels through investment in high-tech technologies, and upgrading the quality of the workforce and managerial capacity in all sectors of the economy.

However, despite continued efforts to modernize industry, up to 70 to 80 per cent of its currently used equipment is obsolete (Nguoi Lao Dong, 2002). Most leading export items (for example, textiles and garments, shoes and electronics) are produced on a subcontracting basis (38 per cent) with low local content and low-level labour input (CIEM, 2003). Comparatively, the gap in economic development between Vietnam and some of the more developed ASEAN countries (i.e. Thailand and Malaysia) could be between 20 to 30 years in some specific production areas, for example, electronic products (Tho, 2001). For example, only 38 per cent of Vietnam's exports are manufactured goods, while the corresponding percentage in China and Thailand is 90 per cent (CIEM, 2003).

Many Vietnamese products do not have a brand or a registered brand, which often leads to disputes over a product's property rights (e.g. Trung Nguyen coffee, Hoa Loc mango, 'dragon' fruit of Phan Thiet, Phu Quoc's fish sauce, An Giang's catfish, etc.). Only 4.2 per cent of enterprises agree that brand is 'a competitive weapon', according to research (Cong nghiep Viet Nam, 2003; Minh, 2002), while 80 per cent of enterprises do not have a brand management strategy (Phan, 2002). Most enterprises, state and private-owned alike, are struggling with a level of low efficiency and effectiveness because of a lack of skilled HR and good management and governance (Tho, 2002).

In fact, these existing features have effectively prevented the country from accelerating the development and integration process at an equal pace with other countries having the same comparable advantages. According to the classification of national competitiveness by the World Economic Forum (WEF, 2009), Vietnam has made relatively no improvement in the ranking in the last five years (see Table 5.7).

To this effect, one survey on the competitiveness of 40 groups of products and services (undertaken by the Central Institute of Economic Studies of the Ministry of Planning and Investment)

Table 5.7 Growth competitiveness comparison index (GCI), 2000–08

	2000 N=75	2001 N=75	2002 N=102	2003 N=102	2004 N=117	2005 N=125	2006 N=125	2007 N=131	2008 N=134
ASEAN									
Cambodia	–	–	–	–	–	111	103	110	101
Indonesia	43	64	69	72	69	69	50	54	55
Malaysia	24	30	30	19	31	25	26	21	21
Philippines	36	48	63	66	76	73	71	71	70
Singapore	2	4	7	6	7	5	5	7	5
Thailand	30	33	37	32	34	33	35	28	34
Vietnam	52	60	62	60	77	74	77	68	70
Vietnam ranking (distance with lowest)	23	15	40	42	40	51	48	63	64

Source: Compiled data from www.weforum.org (accessed 31 January 2009).

Note: The total number of surveyed countries (N=131 in 2007 and N=122 instead of 125 in 2006) was changed and adjusted in the 2008 and in 2009 published ranking report of the World Economic Forum, WEF.

revealed that only 10 products were benchmarked as having major competitive potential (Duc, 2001). Among these were the footwear and garment industries, which focused on high labour intensiveness, low wages and low-level technology (Duc, 2001; Quang, 2001). The situation is alarming enough, as one expert of the Ministry of Trade pointed out (in a meeting with Vietnamese entrepreneurs) that only 28 per cent of the firms had 'exportable' goods, and none of the seven respondent industries in HCMC had electronic products with 'competitive advantage' to compete in the ASEAN market (Lan, 2003).

Improving the overall competitiveness of Vietnamese products and services requires change. This includes combined efforts from the government as well as the entire industry, starting with upgrading the production process with state-of-the-art technology management methods.

Improvement in productivity

To support the 30 per cent GDP growth of future targets (see Table 5.8), there is a need for investment and productivity growth at much higher rates than the average in the 1990s. As a result of unskilled labour, obsolete equipment and weak management, Vietnam could only manage a slight increase in productivity of 2 per cent between 1990 and 1995 and 1.1 per cent between 1990 and 2000, according to estimates (World Bank *et al.*, 2000: 9).

As shown in Table 5.8, Vietnam's competitiveness depends largely on how the country can utilize its available resources (capital, labour and land) in the most productive and profitable way. One solution would

Table 5.8 Investment by source (% of GDP)

Investment source (%)	Actual (1991–2000)	High case (2001–2010)
State budget	5.9	7.0
Investment by SOEs	7.0	7.0
FDI	5.4	3–5
Non-state investment	7.1	11–13
Total investment	25.4	30.0

Source: Adapted from World Bank *et al.* (2000: 6).

be to remove identified impediments to growth in manufacturing and to generate higher value-added service sectors, which will in turn better reallocate under-employed labour in the agricultural sector in a more rational way.

The role of the private sector

Since the Law of Enterprise of 1999 came into effect more than 14,000 new private enterprises were registered in 2000 alone; the majority of them were SMEs. Including those registered at the district level (individual and family), the figure increased to 500,000 (Doanh, 2001). Altogether, SMEs helped to reduce unemployment tension by creating more than 500,000 new jobs and producing different types of commodity goods for the domestic market and export (TBKTSG, 2001).

Although it does not match the size and scope of the SOEs' counterpart, the private sector's contribution to the economy is significant. The private sector generates about half of the national GDP, employed up to 90 per cent of the labour force by 2007 and is by far the fastest growing type of enterprise in terms of numbers (GSO, 2009). However, being latecomers and operating mostly on their own individual capacity, the performance of SMEs is still poor in terms of return on capital, cash flow, sales and liquidity. Obviously, they also need to improve their professionalism in order to be more competitive. The 'level playing field' will further enhance their competitiveness and thereby increase their long-term viability, when all the tariffs are removed as a result of Vietnam's membership of AFTA (2006) and APEC (2015). In 2000, the Asian Development Bank recognized the importance of developing SMEs by providing a US$80 million loan to nearly 15,000 micro and small rural enterprises. It was expected that this loan would accelerate lending to rural businesses and encourage investment by the private sector in new technologies which are crucial for their survival in an increasingly competitive environment (ADB, 2000).

Needless to say, the readiness and capability of the SMEs to face these critical challenges are problematic. In one seminar, where owners of successful private companies gathered to exchange their views on the prospects of integration, the majority admitted that they were not prepared for the battle. The reasons quoted were not surprising: a lack of effective support from the government for each industry, and high prices of utility supplies such as water, electricity, communications, materials, etc. (TBKTSG, 2001).

Nevertheless, considering the positive impact that private SMEs have brought about in only a few years, it is widely believed that greater investment in output by this sector is likely to generate more jobs and growth. Although SMEs often lack initial capital and managerial experience, they are likely to be more sensitive and responsive to the market. However, as long as these constraints in size and capability persist, the majority of local enterprises (SOEs and private enterprises alike) still build their competitive strategy on price instead of a combination of price, quality and diversification, and as a consequence can become prone to foreign competition.

Some of the most urgent and essential aspects for promoting private sector integration can be suggested for future implementation. These include the following (World Bank *et al.*, 2000):

- improving public and administrative attitudes toward private businesses, for example, by official endorsement (as in the case of China);
- ensuring a 'level playing field' for domestic PEs and other players;
- establishing a rule-based business environment for the private sector by a transparent legal and regulatory framework;
- providing necessary credit and capital for business start-up and development;
- promoting good corporate governance on the principles of transparency, accountability and effectiveness for sustainability.

Case studies

The following cases illustrate the benefits in the long run for enterprises (SOEs or PEs of all sizes alike) in having a clear and shared vision and strategy and a clear roadmap to implement and follow it up. The role of effective leadership is also brought to the fore as one of the most critical factors in bringing all the necessary resources (human and material) together to achieve the common goal of stakeholders, even in start-up companies and economies like Vietnam.

Case studies of organizations

Case Study 5.1: An Phuoc Garment Company (APG)

www.anphuoc.com

Small opportunities are often the beginning of great enterprises.

Demosthenes (384–322 BC)

APG provides an interesting example of how a really small Vietnamese company is able to sign a contract with a famous brand name in Europe. The contract of collaboration was signed at a time when APG was still unknown, even in its own domestic market. This family business started in 1992 as a clothes workshop equipped with only 45 sewing machines. The owners soon realized that there was great potential in this business locally and, of course, even more worldwide. So, in order to move in the global direction they decided, in 1994, to create APG. The initial aim of the new company was to provide first to the local market and then to international markets with the largest possible range of fashion products. Thanks to a long-term but clear business vision, APG's leadership has created a successful enterprise in just 15 years, with total revenue of VND139.5 billion (or US$80 million) and a VND3.1 billion profit – a 2.2 per cent revenue/profit ratio in 2008.

At the time at which APG entered the market, the business environment was not favourable for local entrepreneurs. In general, legislation was insufficient and unfriendly, and the country still suffered from a bad reputation for transparency, quality, reliability, etc. Yet, the company's export department learned gradually to expand in size and scope, first to Japan and then to EU countries, being sensitive to market conditions and adopting its strategy. APG can now boast it is one of the most successful garment companies in Vietnam; it is able to ensure stable employment and income for 3,000 workers, maintains a constant average profit/revenue ratio from 1.5 to 3.2 per cent (in 2006–08), owns five factories and 70 outlets nationwide, and in 2008 continued to thrive on an export value of 40 per cent out of its total revenue.

What makes APG different from other local Vietnamese suppliers is its continued drive to build a good image and recognized brand in foreign markets. In this respect, the best strategic decision the company made was to collaborate with France's Pierre Cardin Group. In 1997, a contract was signed for producing clothes 'under licence' for the French brand. This licence arrangement gave both partners the opportunity to produce and retail in Vietnam, Laos and Cambodia. It was an exclusivity contract, allowing the transfer of technology for men's shirts, suits and trousers. The cooperation with Pierre Cardin resulted in an immediate success and today everybody in Vietnam recognizes the An Phuoc brand. This initial strategic step, the basic choice of working under licence, helped APG to improve quality, flexibility and management. The second step required APG staff to work on the tailoring itself and on improving distribution.

APG understood well that the support given by the Pierre Cardin experts had to be exploited to the maximum. The company used this expertise gained from all over the world to analyze the market in Vietnam and other countries under the exclusivity contract. APG then developed its own line and, better still, invested in lines bearing the brand An Phuoc 'made in Vietnam'. The next strategic step was that, instead of focusing on men's fashion, APG decided to invest in all the markets open to them: men's and women's shirts and trousers. In addition, APG went even further by developing lines for polo shirts, shorts, children's clothing and underwear. Now one could buy a whole outfit in just one fashion line: An Phuoc.

What should be the next step for a company that would like to remain in the same business? Copy the techniques, strategies of its model and successful examples of its business partner, Pierre Cardin? APG then started with its own retail shops. It was argued that APG needed to do this powerfully to maximize recognition; it opened 31 shops in Vietnam almost simultaneously so that the visibility of the brand name increased dramatically. This was, and remains, a significant advantage since the visibility is not only important for Vietnamese buyers, but also for foreigners travelling in the country, who can see An Phuoc (linked to the well-known Pierre Cardin brand) for sale all over the country.

As mentioned earlier, together with Pierre Cardin specialists, APG decided to focus on quality, or better still, high quality. To promote its image further, APG regularly participated in various trade shows, fairs and exhibitions, where it has won a variety of top prizes and even the title 'Vietnamese High Quality Goods' (*Hang chat luong cao*). The list of prizes APG has won is very long, especially where the time taken in which to achieve such success has been very short. APG has also obtained ISO 9001–2000 recognition. APG developed quality products with attractive designs by following international trends while, at the same time, keeping its prices reasonable. In this way APG was able to attract more local customers.

Sources: Own deskwork and interviews, September 2008.

Case Study 5.2: Duoc Hau Giang (DHG Pharma)

www.dhgpharma.com

Success has a simple formula: do your best and people may like it.

Sam Ewing

In September 2009, DHG Pharma, a leading JSC in the pharmaceuticals industry, will celebrate its 35th anniversary. DHG Pharma is organized along a matrix structure with four separate product divisions: Pharmaceutical, Herbal, Beauty-spa, and Healthcare. It has a total workforce of 2,135 spread over the whole country, with 47 direct outlets and 20,000 authorized agents. DHG Pharma's competitive advantage rests on its wide distribution network. On average, imported products have occupied only around 7 per cent of the company's total revenue in the last 10 years. Generally, DHG Pharma's products have gained a high reputation for quality, strictly conforming to international standards, such as GLP and ISO/IEC 17025. The fact that 93 per cent of DHG Pharma's products are manufactured locally is considered to be the highest 'local content' ratio in the industry.

DHG Pharma's leading position in Vietnam's pharmaceutical industry can be seen in its total revenue of VND1,450 billion (or US$1.2 million) in 2007, while other competitors could only reach between VND 5–700 billion. DHG Pharma's dividends distributed to shareholders in the 2006–07 period averaged 25 per cent compared to 18–20 per cent for the industry as a whole. In 2008, DHG Pharma's total revenue reached US$1,398,690 and retained a profit/revenue ratio of 11 per cent, one of the highest levels in cross-industry achievement in Vietnam.

To achieve this outstanding performance, DHG Pharma has evolved through several phases of development. To begin with, the company was first established on 2 September 1974 in Ca Mau Province under the name 'Pharmaceutical Factory 2nd September' ('*Xi nghiep duoc 2/9*', the National Day of Vietnam). The company's initial task was to produce the most needed medicines against such diseases as malaria, typhoid and yellow fever, using mainly local herbs and traditional tonics. In 2004 the firm was equitised, with the majority (51 per cent) equity held by the government, under the name of '*Duoc Hau giang*'. Its new mission states that the company 'commits to supplying products of high quality to best serve the needs for the healthcare and happiness of everyone'. To achieve this, DHG Pharma aims to operate on seven adopted core values, which take 'the benefits of the community as fundamental principles for all activities'.

Since then, DHG Pharma has concentrated particularly on developing and modernizing its production lines in parallel with expanding and consolidating its logistics and distribution network. Apart from setting up large-scale warehouses along the south-north national road (using just-in-time principles to ensure timely delivery of suppliers in the value chain and agents and to avoid building unnecessary stock), DHG Pharma also applies a CRM programme very effectively. By this method, not only authorized agents and corporate accounts with outstanding performances are rewarded, but key members of critical customers are also invited to join the company's organized tours in the country as well as abroad.

In 2007 DHG Pharma underwent another change, with a more appealing slogan 'For a healthier and better life', which supports the new vision being built on its core competencies (long experience in the field) and side activities and services (new market development and potential). Toward this end, DHG Pharma launched a two-year campaign, 'DHG Pharma Internal Branding', to communicate, educate and engage employees at all levels with the new direction. All action plans and business strategies are now to be directly linked with the new company's vision to ensure commitment from all sides and cooperation towards achieving the company's ultimate objectives.

It can be said that the new vision and mission has helped DHG Pharma to develop in line with its long-term strategy and, at the same time, prevent itself from expanding its business scope in other increasingly attractive (yet very volatile) businesses, such as real estate and the stock market (with high, short-term ROI) as other companies had done. One such out-of-the-core-business/competency activity is DOMESCO Group, which is led by a pharmacist, but has investments in 11 non-pharmaceutical businesses, which include hotels, restaurants, rental offices and fashion items. Another case is EVN Group (Electricity of Vietnam), which also entered the hotel market in search of quick, short-term profits.

In this respect, DHG Pharma is one of the few companies in Vietnam with a clear and long-term business development strategy that is based on concentric diversification and core business concepts. Also, DHG Pharma has successfully done so even as a SOE with ineffective and inefficient sets of rules and mechanisms, whose hallmarks for operation are governmental control instead of allowing full entrepreneurship to flourish.

DGH Pharma's success is also, to a great extent, attributable to the effective leadership of its CEO, Mrs Nguyen thi Viet Nga, originally a pharmacist but who later developed herself into a fully-fledged business person with a doctoral degree (in economics) and an MBA degree at the age of 50. Using her own example, she has encouraged her staff to take the self-development opportunities offered by the company in an orchestrated effort to enhance the competency of the workforce, and hence the company's competitiveness for sustainable growth in the future. She is also a convincing example of flexible and responsive leadership, who constantly keeps abreast of changes in the market, customers' new requirements, employees' expectations, and the community's concern for environmental protection by practising 'management by walking around' principles. It is expected that her special programme on succession planning to identify and train 'high potential staff' will significantly contribute to sustainable growth and the further success of DHG Pharma in the future.

Sources: Own deskwork and interviews, September 2008.

Case studies of managers

Case Study 5.3: Mr Dang Le Nguyen Vu, CEO, Trung Nguyen

In 2002, a new player came to Roppongi – the pulsating, neon-lit nightclub district in the heart of Tokyo. This is the environment in which a café with humble origins in the forested highlands of central Vietnam opened on a prime piece of real estate this year. With bamboo posts at the door, rattan flooring and conical hats for lamp shades, the café, Trung Nguyen, looks like something out of a mythologized vision of colonial Indochina. That a coffee franchise from a poor, developing country could sprout up in the world's most expensive city is testament to the forces of economic transition in Vietnam, and to the sudden, startling arrival of Vietnam on the international coffee scene and to globalization in general. Most of all, though, it focuses attention on a little coffee start-up from a developing country that is chasing Starbucks' dreams.

Less than six years after it opened its first café in 1996, Trung Nguyen had expanded to more than 400 franchises. That alone is a significant achievement, for regulatory and financial barriers have restrained private enterprise in Vietnam. There are no other franchises, with the exception of the octopus-like businesses of the People's Army. Vietnam is one of the last countries where one still cannot buy a Big Mac. It is remarkable, then, that a small firm started by four medical students from downtrodden Daklak province could grow so large so quickly.

What makes the case of Trung Nguyen intriguing and far-reaching in scope is its counterintuitive global strategy. Typically, successful enterprises from the developed world reach a saturation point in their home countries and begin targeting locations similar to theirs (other developed economies) or places aspiring to be like theirs (emerging markets). To be sure, some obstacles, as well as opportunities, match those of multinationals expanding in the traditional, developed-world-to-developing-world configuration. Success may depend on the nature of the product or service; those that satisfy needs shared across borders are deemed to have the greatest potential for success. The determinant factor can be how the characteristics that differentiate a product, and a firm's strategy for selling it, match new markets that are geographically, culturally and economically distinct from the firm's home base. The cultural and economic gaps between Trung Nguyen's Vietnam and Tokyo's Roppongi could not be wider. But Dang Le Nguyen Vu, the young entrepreneur behind this fledgling empire, has said: 'I want to have the Vietnamese brand name of Trung Nguyen well known in the world. Our coffee is good. There's no reason we can't do it.' His confidence is admirable. But is it realistic? Like the country where he was born, he is up against considerable odds.

In the early 1990s, Mr Vu was a medical student in Buon Ma Thuot, the largest city in Daklak, when he discovered he had more of a bent for business than for surgery. There was then an infectious entrepreneurial spirit sweeping over the country. Public sector jobs, valued under the Communist system because of their stability and the access to power they provided, were now less desirable because of their low pay, rigid rules and corrupt hiring practices. The slight loosening of the government's control on markets unleashed a pent-up demand for private enterprise, personified by young people like Dang. Mr Vu and four friends turned to the ubiquitous beverage of their home town and opened a small processing plant in 1996. With no access to banks or other capital markets for financing, Mr Vu and his partners used a small amount of money they had saved from working at gas stations (less than $1,000 each) and relied on familial connections and home town networks to persuade farmers to sell them unprocessed beans on credit. Later, they used friendships with distributors to buy beans on favourable teams and slowly amass enough capital to import roasting machines from the United States and Taiwan.

Originally, Trung Nguyen was conceived as a processor and exporter. But a marketing problem inadvertently created an opportunity; one that would become the foundation of Trung Nguyen's phenomenal growth. As it tried to sell processed coffee in Ho Chi Minh City (HCMC) – Vietnam's wealthiest and largest city, formerly known as Saigon, and the commercial hub of the South – the company realized it had not adequately marketed its product. So, in 1998, it opened a café, primarily to advertise its brand. Dang employed a triangular approach, opening three cafés within proximity to one another, a strategy that enabled managers to maintain control over the design, service and quality of the cafés, while also keeping inventory and management costs low. As each café became successful, Dang opened additional outlets, one by one, creating new 'triangles' as he expanded.

As the cafés in HCMC thrived, Trung Nguyen decided to expand nationally by franchising. By the middle of 2002, just four years later, there were 422 cafés, at least one in each of Vietnam's 61 provinces. Trung Nguyen established a decentralized network of cafés. Oversight was minimal. The franchising arrangement was simple: in exchange for an upfront investment of about $5,000, a franchisee could use the Trung Nguyen name and its distinctive brown-and-yellow sign with a steaming cup of coffee. Critically, too, franchisees had to buy their coffee, at a 10 per cent discount, from Trung Nguyen. The franchising arrangement made expansion relatively easy and required little investment from Trung Nguyen, or from the café operators. This helped Trung Nguyen rapidly grow and quickly sell and promote its coffee across the country. However, the laissez-faire arrangement also surrendered considerable control over the style, quality and service, which put Trung Nguyen at risk of having its name attached to poorly run cafés. Cafés targeted young, upwardly mobile professionals – the new middle class that was emerging in modern Vietnam. In a country with a per capita annual income that is still below $300, Trung Nguyen was focusing on the nouveau riche who thought nothing of paying nearly $1 for a cup of coffee.

The company did not open cookie-cutter branches. Each café has a distinct style and atmosphere, usually reflective of the local community and region. So cafés in the centre of HCMC are aimed at a young, hip crowd, with a Popsicle-coloured decor and loud, blaring pop music. Cafés in conservative Hanoi, on the other hand, have a more languid, traditional atmosphere with waitresses dressed in *ao dai* (the traditional flowing tunic of Vietnamese women), soft flute music and rustic, bamboo-and-rattan decor.

The cafés are a key ingredient of brand stewardship. Trung Nguyen is a well-known name in Vietnam, referring to a geographic sub-region within the Central Highlands. The company devotes considerable energy to cultivating an image of quality, both in the cafés and in the coffee itself. Dang conducted his own research to develop 30 styles of coffee roast and nine distinctive flavours. The coffee is served in the traditional Vietnamese style, in individual-sized tin filters over espresso-sized cups, often complemented with sweetened condensed milk in a drink called *ca phe sua da* (iced coffee – the French introduced this recipe because Vietnam had little refrigeration at the time).

Trung Nguyen has engaged in extensive vertical integration. It processes, packages, develops product, exports, operates cafés, runs some small farms to grow coffee and even has a training institute for hospitality business workers. Its diversified business and its position as a private enterprise in an industry dominated by the state sector give it both advantages and disadvantages. Because all facets of the industry are dominated by the state sector, Trung Nguyen is in a weakened position: the government can, and does, give preferential treatment to state coffee companies. Overabundant supply mitigates that factor because price reductions benefit Trung Nguyen. In addition, farmers have little leverage over negotiating prices. But, because of the company's concern for quality and because the bulk of Vietnamese coffee is not of a high grade, Trung Nguyen pays a slight premium for better-grade coffee to establish loyalties with individual growers. The company's domestic sales, including its cafés, are also shielded from foreign competition by a 50 per cent tax on imported roast coffee.

The rapid expansion of Trung Nguyen has nearly saturated the market of its target customers, so the company is putting the brakes on further domestic expansion and investing in upgrading its facilities – a defensive posture to protect itself from potential new entrants to the markets. It is also aggressively challenging and shutting down copycats – companies that imitate the Trung Nguyen name and appearance. Issues of trade mark protection are a persistent problem in Vietnam, which has not yet developed a sophisticated legal environment. 'We will be downsizing our strategy for large-scale development and concentrating more on quality control,' said Dang. 'Our upcoming target is to reaffirm the special identity of each cup of our coffee.' The company hired a New Zealand–based consultant and is investing $5 million to make the franchises operate more professionally and more consistently, to ensure the unity of brand and service. The company also is building an instant-coffee factory to diversify its export business (currently just 5 per cent of Vietnam's coffee exports are processed). But its founder also thinks Trung Nguyen has outgrown Vietnam. 'The key is to invest in brand and overseas,' said Dang. In 2002, Trung Nguyen opened its first café in Tokyo. 'This is a very important step,' said Toshihiko Mizuno, managing director of Daitsu Inc., a coffee retailer that is Trung Nguyen's Japanese franchisee. 'If we succeed in Tokyo, that will accelerate Trung Nguyen's expansion plans abroad.'

Trung Nguyen's success at home in Vietnam parallels the Starbucks experience in the United States. The most fundamental difference is that Trung Nguyen uses franchises (both in Vietnam and outside) to expand, while Starbucks owns and operates its cafés and establishes joint ventures in some countries, like Japan. While both companies face the hurdles of introducing a new brand and, in some cases, a new product category to foreign markets, Starbucks has an established, global identity, while Trung Nguyen is unknown outside of Vietnam. Starbucks spends just $30 million annually on marketing and advertising (about 1 per cent of revenues), compared to the $300 million spent every year by McDonald's. Trung Nguyen does not have the resources to spend on a vast marketing campaign, yet it does not have the brand name recognition of Starbucks either. It will have to rely on a word-of-mouth campaign among emigrants and hope that spreads to a wider audience. Brand recognition can work both ways, however. Trung Nguyen's reputation has not suffered the beating that Starbucks has taken as a symbol of a negative side to globalization.

Sources: Own desk work and interviews, February 2009.

Case Study 5.4: Mr Nguyen Thanh My, CEO, My Lan Chemicals (MLC)

Workers at MLC are becoming used to the familiar figure of a white-haired, casually dressed man with a stout body. He sometimes appears suddenly just to give some instructions, smile at the cook or say 'hello' to a worker. The man is Nguyen Thanh My, a well-known businessman in Canada and now the CEO of My Lan. Mr My has a doctorate in chemistry and 50 internationally recognized inventions of his own.

When Mr My first set foot on Travinh to start his business, some locals viewed him with doubtful eyes. 'Product chemicals are kind of causing pollution like Agent Orange during the Vietnam War [see also Case Study 5.2 above]. So that *Viet kieu* (overseas Vietnamese) should have to move somewhere some time.' Some local officials were also concerned and asked the Canadian Embassy to provide some information about Mr My and his company in Canada. When Mr My learned about this, he said, 'I and my workers live and work here. If we cause pollution, it's a way to kill ourselves first.'

Some years after his company started operation, nobody sees smoke, dirt or polluted waste water. Mr My's assistant, Tran The Tuong, explained that the company had strictly observed environmental

> protection rules and, as such, waste from production is collected and treated by an environmental treatment company in HCMC. For the printing material factory, 70 per cent of its waste water will be re-used and the rest will be fully treated before being discharged into the environment.
>
> MLC produces chemicals used in the printing and television industries. More than 90 per cent of its output is exported to industry giants such as Epson, Samsung and Toshiba. In Vietnam, MLC holds more than 50 per cent of the market for printing plates using its technology. Despite being a young company, MLC has achieved a high return on investment. Sales in 2007 reached VND23.9 billion, and pre-tax profit made up VND9.7 billion. Mr My explained his success formula in a simple way: 'In business, you should not stick to sales and a large workforce, but you must seek to make products that have high value and generate large profit.' With the profits earned, Mr My invested heavily in the welfare of his workers. The company premises have greenery, orchids, a football field, a tennis court, a refectory and steam bath, and haircut rooms. Mr My also plans to develop a compound of 40 houses for staff. 'Every service here is free. Workers can enjoy what I can,' he proudly said. As a result, all workers see MLC as their home, and try their best to contribute to the growth of the company.
>
> Source: Adapted from Ho Hung (2009).

Challenges

> *Wise are those who learn that the bottom line doesn't always have to be their top priority.*
>
> William A. Ward

The streamlining of the administrative and legal systems to further improve the business environment and competitive position of Vietnam in global markets continues to be the most critical area to be tackled in the years to come. The government's supportive and active role is pivotal in helping enterprises to make inroads into international markets. The focus of this active support policy to ensure quick and effective integration should be concentrated on creating a 'level playing field' for all economic sectors and helping enterprises to develop critical marketing skills and institutions (i.e., trade promotion and distribution networks) in foreign markets, especially sophisticated ones (such as the EU, the US and Japan).

To make this policy change, Vietnam needs to develop new and effective institutional arrangements for implementation. Some of the key government measures to help producers establish, develop and maintain their footholds in foreign markets and consolidate their home bases against foreign exporters need to be done, especially with regard to easing customs procedures, setting up logistic facilities (packaging, storage), establishing support and promoting institutions (e.g., Bank for Investment and Export Promotion), and develop a 'made-in-Vietnam' brand (Quang, 2001; Minh, 2002).

These policy-oriented priorities will arguably be instrumental in building a more favourable foundation for the economy to develop more sustainably. Nevertheless, such measures go together with a series of concrete actions in order to ensure a synchronized development at both macro and micro levels. More importantly, the 'internal strength' of the country will only be unleashed and utilized under a condition in which a good level of professionalism (*tinh chuyen nghiep*), entrepreneurship (*tinh than doanh nghiep*) and good governance (*quan tri kien hieu*) are well developed and established (Quang, 2000).

In the final analysis, complex issues need not only a series of temporary solutions, but also well-designed and coordinated strategies (Quang, 2000). Vietnam is at the threshold of a new phase in its development process and has the potential to overcome many impediments on the way to further development and integration. Based on the stable growth rates of the past decades, Vietnamese leaders set forth an ambitious objective to turn the country into an 'industrialized country' (*mot nuoc cong nghiep*) by 2020 (CPV, 2001). According to some estimates, this requires a consistent average growth rate of 7–8 per cent annually and a 25 per cent growth rate in exports over the next two decades (Lai, 2001). Certainly, the realization of such an ambitious target relies a great deal on government (macro) and enterprise (micro) capability to deliver and to cope with the new conditions in world markets.

There is evidence that Vietnam is getting better at preparing a firm ground for the challenges ahead, albeit with due caution (Ping, 2009; De Ramos, 2009). Before facing the post-2008 global financial and economic recession, the economy had been growing steadily, foreign investors returned in high numbers in response to the more favourable and responsive business environment and the 'internal strength' had started to be unleashed by a surge of dynamic and ambitious local entrepreneurs. In particular, the government has issued a series of measures to promote manufacturing and processing for export and the local sale of consumer goods (Cohen, 2003); to provide more concrete and active support for trade promotion, such as involving overseas embassies in the process (TBKTSG, 2003); to set up information centres; to initiate regular dialogue with the business community (Lan, 2003), and to establish a central coordinating body for integration.

Vietnam should continue to carry out concrete measures that aim to improve the competitiveness of products and the integration process, such as terminating the privileged regime given to SOEs, improving the quality of export products, increasing market shares in 'traditional markets' (e.g., the southern part of China, Laos, Cambodia and former socialist countries), creating awareness and practising corporate social responsibility to ensure the quality, safety and friendliness to the environment of products, focusing on education and T&D to raise the quality of the workforce in terms of more adequate curriculum and training directed to the needs of the market, and utilizing the potential (capital, professional knowledge, skills and experience) of overseas Vietnamese to bridge the gap currently facing local workers.

Conclusion

> *The point, as Marx saw it, is that dreams never come true.*
> Hannah Arendt

As presented in this chapter, the success of Vietnam's drive to becoming a 'middle income' country depends largely on the country's capacity to translate into practice the measures to improve the country's competitiveness. In this regard, a well-designed and coordinated implementation plan with special focus on unleashing the 'internal strength', improving the efficiency and effectiveness of SOEs, promoting the potential of SMEs, building appropriate professionalism for HRs, elaborating a friendlier and effective legal framework and developing a more transparent and supportive government apparatus will be required.

At the macro level, the government needs to focus on balancing the economy's fundamentals to ensure the quality of growth by being less export- and more import-oriented (direct markets, capacity building, higher value content to products and services, and more socially responsible), rather than trying to achieve high but unrealistic GDP growth targets every year (EIU, 2008; Tho, 2008; Straight Times, 2008). At the micro level, cross-sector enterprises should reposition themselves strategically (e.g. market, product portfolio, quality delivery, image building, customer retention, commitment to the welfare of the community and sustainability of the living environment). Without these strategic and operational adjustments to turn short-term challenges (high inflation, export decline, social unrest and world economic downturn) into sustainable opportunities (Straight Times, 2008; Doan, 2008), the ambitious objective of the leadership to turn Vietnam into an 'industrialized country' by 2020 will remain a mere dream.

Bibliography

ADB (2000) Asian Development Bank, 'Rural credit project in Vietnam will enable poor to start enterprise', *ADB News Release*, No 147/00, 12 December.

Bekefi, T. (2006) 'Viet Nam: Lessons in building linkages for competitive and responsible entrepreneurship', UNIDO and Kennedy School of Government, Harvard University.

Beresford, M. (2008) '*Doi Moi* in review: The challenges of building market socialism in Vietnam', *Journal of Contemporary Asia*, 38, 2, 221–43.

Cheshier, S. and Penrose, J. (2007) 'The Top 200: Industrial strategies of Vietnam's largest firms', United Nations Development Program, October.

CIEM (2002) Central Institute for Economic Management, 'Vietnam's economy in 2001', Hanoi.

CIEM (2003) Central Institute for Economic Management, 'Economic integration', 22 January. Available at http://www.ciem.org.vn/index.php?newlang=english

CII (2002) Confederation of Indian Industry, 'Business Services: FDI in Vietnam'. Available at http://www.ciionline.org/busserv/international/countries/2002/Vietnam/FDI.html

Cohen, M. (2003) 'Vietnam: new and improved', *Far Eastern Economic Review*, 30 January.

Cong Nghiep Viet Nam (2003) 'Khoi dong con tau thuong hieu (Starting the locomotive of brands)', 1 February.

CPV (2001) Communist Party of Vietnam, 'To promote the entire nation's strength, continue with the renewal process, step up industrialization and modernization, build and safeguard the socialist Vietnamese homeland', *Political Report of the Central Committee*, 9th National Congress, April.

De Ramos, A. (2009) 'Southeast Asia's wounded tigers', *Far Eastern Economic Review*, 20 January.

Doan, T. (2008) 'Khung hoang cung la co hoi doi moi (Crisis is also an opportunity for reform)', *Thoi bao kinh te Sai Gon* (Saigon Economic Times), 49, 13 and 64.

Doanh, L.D. (2001) 'Chan dung doanh nhan moi o Viet Nam (Profile of the new entrepreneur in Vietnam)', *Nguoi Lao Dong*, 18–20 May.

Duc, H. (2001) 'So canh tranh duoc chi dem tren dau ngon tay' (The competitive products are just a handful)', *Thoi bao Kinh te Sai Gon*, 20, May.

EIU (2008) Economist Intelligence Unit, 'Country Briefings: Vietnam, Factsheet', 25 November. Available at http://www.economist.com

Gates, L. C. (2000) 'Vietnam's economic transformation and convergence with the dynamic ASEAN economies', *Comparative Economic Studies*, XLII, 4.

GSO (2008) General Statistical Office, *Statistics Yearbook 2007*, Hanoi: Statistical Publishing House.

GSO (2009) General Statistical Office, 'Statistical Data'. Available at http://www.gso.gov.vn/default_en.aspx?tabid=467&idmid=3 (accessed 19 March 2009).

Harvie, C. (2001) 'Competition Policy and SMEs in Vietnam', Working Paper Series 2001, Department of Economics, University of Wollongong.

Ho Hung (2009) 'Sharing with others', *The Saigon Times*, 5–6, 9, 20 and 50.

Kamoche, K. (2001) 'Human resources in Vietnam: The global challenge', *Thunderbird International Business Review*, 43, 5, 625–50.

Lai, L. (2001) 'Doanh nhan, ong la ai? (Entrepreneur, who are you?)', *Tuoi Tre*, No 20, May.

Lan, P. (2003) 'Thu tuong se doi thoai voi doanh nghiep vao thang ba (The Prime Minister will have a dialogue with the business community in March)'. Available at http://Vnexpress.net/vietnam/kinhdoanh (accessed 7 February 2003).

Martin, J. R. (2002) 'World Competitiveness Reports'. Available at http://www.maaw.info/WorldCompetitivenessReports.htm (last revision 24 May 2002).

Minh, K. (2008) 'Nguon noi luc la yeu to quyet dinh (Internal strength is the critical factor)', *Thoi bao kinh te Sai Gon*, 11 March, 46, 32.

Minh, N. (2002) 'Lien ket de phat trien va hoi nhap (Joint force to develop and integrate)', *Dien dan Doanh nghiep*, 19, 3 March.

MPI (2006) Ministry of Planning and Investment, 'The five-year socio-economic development plan 2006–10', March, Hanoi.

Phan, L. (2002) 'Cham, con hon khong (Late, but better than never)', *Thoi bao Kinh te Sai Gon*, 50, 5 December.

Ping, O.B. (2009) 'Outlook for Vietnam still bright', *The Business Times* (Singapore), 24 February.

Quang, T. (1997) 'Sustainable economic growth and human resource development in Vietnam', *Transitions*, 18, 1&2, 256–80.

Quang, T. (2000) *Vietnam: Challenges on the Path to Development*, Bangkok: SAV-SOM Joint Publishing.

Quang, T. (2001) *Vietnam: Gearing Up for Integration*, Bangkok: SAV-SOM Joint Publishing.

Quang, T. (2006) 'Human resource management in Vietnam', in A. Nankervis, S. Chatterjee and J. Coffey (eds.) *Perspectives of Human Resource Management in the Asia Pacific*, pp 231–52. Sydney: Pearson Australia.

Runckel and Associates (2005) 'Vietnam: Overview of the seven biggest currency earners in 2005'. Available at http://www.business-in-asia.com (accessed 27 November 2008).

Straight Times (2008) 'Vietnam walks tightrope', 16 November. Available at http://www.strighttimes.com

Tai, T.V. (2001) 'The US–Vietnam Trade Agreement', *Harvard Asia Quarterly*. Available at http://www.fas.harvard.edu/~asiactr/haq/200101/0101a008.htm

TBKTSG, Thoi bao Kinh te Sai Gon, Xuan Qui Mui 2003; Tuoi Tre Journal; Nguoi Lao dong Journal, Thanh nien Journal; various issues.

Thai, T. (2003) 'Nam nang cao chat luong hang xuat khau (The year to increase the quality of exported goods)', *Thoi Bao Kinh Te Sai Gon*, 5, 23 January.

Thiem, N.T.T. (2006) *Market, Strategy and Structure: An Added Value Approach* (6th edn). HCMC: Youth Publishing House/Saigon Economic Times.

Thiem, N.T.T. (2008) *Branding: Equity and Values* (3rd edn). HCMC: Youth Publishing House/Saigon Economic Times.

Tho, T. V. (2001) 'Kinh te Viet Nam buoc vao the ky 21: hai kich ban tang truong' (Vietnam's economy at the threshold of the 21st century: Two growth scenarios)', *Thoi bao Kinh Te Sai Gon*, 20 May.

Tho, T.V. (2002) 'Mui dot pha chien luoc cho cong nghiep hoa (The breakthrough for industrialization)', *Thoi bao Kinh te Sai Gon*, 12 December.

Tho, T.V. (2008) 'Tu cai cach tiem tien den xay dung co che chat luong cao: dieu kien de phat trien ben vung o Viet Nam (From gradual reform to building a high quality mechanism for sustainable development in Vietnam)', *Thoi dai moi (New Era)*, 14 July.

Tri, V.N. (1990) *Vietnam's Economic Policy since 1975*, Singapore: Institute of Southeast Asian Studies.

Tyers, R. and Rees, L. (2002). '*Trade Reform and Macroeconomic Policy in Vietnam*', Working Paper No 419, Austrian National University.

US Department of State (2009) 'Background Note: Vietnam'. Available at http://www.state.gov/r/pa/ei/bgn/4130.htm (accessed 18 March 2009).

VVG (2008) Vietnam Venture Group, Inc., 'Foreign investment by sector', *Current Report of Vietnam's Economic Indicators*. Available at http://www.vvg-vietnam.com (updated 18 November 2008).

WEF (2009) World Economic Forum, 'Vietnam Competitiveness Profile'. Available at http://www.weforum.org (accessed 31 January 2009).

World Bank, Asian Development Bank and UNDP (2000). 'Vietnam 2010: Entering the 21st century', Vietnam Development Report No 21411-VN, December 14–15.

6 The changing face of foreign direct investment management in Vietnam

Clemens Bechter, Chris Rowley, Katharina Kühn and Oliver Massmann

- Introduction
- Key issues and new developments
- Case studies
- Challenges
- Conclusion

Introduction

There are several aspects to the critical area of the management of FDI. These include those concerned with the role of FDI, together with its impact and importance, growth and levels, both promised and actually delivered. The sources of FDI funds, as well as sectoral destinations, are also of importance. FDI also faces challenges.

Vietnam shares many similarities with China as a consequence of its recent industrial development, although the country's transition from a centralized state to a market economy has been slower than that of its neighbour. Vietnam has become Thailand's main rival in rice and aquaculture exports, Brazil's in coffee and may become India's in software development (UNCTAD, 2006). The country is one of Asia's most open economies: two-way trade is around 160 per cent of GDP, more than twice the ratio of China and over four times that of India (UNCTAD, 2007a). The economy had been growing at 7–8 per cent annually, peaking at 8.5 per cent in 2007 (see also Chapter 1). Within this performance FDI has a key role and impact.

FDI's growing role in Vietnam is covered in the following sections. This is in terms of key issues and developments, such as WTO membership, FDI entry modes and flows. Organizational and manager cases and vignettes are also provided, and the challenges to be faced are detailed; these include those involving labour productivity, real estate, industrial parks and labour relations.

Key issues and new developments

There are a range of key issues and developments that impinge on the area of the management of FDI. They include the following factors. Since the launch of the *Doi Moi* reforms in 1986, FDI has performed very well with close to 10,000 FDI projects and a total investment capital in excess of US$100 billion (Vietnam Economic Times, 2008). In 2007 alone FDI commitment amounted to US$21.3 billion and foreign and domestic investment combined accounted for 44 per cent of GDP. Vietnam envisaged a balanced ratio structure for drawing in FDI capital to promote continued economic growth as 50:30:20–50 per cent from the private sector, 30 per cent from the public sector, 20 per cent from FDI (Minh, 2008).

However, less than half (45.6 per cent) of the total registered capital of FDI was implemented (see Table 6.1) by 2007 (GSO, 2009). This slow rate is, according to some observers, a direct result of the country's low ability to absorb the funds and the poor conditions to support the implementation of the projects. The three main 'bottlenecks' are (1) poor and inadequate infrastructure; (2) a serious shortage of labour, especially high-end workers, and inappropriate administrative regulations, including lengthy procedures; and (3) harassment or corruption (Minh, 2008). As a result of these constraints, many large projects – such as new city development, housing, office building, chemicals and tourism – cannot be implemented, especially in the centre of the country.

The inflows of FDI, ODA and overseas remittances for 2008 were estimated at US$30 billion. The figure exceeds the trade deficit of US$20 billion. FDI commitments for 2008 reached a new record high of US$47 billion for the first eight months, a year-on-year increase of 300 per cent (GSO, 2009). However, Vietnam's economic and business risks – such as inflation, corruption and poor infrastructure – could worry and frighten foreign investors and alter these capital inflows. Nevertheless, the World Investment Report (UNCTAD, 2007) gave an optimistic forecast with regard to Vietnam's FDI. Some 11 per cent of

Table 6.1 Vietnam's FDI registered capital, 1988–2007 (US$ million)

Year	Number of projects	Registered capital	Implemented capital
1988	37	341.7	N/A
1989	67	525.5	N/A
1990	107	735.0	N/A
1991	152	1291.5	328.8
1992	196	2208.5	573.9
1993	274	3037.4	1017.5
1994	372	4188.4	2040.6
1995	415	6937.2	2556.0
1996	372	10164.1	2714.0
1997	349	5590.7	3115.0
1998	285	5099.9	2367.4
1999	327	2565.4	2334.9
2000	391	2838.9	2413.5
2001	555	3142.8	2450.5
2002	808	2998.8	2591.0
2003	791	3191.2	2650.0
2004	811	4547.6	2852.5
2005	970	6839.8	3308.8
2006	987	12004.0	4100.1
2007*	1544	21347.8	8630.0
Total 1988–2007		99596.2	46044.5

Source: Adapted from GSO (2009).
Note: * preliminary data

the surveyed transnational groups confirmed that Vietnam would be their most attractive market in the coming years. As a destination Vietnam ranked sixth, behind China (52 per cent), India (41 per cent), the US (36 per cent), Russia (22 per cent) and Brazil (12 per cent).

In terms of sources of FDI Asian countries contribute the lion's share of FDI into Vietnam (see Table 6.2). In 2007, South Korea became the largest investor with 240 projects (almost 15 per cent of the total), with Singapore second and six Asian countries were in the top 10, and they accounted for over 59 per cent of the total. Registered future projects amounted to US$50 billion across 50 projects. These included a US$3.8 billion power plant by Japan's Sumitomo Group, a US$2.5 billion cultural and trading centre by Kumho Asiana, a US$9 billion Trustee Swiss Group project on Phuquoc, and a US$3.5 billion international university township in HCMC by Malaysia's

Table 6.2 Vietnam's top ten investors by country, 1988–2007* (US$ million)

Ranking	Country	Number of projects	Registered capital	% total
1	South Korea	1,861	14,647.3	14.7
2	Singapore	632	12,575.2	12.6
3	Taiwan	2,003	12,200.2	12.2
4	Japan	997	9,783.5	9.8
5	British Virgin Islands	389	9,771.5	9.8
6	Hong Kong	621	7,007.7	7.0
7	USA	440	3,509.6	3.5
8	France	258	3,128.7	3.1
9	Malaysia	285	3,036.4	3.0
10	Netherlands	104	3,001.9	3.0
	Total (1988–2007)		99,596.2	

Source: Adapted from GSO (2009).

Note: * preliminary data

Berjaya Land Berhad. These projects will be carried out during 2008–20 (Vietnam Economic Times, 2008). In the first half of 2008, Taiwan took the lead with US$8.2 billion of committed FDI, followed by Japan, US$7.1 billion and Canada with US$4.2 billion. Again, very large projects are behind such high commitments, and include those in steel, oil refinery and real estate (Vietnam Economic Times, 2008).

However, less than 50 per cent of Vietnam's officially published FDI figure actually finds its way into real disbursement. Figure 6.1 (below) shows that over the last ten years South Korea, Singapore and Taiwan were major investors but disbursement has been well below 50 per cent (see Figure 6.1) (UNCTAD, 2007a).

In terms of the protection of investors, this has been improved and the legal framework has become more favourable and comprehensive (see also Chapter 4). FDI has, thus, been a major driving force for both economic transformation and poverty reduction and played a major role in the industrialization process (UNCTAD, 2006).

Implications of WTO membership

Vietnam joined ASEAN in 1996 and the WTO in 2007 and while the reform of the regulatory framework towards a market economy

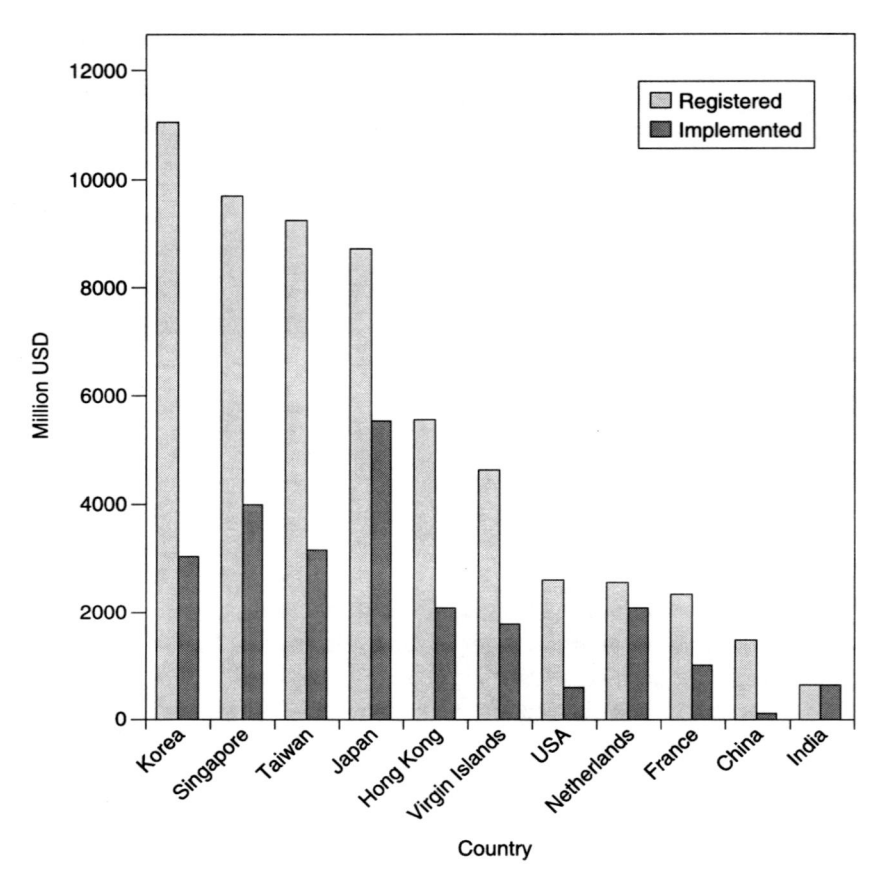

Figure 6.1 Vietnam FDI – registered vs implemented, 1998–2007.
Sources: Adapted from GSO (2009) and http://www.unctad.org.wir (2008)

formally began in 1986, it was only the beginning of the WTO accession negotiations in 1995 that really started the adoption of substantial changes. WTO membership was the result of changes in the theory underlying the Vietnamese economic and legal system since the beginning of the *Doi Moi* policy. The lengthy accession process of 11 years for a country with relatively little economic power illustrates both the interest in the Vietnamese market and the high level of reform required. In addition, the failure of other accession countries (especially China), to successfully implement WTO commitments posed additional challenges for Vietnam and led to a number of reforms prior to WTO membership.

Changes undertaken following membership of the WTO have affected a wide number of areas in relation to FDI, such as trading. The single most important shift for companies was marked by the adoption of the LOI and the LOE (in 2005), which provided a common framework for both foreign and domestic investors (see also Chapter 4). These laws also put private and public companies legally on the same level.

Challenges remain from a practical point of view, and the reform process towards the establishment and management of the market economy is not complete. In particular, the legal system is still burdensome and complex, and the regulatory bias is to 'direct and control' rather than 'regulate, monitor and enforce', as in market economies. A further major problem is the proper implementation of existing laws and regulations (UNCTAD, 2007b).

Despite the fact that the WTO does not include a specific investment regime, there are investment regulations spread over various agreements that directly influence the regulation of investment. The Agreement on Trade Related Investment Measures (TRIMS) clarifies the applicability of the GATT rules on national treatment and the prohibition of quantitative restriction in certain investment measures (De Sterlini, 2005). Most importantly, the new agreements require the removal of performance and local content requirements in order to foster a more compatible trade environment. Foreign investors will, especially in the automotive industry, benefit from these changes. For example: 'Local content requirements have vanished, but in turn the special consumption tax has been increased from 5 per cent to 50 per cent for completely knocked down cars. For most automotive manufacturers it is not economical to produce locally because the market is fewer than 120,000 car sales annually. Within five days, more cars are sold in the US than the whole year in Vietnam,' says Mr Tran Duc Kien, Supply Operation Manager, Ford Vietnam (fieldwork interview).

WTO accession resulted in an array of investment possibilities for foreign investors, including in politically sensitive sectors such as financial services. A further impact can be seen in greater protection of intellectual property rights by a legal circular issued in 2008. However, the threshold that constitutes a violation of rights remains extremely high, penalties do not have a sufficiently deterring effect and an efficient enforcement system is not yet in place.

Overall, accession to the WTO has contributed to foreign investors' trust in Vietnam. Thus, FDI commitments from 2006 to 2008 were higher than the previous 20 years combined. In turn, foreign investors have also played their part in integrating Vietnam into the world economy.

Entry modes

While huge progress has been made in terms of openness to FDI, hurdles still remain and the FDI entry regime is far from being liberal in comparison to other developing countries. The government has, instead, consciously chosen a gradual approach towards further liberalization and still aims to steer investment into particular sectors. Hence, stringent conditions for many sectors have been maintained, an approach which reflects the influence of the former planned economy system. The conditions for FDI entry are laid out in the LOI and its implementing decrees, in sectoral laws and regulations, and in the WTO schedule on services and legal regulations on mergers and acquisitions (M&A). The LOI defines four broad categories for investment projects: (1) prohibited sectors; (2) conditional sectors for both foreign and domestic investors; (3) conditional for foreign investors only; and (4) sectors not listed under any of these categories are considered to be unconditional.

While a wide range of sectors are listed as conditional, these are subject to stringent conditions in most countries. Important sectors of interest to foreign investors that are listed as strategic (*chien luoc*) include telecommunications, banking and finance, trade and distribution, education, media and real estate. The precise nature of conditionality is mostly laid out in specific laws and regulations for each sector and includes caps on foreign ownership, cooperation requirements and restraints on operations such as limiting the provision of services to other FIEs. Many service restrictions that are in place do, however, have clearly stated phase-out periods under the WTO commitments on services.

In the initial stage, many foreign investors chose to enter the Vietnamese market with a RO. The registration process for ROs is the easiest and quickest of all the registration procedures, but the permitted scope of business is consequently very restricted. A RO is of use mainly to identify possibilities in the market and prepare the ground for deals with an offshore entity.

When deciding to operate formally in the Vietnamese market, an investor has the choice of setting up a wholly or partially FOE in the form of a LLC or a JSC (as seen in Figure 6.2). The LOI does not contain the form of a JVE; instead, it addresses LLCs with foreign and domestic shareholders. A one-member LLC is the standard entity for a fully foreign investment project and is owned by an individual or organization. A JSC is defined in the LOE as an enterprise whose charter capital is divided into equal portions known as shares. Like the LLC, the JSC is a juridical person with its own charter. JSCs can either be listed formally on the stock market or operate as unlisted companies. The regulations in the LOE apply equally to both forms. Shareholders can be organizations or individuals and the minimum number of shareholders is three. Debts and other liabilities of the JSC are the liability of the shareholders within their contributed amount of capital. A JSC is entitled to issue bonds or additional shares in order to mobilize capital. This complex process is shown in Figure 6.2.

Apart from establishing a Vietnamese company, a BCC is also a potential investment vehicle. The BCC is not a company form, but

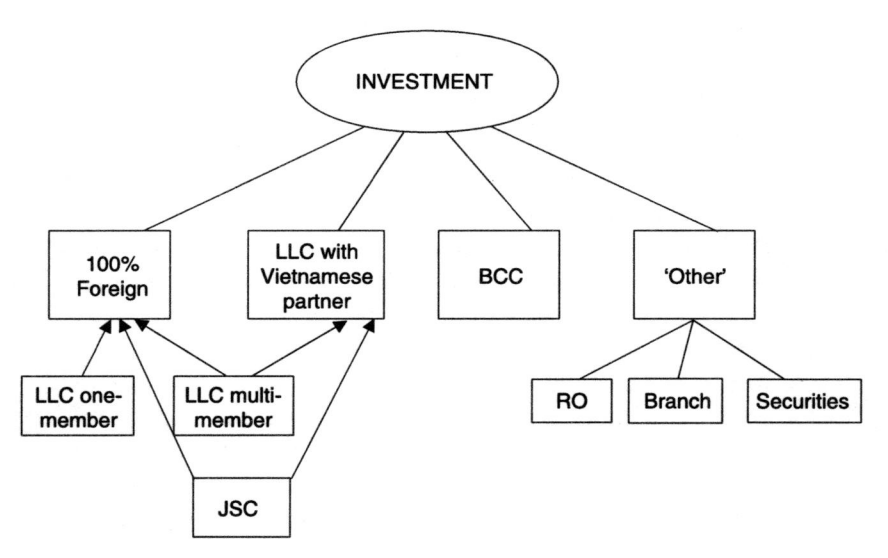

Figure 6.2 Types of FDI in Vietnam.

a contractual relationship in which a foreign and a domestic investor agree to implement a specific investment project in Vietnam and obtain a licence. The BCC is a very flexible instrument: the sharing of profits can be regulated by the parties in the BCC contract independently from the contributed capital share. However, in a BCC the investors are exposed to unlimited liability, though a foreign investor can form a LLC abroad to enter into a BCC.

For investment projects in infrastructure, the form of a BOT project is still the main instrument. Like a BCC, a BOT project is not a company form but rather a contractual partnership for the implementation of a specific project. The idea is that the foreign investor agrees to set up an infrastructure project, receives the licence to operate that project in order to generate profits for a limited period of time, usually 50 years, and then transfers it to the Vietnamese state without compensation. The partner in a BOT project is the corresponding Vietnamese authority. BOT projects allow the state to build infrastructure with foreign capital while retaining high levels of control. Vietnam has a huge demand for investment in infrastructure; it is estimated that US$1.5 billion annually between 2007 and 2017 is needed in the power sector alone (EAI, 2007). Therefore, investors in BOT projects have the most favourable investment conditions, such as free land use rights and the lowest tax rates. Although there is a desire to open the market for investment in infrastructure, the BOT contract will remain an important form in the foreseeable future.

The right of establishment of foreign corporations is highly regulated or is in the planning stage to be regulated. For all investment forms, the intended scope of business should be formulated as broadly as possible, as the company will be allowed to act only within that defined scope and the extension of that scope is a cumbersome process. Of significance for foreign investors is that contractors can also specify foreign law as the governing law in the project contract and other contracts relating to the project provided that such foreign law is not contrary to fundamental principles of Vietnamese law. Moreover, arbitration can be placed with an international dispute settlement body, such as the Singapore International Arbitration Centre.

There is discussion about the participation of foreign investors as strategic partners in SOEs in the equitisation process. In sectors such as telecommunications, memoranda of understanding for partnerships have been signed. Under WTO rules, foreign companies that provide mobile and other services without their own network infrastructure are allowed to set up LLCs with domestic telecommunications suppliers.

In general, granting an investment licence has become easier. When asked about his experience, Mr Don Tran, an overseas Vietnamese and general director of Global Equipment Services (GES) Vietnam said: 'It was really a nice surprise for me. Thanks to assistance from HCMC People's Committee and the SHTP, we didn't encounter any trouble with administrative procedures. Of course, we had a long time to study and prepare, but I can say the time for us to get a licence was quicker than in Japan and the Republic of Korea' (Vietnam News, 2007). To stimulate further FDI, Vietnam will open up new investment promotion offices in Japan, Singapore and the US.

Modes of FDI

LLCs and former JVEs have been an effective means of FDI. Managing JVEs often encountered problems usually stemming from an ineffective legal system, red tape, bureaucracy, frequent regulation changes, protectionism and corruption (Swierczek et al., 1998; Quang, 1998; Sheridan, 1998). Additional problems arise from a lack of management skills, cultural differences, mistrust and contradictory interests. Therefore, not surprisingly, for the period 2004–06, nearly 1,000 FDI projects (20 per cent of the total) were prematurely terminated (UNCTAD, 2007a). A study (covering 551 JVEs in Vietnam) came to the conclusion that goal clarity and conflict management are key factors influencing the success of JVEs (Thuy, 2005); cultural sensitivity and information exchange, however, do not have significant effects. The study also shows that flexibility, in terms of the willingness to modify agreements in response to unforeseen circumstances, is the most important JVE success factor. Trust is also an important factor, as indicated by the following quote: 'Our company has two joint ventures in Vietnam: one for trading with Vinatobacco and the other one with Vietnam National Tobacco Corporation for leaf development. Flexibility and mutual trust form the basis of our cooperation,' says Ms Dang Thi Ngan, British American Tobacco (fieldwork interview).

One reason for the existence of JVEs was that foreign investors could not own land, but SOEs could provide it as their capital contribution. Foreign investors also felt safer investing in the protected SOE sectors. In 2004, for example, there were 821 FDI based JVEs. However, foreign investors increasingly preferred total ownership. Thus, between 2000 and 2004, the share of JVEs declined from 44 to 26 per cent of the number of FIEs, from 70 to 53 per cent of foreign capital formation and from 30 to 17 per cent of employment in FDI enterprises (GSO, 2007). However, under the new LOI, those JVEs with more than 51 per cent of domestic capital ownership face the same conditions as domestic investors.

To avoid the pitfalls of LLCs, some companies have M&As as their entry strategy (Zhan and Terutomo, 2001). Acquiring an existing company is an investment option for both foreign and domestic investors seeking to increase market share quickly. For example, Asia Pacific Breweries Ltd, a Singapore-invested firm that owns Viet Nam Brewery Ltd (VBL), expanded its capacity by acquiring an 80 per cent interest in Quangnam VBL Ltd, while Viettel bypassed the need to develop an outlet network by acquiring Nettra's existing network (Massmann, 2008).

There are a variety of factors that push a company to purchase another. Some takeovers are opportunistic and encouraged by the target company's reasonable price, or the acquiring company expects to increase its bottom line with the acquisition. Other takeovers are considered to be a strategic necessity for the company to enter into a new market without undue risk or the time and expenses needed to start a new business. The company may also aim to eliminate or reduce competition. Also, M&A may also be the only practical means of doing business in a number of sectors. For example, the Law on Real Estate Transactions (2006), places conditions on legal capital with regard to entities wishing to operate in this sector. A few, however, have found a way to bypass this obstacle by acquiring an existing company already registered to conduct business in this sector.

Procedures for acquiring a company are specified in the Law on Competition (2004), Decree No 116/2005/ND-CP (2005) and Article 56 of Decree No 108/2006/ND-CP (2006), which details and guides implementation of the LOI. Established M&A law in other countries classifies acquisitions into two types: (1) share purchase, under which the target company itself is acquired and (2) asset purchase, under which assets of the target company are acquired but not the target company itself. The Vietnamese laws on M&As are not yet perfected, and even the definition of an acquisition is vague. Article 17.3 of the Law on Competition comes closest, stating: 'Acquisition of enterprises refers to an act whereby an enterprise acquires the whole or part of the property of another enterprise sufficient to control or dominate all or one of the trades of the acquired enterprise.' According to Decree No 116/2005/ND-CP, control or domination is given if the acquiring company holds more than 50 per cent of voting rights at the general shareholders meeting or on the board of management or otherwise, in accordance with the charter of the acquired company, or can control or dominate the financial policies and operations of the acquired company. The law, in other words, was silent on the issue of acquisition by means of asset purchase.

Decree No 108/2006/ND-CP sets out some procedures for a foreign investor to obtain official approval of an acquisition. However, the approval process for obtaining an investment licence is ambiguous. Some foreign investors may run into problems when authorized state or local authorities delay approval of acquisitions while they await guidelines. M&A deals may also be examined with respect to competition rules regarding monopolies or economic concentrations, a process that may be hampered or delayed because of the lack of official data on the market and the market share of enterprises. No matter whether a company chooses a LLC or M&A, it requires financial resources as well as HRs. Indeed, relational capital – which is defined as trust, mutual respect, understanding and close relationships between individuals in a business partnership – are important success factors here (Thuy and Quang, 2005).

Flows of FDI

Geographically, FDI is concentrated around HCMC and Hanoi. In 2007, US$12 billion in FDI was directed towards 900 new projects, while US$9 billion, and remaining capital, went to 250 existing projects. The industrial sector attracted the largest chunk of FDI, a total of US$5 billion (Vietnam Economic Times, 2008). Vungtau, a coastal city near HCMC, attracted the largest amount of FDI in 2007, with more than US$1 billion. Cities that ranked second and third are Hanoi and HCMC, with close to US$1 billion of FDI. How fast the pace is going can be seen in HCMC: in the first six months of 2008 alone the city attracted US$1 billion of FDI.

From 1988 to 2007, HCMC received close to US$20 billion worth of FDI projects. The whole Red River Delta, including Hanoi and Haiphong, received a similar amount, and was followed by South Central with Danang and Quangngai (GSO, 2009) in levels received (see Table 6.3). There was hardly any FDI in the North West, North Central, South Central, Central Highlands, River Delta areas, and only a limited number in the North East, mainly in Quangninh. Including the cities of HCMC, Binhduong, Baria-Vungtau and Dongnai; the South East is the centre of FDI, with over US$ 42 billion (see Table 6.3).

In terms of destination sectors for FDI, the following is noted. As a result of its fast economic growth, Vietnam is struggling to generate enough power to fuel that growth. Half of Vietnam's domestic energy consumption comes from oil, with hydropower (20 per cent), coal (18 per cent), and natural gas (12 per cent) supplying the remainder.

Table 6.3 Licensed FDI projects, by major cities/provinces, 1998–2007 (US$ million)

Rank	City/province	Number of projects	Registered capital	% of total
1	Ho Chi Minh City**	2,816	20,174.2	20.2
2	Hanoi	1,183	15,085.6	15.1
3	Dongnai	986	12,824.2	12.9
4	Binhduong	1,607	8,958.1	9.0
5	Baria-Vungtau	222	7,520.1	7.5
6	Haiphong**	321	3,188.1	3.2
7	Danang**	148	2,478.0	2.5
8	Quangngai**	21	2,191.9	2.2
9	Vinhphuc	164	2,060.9	2.1
10	Hatay	97	1,991.7	2.0
Total			99,596.2	

Sources: Adapted from GSO (2009).
Note: *preliminary data; **cities with naval ports

To ease the situation the government invited foreign companies to invest in this politically sensitive sector (EAI, 2007).

Case studies

The following case studies and vignettes demonstrate that Vietnam is trying hard to open up to FDI as a result of *Doi Moi*, especially in economically critical sectors, such as finance and energy, and at the cost of the centrally planned economy in order to accelerate economic growth. The cases of individual managers show how foreign investors have tried to cope with the local reality in order to achieve their FDI objectives.

Case studies of organizations

Case Study 6.1: DKSH: A Swiss business with strong Asian roots

In the 1860s, three Swiss entrepreneurs sailed east to Asia. Independently and within a few years of each other, Wilhelm Heinrich Diethelm set off for Singapore, Edward Anton Keller for the Philippines and Hermann Siber for Japan. Over the years, they established flourishing trading houses, which over decades evolved into major players in South East Asia, China, the eastern Asian Pacific region and Japan. With a reputation as reliable business partners possessing a superior understanding of their markets, they earned the respect and trust of major international companies and local business communities alike. The Diethelm Group and the Keller Group formally joined forces in 2000. In 2002, Diethelm Keller Services Asia came together with SiberHegner to create a global marketing, sales, logistics and distribution company with a unique pan-Asian network: DKSH was born.

DKSH is a market and business expansion service group. It enables and supports companies in expanding their businesses in existing markets and launching into new ones – market expansion services. It combines sourcing, marketing, sales, distribution and after-sales services and provides its partners with fundamental expertise and on-the-ground logistics, covering the world's most complex and demanding growth markets. It offers market, product and application understanding and a pan-regional network. It is a trusted link, connecting suppliers to customers along the entire value chain. Providing tailor-made services for customers and suppliers, covering all their needs and requirements, DKSH builds partnerships. Deeply rooted in communities all across Asia, its network of business relationships has been built over the course of a corporate history lasting 150 years.

In terms of the organizational structure of DKSH, business activities are managed through four highly specialized business units, each servicing specific industry sectors. Country organizations implementing business unit strategy enable region-wide coverage, while a head office provides cost-effective services and state-of-the-art, group-wide infrastructure. Uniting diverse expertise with wide-ranging intercultural competence, the Executive and Business Management teams enable them to respond swiftly, proactively and flexibly to new challenges and opportunities.

DKSH generates annual gross revenues of more than CHF8,700 million and employs over 22,000 specialized staff incorporating no less than 48 nationalities. The Group operates in 35 countries through a coordinated network of 440 business locations across Asia and another 15 in Europe and the Americas. Ranked by sales and number of employees, DKSH (which is headquartered in Zurich) is among Switzerland's top 20 companies.

DKSH's Asian history dates back to 1890 when it started up activities in Saigon and Haiphong but withdrew from the north in 1954 and from Saigon in 1955. During those 60-plus years, the company was active in the import business for consumer and pharmaceutical products and also represented shipping lines and insurance companies. The company re-entered Vietnam in 1991 more than 100 years after its initial entry. The government's 'open door' policy in the early 1990s attracted the company back and in the 1990s it succeeded in obtaining an operating licence as a fully FIE providing sales, marketing and logistics services. 'The first positive change came with *Doi Moi* followed by WTO and the new Law on Investment', it has been asserted. From the 2000s, in particular, the business of DKSH has rapidly evolved.

Furthermore, 'the WTO brought many changes. Trading is far easier than it was before. On the other hand it also brought in more competition from abroad,' says Mr Trinh Quang Thanh, Director of DKSH. In 1997, the company spent more than US$4 million to scale up its operations which includes logistics and trading. The Swiss parent company of DKSH employs 10,000 people in Thailand, 3,000 in

Malaysia, followed by Singapore and Vietnam with more than 2,000. DKSH Vietnam mainly operates through four business units, which are supported by the support functions of logistics, finance, HRs and IT.

Source: Authors' study; fieldwork interviews (2008); company websites.

Being forced to import electricity, the government has opened the energy sector to FDI by entering into LLC agreements. One such energy cooperation has been formed between Petrovietnam and the US oil company Chevron (formerly Texaco).

Case Study 6.2: Organizations in the energy sector

Vietnam's energy sector is dominated by Petrovietnam and Electricity of Vietnam (EVN), both under the control of the Ministry of Industry; although, in practice, the two national companies are also directed by the Politburo and other central government planning agencies. Petrolimex, a unit of Petrovietnam, operates 300 miles of oil pipeline, although much of the country's fuel supply is transported by road.

Vietnam exports all of its crude oil output and has to import all petroleum products for domestic consumption. The country's complete reliance on imported petroleum products is expected to cease when its first oil refinery becomes operational in 2009. Dung Quat Oil Refinery will be capable of refining more than six million tonnes of crude oil a year. Petrovietnam exported 15.72 million tonnes of crude oil, bringing in US$8.8 billion in 2007. Chevron, which holds a 43 per cent stake in the offshore development off the south west coast of Vietnam, is planning a US$4.3 billion project and is willing to take stakes in all parts of integrated gas development, from exploration to power plants. Such a deal would break with Chevron's usual reluctance to invest outside its core business. Chevron has recently been under attack for human rights violations and environmental neglect.

Historically, the government urged upstream firms, such as Chevron, to invest in downstream infrastructure. In return, foreign partners could expect to secure a market for their resources by investing in power plants and other downstream facilities. State-owned EVN dominates downstream generation, transmission, distribution and sale of electricity in Vietnam. This makes a partnership difficult. The participation of foreign and private companies has been permitted since 2002, but the lack of a regulatory regime has inhibited investment. In the past, coal-fired and hydroelectric power plants have supplied the majority of electricity in Vietnam. However, in recent years natural gas-fired power plants have emerged as a new source of electricity. EVN has outlined plans to build 74 new power stations by 2020. The relationship between the two SOEs, EVN and Petrovietnam, is complex and influenced by politics. For example, EVN's electricity retail prices are fixed by the government and it has to supply it at any cost. In 2008, in a bid to limit the electricity shortage in the start of the dry season, EVN had to buy back electricity produced by Petrovietnam and resell to customers at a VND3 billion (US$17.2 million) loss due to the fact that Petrovietnam benefited from sharp increases in oil prices but EVN had to keep electricity prices stable. More recently, Petrovietnam has moved into the power generation business itself, competing against EVN.

According to estimates, the Chevron–Petrovietnam project should produce more than 500 million cubic feet of gas per day, expected to be reached within five to seven years of commencing operation, which in turn would represent about 70 per cent of Vietnam's gas production. The initial projected cost of US$4.3 billion will include the offshore part and pipeline to the power complex, though not the power plant itself. Engineering and construction costs for upstream projects have risen significantly over the past few years in line with rising costs of labour and steel.

Sources: Authors' study; Tegel and Koenig (2007); EAI (2007).

Case studies of managers

Case Study 6.3: Mr Mark Schiller, Managing Director, Shipbuilder Strategic Marine (SSM)

One of the reasons that SSM from Australia picked Vietnam was its HR. According to Mr Schiller, SSM's Managing Director, the skills, work ethics and attitude to life of the Vietnamese people fit the culture of SSM that is very much a family business. Also, within Vietnamese culture, he observes, you live as a family and are very happy and very hard working.

Regarding Ba-Ria Vung-Tau province as the place for investment, Mr Schiller explains that the local government was very welcoming, helping the company to process the necessary procedures in a short period of time and offered several attractive options. There is reasonable skilled labour in the region as a result of of the oil industry, where some potential customers for SSM can be expected to come from.

Starting with an initial total investment of US$25 million, SSM employs 1,100 people on a full-time basis and commits to contribute significantly to the economy of the region as well as to Vietnam as a whole. Besides offering sizeable job opportunities to local people, SSM also has over 100 subcontractors and suppliers of materials, machines, clothing and shipyard operations. SSM contributes greatly to the transfer of technology as it has a very strong management system, implementation and technical know-how from top-notch engineers assigned from Australia. Thus, as Mr Schiller said in an interview: 'There is no doubt our investment will benefit Vietnam not only in this yard but also, as time goes on, we will develop skills and technology around Vietnam.' SSM's intention is to have a mixed management team, consisting of 20 Vietnamese and 10 Australian managers to facilitate the process of transfer of management skills and technology to Vietnam and, at the same time, to maintain its international business and world safety standards.

Initially, SSM's five-year investment plan called for the company to be established in 2009. Its medium-term plan is to develop the waterfront two years after that so that the yard will be able to carry out repair work within three to five years. To be ready for that, SSM has set up a two-year in-house T&D programme in specific knowledge for its future development business for 50 local people.

Of course, SSM has felt some impact from the post-2008 global financial crisis, but Mr Schiller believes that the company's core products and services are in special areas that are always needed. SSM is operating on an international scope and concentrates on the market for high-speed, high-tech quality vessels for the oil sector, which is still strong. National security, and the vessels required for it, is also a SSM market as governments worldwide still want to secure their countries and people, as Mr Schiller pointed out.

Source: Adapted from Tu Tam (2009b).

Case Study 6.4: Mr Takashi Fujii, General Director, Dai-Ichi Life Insurance Company of Vietnam Ltd (DIIVN)

The post-2008 global credit crisis has impacted on Vietnam's economy but, compared with others in the region, General Director Fujii of DIIVN believes that his company has experienced a less severe influence because Vietnam's exposure to the crisis is still limited. The local financial sector is still in the development phase and has yet to suffer like that of the rest of the world.

According to Mr Fujii's reasoning, insurance is, in reality, a tool for protection, hence when the market goes down, the role of insurance can become even more important and a better tool to protect investors. Hence, the crisis is a good time for investors to become aware of the real function of insurance. So, Mr Fujii believes that the local slowdown can even stimulate market growth for his company.

Mr Fujii's unconventional thought has some sound underpinning and rationale. In 2008, DIIVN reached over 1,200 per cent in terms of liquidity and this turned the company into the leader in the insurance market in Vietnam. For new contracts, DIIVN's revenue accounted for VND190.9 billion, an increase of 51 per cent compared with 2006 when the company first started its business. During 2007–09, the growth rate in exploiting new markets increased by nearly 30 per cent per year on average, which allowed DIIVN to increase the number of its offices in the country to 52.

Mr Fujii is quite optimistic about the future business opportunities for his company. With a population of more than 85 million, of which only about 5 million have insurance policies, he firmly believes that there is still a lot of room for business expansion, and the industry is expected to grow at 20 per cent a year on average. To make full use of these business opportunities, Mr Fujii plans to focus especially on building this company's brand recognition, being fair to its clients, expanding the agent network to reach out to potential customers in remote areas, training employees and diversifying its product offerings to meet the increasing demand in these areas.

Source: Adapted from Tu Tam (2009).

Challenges

Vietnam will face the following challenges in the future to make the country a continuingly attractive destination for FDI. These challenges arise particularly in the areas of labour productivity, real estate, industrial parks and labour relations.

Labour productivity

Foreign investors were eager to invest in Vietnam, although as was noted earlier, real disbursement does not always match the promised funds. In some areas, such as real estate development, conflicts between FDI projects, local projects and farmers exist. For example, although vocational T&D programmes are in place, farmers are often considered to be not good enough to work in hotels or insufficiently qualified to become skilled workers; or the farmers themselves do not want to work in factories because of the low salaries. FDI projects are, therefore, hampered.

The cost of labour is often important to FDI. However, Vietnam's relative advantage in lower wage costs does not extend to other categories of costs. Vietnam has higher shipping costs than Thailand – for example, sending a 40-foot container to Europe from Vietnam costs US$ 4–500 more than from Thailand or China. Thailand is also cheaper in terms of office rental and housing for expatriates. Thailand also offers cheaper electricity and water, although more marginally. Compared to Vietnam, Thailand's infrastructure, transportation, electricity and water supply are more stable and better managed.

Power issues are a key concern for all industrial parks in Vietnam and one that has received considerable attention from the government because of a foreseeable power shortage. Compared with the daily electricity demand, EVN lacks between 1,500 to 2,500 MW every day during peak hours (EAI, 2007). However, the rule of law, intellectual property protection, and a generally better quality of life for expatriate managers are all factors that draw companies to Vietnam instead of Thailand.

Real estate

The real estate sector has attracted a wave of FDI interest. Hotels and property development were initially the main sectors for investment in the early 1990s, but it was the real estate bubble that accounted for the downturn in FDI between 1997 and 2004 (Masina, 2006). Yet, in 2008, many new real estate projects were signed, such as the university township development in Hanoi.

Real estate prices were growing steadily, driven by stock market volatility, improving living standards, and revised legislation opening up the sector for foreign investors. One example is given in Text Box 6.1. In addition, FDI itself has played a major role in driving up demand for high-quality property, especially in the office segment. Difficulties faced by real estate developers are land clearing procedures and lack of adequate infrastructure.

Text Box 6.1: North Red River new residential area, Hanoi

A consortium of three investors, led by Switzerland's Tradco Global Engineering and Construction SA, plan to invest US$3 billion in a residential and commercial complex in Hanoi. The complex includes a six-star hotel and a few four- and five-star hotels that will be linked with office and trading centres. In the first phase the six-star hotel, an 18-hole golf course, water park and modern villas will be built. The residential area, which will be finished by 2012, will supply around two million square metres of accommodation. Schools and a hospital will be developed in the last phase, by 2013.

Urbanization in Hanoi has brought about better living conditions for those living nearby but it has also taken agricultural land from them. Consequently, many farmers suddenly became unemployed. From 1998 to 2003 some 7,000 hectares of agricultural land were converted to urban use. The official plan for 2020 states that another 12,000 hectares of agricultural land will be used for constructing new residential buildings, roads and industrial zones. Of the 12,000 hectares, 75 per cent will be from the north side of the Red River.

Sources: Authors' own study; GSO (2007).

Industrial parks

Many SOE's, such as EVN, continue to survive through protection from international competition and provision of low interest loans. The government has failed to invest in SOEs to upgrade technology to make them more competitive. Foreign investors, especially those residing in industrial parks, are expected to bring T&D and technological upgrades. 'We are not only providing buildings and infrastructure but also vocational training. This way we contribute to the upgrading of human resource skills,' says Mr Pham Van Tinh from the Corporation for the Development of Bien Hoa Industrial Zone (fieldwork interview). The Vietnamese government has created many legal and financial advantages for industrial parks and their resident firms. One example can be seen in Text Box 6.2.

Text Box 6.2: Amata

Amata is a Thai company that established its Vietnamese JVE in 1994. It is located in Dong Nai province very close to the city of Bien Hoa on land that was part of the US army headquarters Long Binh base during the Vietnam War. The duration of the JVE is 50 years with a legal capital of US$17 million contributed by both parties as follows: the Vietnamese party contributed US$5 million of legal capital in the form of land use rights on an area of 100 hectares; the foreign party contributed US$12 million in cash. A benefit of the Amata site is that it is close to the new deep-water port that is soon to open and to the site of the new airport, the opening date of which is still unclear.

The government has provided corporate income tax incentives for new service enterprises paying tax rates of 15–20 per cent, as opposed to 28 per cent outside the industrial zone. Also, new manufacturing enterprises inside industrial parks are entitled to the rate of 15 per cent, instead of the standard 28 per cent. Enterprises outside industrial parks often have to go to different authorities to carry out licensing procedures, such as the Department of Trade for import licences, the Department of Investment and Planning for key personnel registration, and the Department of Labour for foreign labour permits. In contrast, the Provincial Management Boards of industrial parks are authorized to review and decide on all of these issues, from granting and amending investment licences and approving import plans to granting work permits for short-term foreign staff. In contrast to Board of Investment (BOI)-approved industrial parks in Thailand, a

> company cannot own land in Vietnam; this is a clear disadvantage because land usually appreciates in value, while a leasehold is a depreciating asset.
>
> Many well-established companies have chosen the Amata site – namely, Akzo Nobel, Bayer, Bosch, Kao, Nok, San Miguel and Shiseido. Dr Phien of Amata Vietnam notes that 'most foreign companies seemed pleased with the quality of the work produced by their Vietnamese workers, generally rating the quality of work higher than in similar Thai or Chinese operations. Vietnamese workers are fast learners and willing to work overtime'.
>
> Source: Authors' own study; interviews (2008).

Labour relations

The FDI-invested sectors are the most dynamic areas in terms of generating GDP growth, and exports are also heavily dominated by FDI enterprises (GSO, 2007). The most rapidly expanding sector is low-wage, export-orientated manufacturing in which women workers predominate. Indeed, studies have shown that women are the real work horses of the Vietnamese economy (Desai, 2000). Women's share of employment in the FDI sector has risen, while in SOEs and domestic non-state firms it fell.

Labour strikes are common in labour intensive industries, primarily affecting subcontracting companies owned by South Korean, Taiwanese or Hong Kong-based firms (Quang et al., 2008). The causes of these strikes are almost always low pay rates. South Korean-owned facilities have incurred considerable bad feelings not only because of low pay, but also because of previous incidents in which South Korean managers were insensitive to Vietnamese staff and carried out disciplinary actions that were seen as not in line with the misdemeanour. These events created environments in which little trust often exists on either side and small differences can quickly blow up into major controversies (Quang et al., 2008).

According to statistics from the General Confederation of Labour (2008), 1,290 strikes took place nationwide between 1995 and 2006, most of which were spontaneous and not led by any trade union organization or labour representatives. The peak period for strike action was the first two months of each calendar year, which coincided with the Lunar New Year festival (*Tet*) when employee discontent with wage and bonus policies often arose. For example, the first quarter of 2007 alone saw the participation of 62,700 employees in 103 strikes (in 14 provinces and cities), of which 79 were in FIEs, 23 in domestic PEs and one in a SOE. Most strikes were in textile, garment and footwear companies. Text Box 6.3 provides an example of such conflict.

Text Box 6.3: Nike

Nike's Taiwanese subcontractor produces around 10 million pairs of shoes in Vietnam. However, as a result of low pay (about US$60 per month) 20,000 workers demanded a 20 per cent pay increase and better canteen food in April 2008. After their demands were not met they went on strike. Such unorganized labour unrest is becoming more common as inflation rates (15 per cent in June 2008 and higher since) and living costs have surged. Similar strikes at other Nike factories took place in 2007.

One report highlights violations of labour law and poor working conditions as well as health and safety practices and sexual harassment. 'Workers cannot go to the bathroom more than once per eight-hour shift and they cannot drink water more than twice per shift. Forced and excessive overtime to meet high quotas is currently the norm at Nike factories. During January 1997, we found workers who worked over 80 hours of overtime and in February, which was a short month because of the national four-day holiday for Lunar New Year, they were forced to work over 70 hours of overtime' (VLW, 1998). Not surprisingly, looking at the above conditions, the relationship between factory managers and workers has been extremely tense for years.

Source: Authors' own study; World Bank (2008); Vietnam Labour Watch (1998).

In the first two months of 2008, another series of unlawful strikes took place. On a single day, 8 January 2008, there were three strikes in the Tan Thuan Export Processing Zone. There were also strikes recurring one year after they first took place as a result of the failure of employers to realize their commitments (e.g., a strike against SH Global Export Garment Co in Quoc Oai District, Hatay Province).

Under Decree No 11, if a strike led by representatives of a labour collective is regarded as unlawful and harmful to the interests of the employer, those representatives and striking workers themselves will bear personal responsibility according to their respective roles in the strike for paying a share of damages to their employers. Employers are required to request payment of damages from trade union organizations or representatives of labour collectives and labourers involved in a strike within one year of the court ruling declaring the unlawfulness of the strike. Decree No 11 aims to reduce the number of unlawful strikes, contributing to stabilizing the economic and political situation in industrial parks, and protecting the interests of enterprises. However, the enforceability of the decree remains questionable.

Grass-roots trade union organizations at enterprises are bound by many unfavourable regulations. For instance, one requires union leaders to obtain a 51 per cent vote of trade union members before striking. This requirement is impossible to meet because employees cannot leave their work to go around asking other employees or show their support for a strike as they risk being sacked. Furthermore, most employees do not trust trade union leaders when they are urged to take action. Other reasons include the cumbersome procedures for striking lawfully, which require approximately 20 days to complete, during which time disputes may develop into open conflict. Needless to say, improved working conditions might be the single most effective means to limit the risk of unlawful strikes.

Conclusion

Vietnam has come a long way from a war-torn and isolated communist country to a more market-oriented economy that some foreign investors have considered to be 'flavour of the month' for some time. In addition, despite its success, Vietnam has the potential to attract even higher levels of FDI (UNCTAD, 2007b), for example, by encouraging investors to diversify into sectors that are still closed. Here, the WTO commitments in the services sector will provide for additional opportunities once the phase-in periods have expired. Areas for further liberalization should be given careful consideration, and infrastructure and education especially could benefit from higher levels of openness to FDI (UNCTAD, 2007b).

However, like many other emerging countries, Vietnam can no longer hope to be an attractive country to investors across all business sectors. Instead, the country needs to find its market niche in the global marketplace (Michalet, 1997) and to seek to establish a presence with a small number of countries, with world-competitive facilities that together strengthen their regional or worldwide competitive advantages. Vietnam has already tried to position itself against China, India and Thailand. A draft law intends to lower the basic corporate tax rate from the current 28 per cent to 25 per cent – a move intended to make Vietnam an even more attractive destination to FDI than its neighbours in the ASEAN region.

MNCs are continually moving their portfolios of mobile assets (e.g., intellectual property, know-how) across the globe to find the best match with the immobile assets of different locations (Lall, 2000). The ability to provide the necessary immobile assets thus becomes a critical part of an inviting FDI strategy. Immobile host country assets include the labour force, infrastructure, supply networks and legal system. Vietnam, with excessive and often contradictory regulations, red tape, inadequate infrastructure, poor legal enforceability, weak banking system (see Chapter 4), privileges still enjoyed by SOEs, high land and rental costs, corruption, poor protection of intellectual property rights and currency controls, is not well positioned to provide such immobile assets. Although progress has been made in recent years, Vietnam still has a long way to go to match a country like Singapore. Indeed, the lack of qualified HR is also becoming a critical element (see Chapter 2). Therefore, as one response, the 3 per cent limit on foreign workers was lifted in 2008 to open up the labour market.

Attracting FDI on the grounds of cheap labour causes labour disputes and cannot be a long-term strategy. However, Vietnam has a young workforce and strong economic growth; by respecting intellectual property rights it could position itself against China; with a more flexible labour market and political stability it could compete against Thailand and, with an overall more market-oriented policy and less red tape, differentiate itself from other Asian countries. Even if not all registered capital is disbursed, Vietnam's FDI growth rate has been impressive. In short, the changing face of management in this area has several underpinnings, as outlined, and is complex.

Bibliography

Beresford, M. (2008) 'Doi Moi in review: the challenges of building market socialism in Vietnam', *Journal of Contemporary Asia*, 38, 2, 221–43.

Chau, Ngoc (2008) 'Moi truong kinh doan dam chan tai cho (Investment environment has not changed)', *Vnexpress.com.vn*, 10 September.

Desai, J. (2000) *Vietnam Through the Lens of Gender: Five Years Later. Results from the Second Vietnam Living Standards Survey*. Bangkok: Food and Agriculture Organisation, United Nations Regional Office for Asia and the Pacific, November 2000.

De Sterlini, M.L. (2005) *The Agreement on Trade Related Investment Measures, the World Trade Organization – Legal, Economic and Political Analysis*. Free Press: New York.

Doanh, Le Dang (2002) Foreign direct investment in Vietnam: Results, achievements, challenges and prospects, International Monetary Fund, Conference on Foreign Direct Investment, Hanoi, 16–17 August, 2002.

EAI (2007) Energy Administration Information, 'Country Analysis Briefs: Vietnam'. Available at http://www.eia.doe.gov/emeu/cabs/Vietnam/Full.html (accessed 2 April 2008).

General Confederation of Labour (2008) Available at http://www.congdoanvn.org.vn (accessed 7 July 2008).

GSO (2007) 'Statistical Data: Investment'. Available at http://www.gso.gov.vn/default_en.aspx?tabid=491 (accessed 1 May 2008).

GSO (2009) 'Statistical Data: Investment'. Available at http://www.gso.gov.vn/default_en.aspx?tabid=491 (accessed 20 March 2009).

Lall, S. (2000). 'FDI and development: Research issues in the emerging context'. Paper presented at the Asian Development Forum, Singapore, 5–8 June, 2000.

Masina, P. (2006) *Vietnam's Development Strategies*. Abingdon: Routledge, UK.

Massmann, O. (2008) 'Vietnam Economy'. Available at http://www.vietnam-trade-investment-law.sino.net (accessed 1 April 2008).

Michalet, C.A. (1997) 'Strategies of multinationals and competition for foreign direct investment: The opening of central and eastern Europe', Washington DC: Foreign Investment Advisory Service, Occasional Paper 10, 31–32.

Minh, Q. (2008) 'Vi sao giai ngan von FDI thap (Why disbursement of FDI capital is low)', *Thanh Nien*, 5 September, 1 & 6.

Ministry of Foreign Affairs (2008) 'Projects worth 40 billion US$ expected'. Available at http://www.mofa.gov.vn/en/nr040807104143/nr040807105039/ns070820163008 (accessed 1 May 2008).

Ngoc, Minh (2008) 'Thay gi tu FDI (What we see from FDI)', *Thanh Nien*, 22 April. Available at http://www.thanhnien.com.vn.

Quang, T. (1998) 'A case of JV failure: Procter & Gamble vs. Phuong Dong in Vietnam', *Journal of Euro-Asian Management*, 4, 2, 85–101.

Quang, T., Thang, L.C. and Rowley, C. (2008) 'The changing face of human resource in Vietnam', in, C. Rowley and S. Abdul-Rahman (eds.) *The Changing Face of Management in Southeast Asia*, pp 185–220. London and New York: Routledge.

Saigontourist (2008) 'Phu Quoc island to house US$9 billion resort complex'. Available at http://www.saigon-tourist.com/news/detail_en.asp?id=12970 (accessed 1 May 2008).

Sheridan, N.P. (1998) 'Opportunities and challenges to joint ventures in Vietnam. A case study of the origin of a basic problem: lack of trust'. Available at http://www.vvg-vietnam.com/jointventures.htm (accessed 1 March 2008).

Sidhu, K. (2004) *Die Regelung von Direktinvestitionen in der WTO*. Göttingen, Germany: V&R Unipress.

Sornarajah, M. (2004) *The International Law on Foreign Investment*. Cambridge, UK: Cambridge University Press.

Swierczek, W.F., Hirsch, G. and Muoi, L.T. (1998) 'International business negotiation: A comparison between international and Asian negotiation styles in the Vietnamese context', *Journal of Euro-Asian Management*, 4, 2, 1–22.

Tegel, S. and Koenig, K. (2007) 'Chevron's human rights problems span three continents'. Available at http://www.chevrontoxico.com/article.php?id=377 (accessed 2 April 2008).

Thuy, Lai Xuan (2005) 'Relational capital and performance of international joint ventures in Vietnam'. PhD thesis, Asian Institute of Technology, Thailand.

Thuy, Lai Xuan and Quang, Truong (2005) 'Relational capital and performance of international joint ventures in Vietnam', *Asia Pacific Business Review*, 11, 3, 389–410.

Tu Tam (2009) 'Life insurer to become more dynamic', *The Saigon Times*, February 21, 9, 9, 7.

Tu Tam (2009) 'The labour force attracts us', *The Saigon Times*, March 7, 11, 9, 7.

UNCTAD (2006) *World Investment Report 2006: FDI from Developing and Transition Economies: Implications for Development*. New York/Geneva: United Nations.

UNCTAD (2007a) *World Investment Report 2007: Transnational Corporations, Extractive Industries and Development*. New York/ Geneva: United Nations.

UNCTAD (2007b) *Investment Policy Review Viet Nam – Draft Report*. New York/ Geneva: United Nations.

Vietnam Economic Times (2008) 'Foreign investment portal'. Available at http://www.gda.com.vn/?page=statistics (accessed 7 March 2008).

Vietnam Labour Watch (2008) 'Nike labour practices in Vietnam'. Available at http://www.saigon.com/~nike/reports/report1.html (accessed 1 May 2008).

VietnamNews (2007) 'First semiconductor parts factory to open'. Available at http://vietnamnews.vnanet.vn/showarticle.php?num=01TAS260707 (accessed 6 July 2008).

Wiemann, J. et al. (2006) *Vietnam, the 150th WTO Member: Implications for Industrial Policy and Export Promotion*. Bonn, Germany: German Development Institute (DIE).

World Bank (2008) 'Nike in Vietnam: the Tae Kwang Vina Factory'. Available at http://siteresources.worldbank.org/INTEMPOWERMENT/Resources/14826_Nike-web.pdf (accessed 1 May 2008).

Zhan, J. and Terutomo, O. (2001) *Business Restructuring in Asia: Cross Border M&As in the Crisis Period*. Copenhagen: Copenhagen Business School Press.

7 The changing face of public sector management in Vietnam

Truong Xuan Do and Quang Truong

- **Introduction**
- **Key issues and new developments**
- **Case studies**
- **Challenges**
- **Conclusion**

Introduction

Vietnam's recent socio-economic development has been remarkable. Poverty was cut from 58 per cent in 1993 to 18.6 per cent in 2006, and the average income per capita grew from US$288 to US$712 during the same period (ADB, 2007). To sustain this pace of economic growth and further reduce poverty, the country's Socio-Economic Development Plan (SEDP) for 2006–10 stresses the need to strengthen the current governance system to ensure that public resources are utilized more efficiently and effectively, to reduce misuse of public resources and to control corruption (World Bank, 2006).

In 2007 Vietnam entered into a new phase of economic development with deeper integration into the global economy that was marked by WTO membership. The benefits of global integration, however, accrue to economies whose competitiveness is not undermined by the high transaction costs of red tape and inefficient administration in general. In a dynamic and challenging context, Vietnam's public administration system must contribute more effectively to the country's transformation into an industrialized and modern state as it wishes to be by 2020 (United Nations, 2005).

Against this backdrop, this chapter first provides an overview and highlights key issues of public administration, including the management of SOEs in Vietnam. These issues are then illustrated by two case studies that illustrate how change and reform are implemented in the public sector at both local and central government level. It concludes with a discussion about the main challenges that public administration is facing now and in the foreseeable future.

Key issues and new developments

As defined by the 1992 Constitution (amended in 2001), the formal government apparatus is distinct from that of the political party in power, the CPV. Nevertheless, the Constitution asserts the supremacy of the CPV as 'the force assuming leadership of the state and society' (Article 4). Consequently, the state (or government, *Nha nuoc*) is practically under the control of the party through an interlocking system of parallel hierarchies, extending down into the lowest government units, especially when a party leader and government official is the same person. As a result, high-ranking CPV members often hold key positions in the central government. This stereotype is to be seen in the CPV's lower committees at the local level (Quang, 1981). It is the overwhelming position and the unclear relationship between the CPV Central Committee and the legislative and executive branches that remain the most extraordinary characteristic of the SRV's power structure (see Figure 7.1).

As illustrated above, the dividing line between policy making and policy execution is blurred in Vietnam, as in other socialist countries. Because of its pervasive role, the CPV often overshadows its counterparts in the state organ in terms of number and quality of personnel and emerges as the most monolithic and bureaucratic system of its kind. In practice almost all members of the state hierarchies are also members of the CPV (they are all called 'cadres' or '*can bo*') and, therefore, are subject to its own system and discipline. By creating such a close-knit system (party–state–mass organizations), the CPV is involved not only in decision-making processes but also in the day-to-day activities of the parallel organizations.

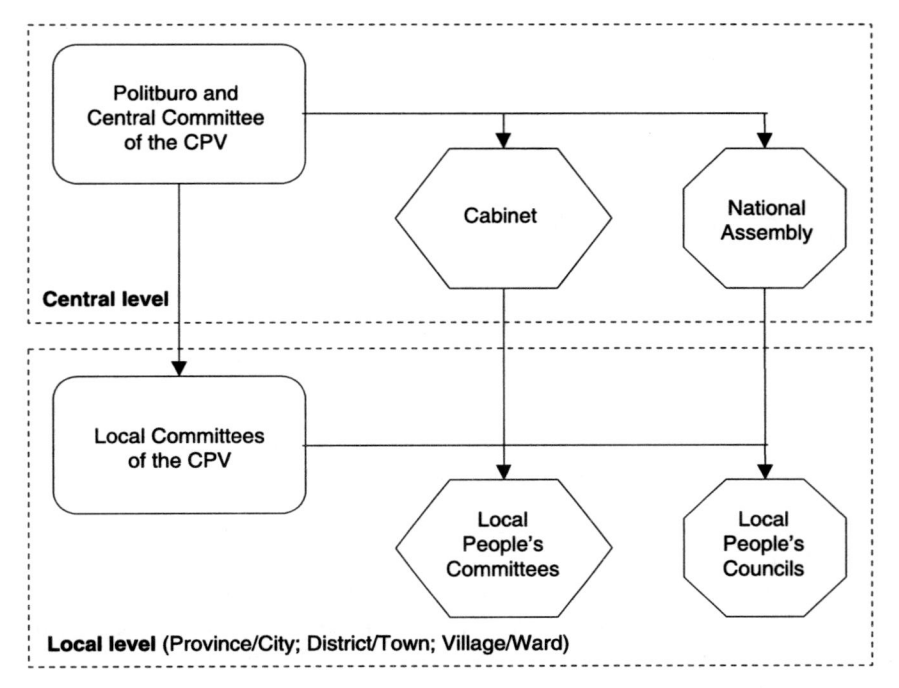

Figure 7.1 Relationship between the CPV and executive and the legislative branches.

Public sector reforms

The following section highlights the key issues and developments in public administration in Vietnam. These issues include (1) public administration reform (PAR), (2) the regulatory framework, (3) the management of civil servants, (4) corruption and (5) the reform of SOEs.

Public administration reform (PAR)

PAR is the theme by which changes in public management in Vietnam have been made since the late 1990s. The PAR Master Plan for the 2001–10 period provides a comprehensive framework for the reform of the public administration of Vietnam. The Plan covers four reform areas: (a) institutional reform, (b) organizational structure, (c) HR, and (d) public finance. In practice, however, the Plan is structured around seven programmes concerning:

- developing and issuing normative legal documents;
- revising tasks, functions and organizational structures;
- modernizing administrative systems;
- staff downsizing;
- improving the quality of cadres and civil servants;
- salary reform; and
- improving the financial management mechanisms for the administrative and public service delivery agencies.

The implementation of the Plan was led by the Ministry of Home Affairs under a steering committee which included members from various ministries (World Bank, 2004).

Initially, substantial progress was made in all four areas of PAR. Notably, the legislative process has increased and improved in quality. The capacity and quality of the law-making process at the NA is steadily increasing. The content of the laws is increasingly in accordance with international standards (World Bank, 2004).

In the area of organizational reform, reorganization of state agencies was carried out. The number of governmental bodies was reduced to 18 ministries and four equivalent agencies. Their working procedures, functions and responsibilities were better clarified. Decentralization of central management to local governments has been made in the areas of economic management, organization and personnel, culture, society, health and education (World Bank, 2006).

The amendment of the Ordinance on Cadres and Civil Servants in 2003 established a new framework for civil service management. One of its key features was the clear distinction between administrative civil servants, public servants working in public service delivery agencies and government officials working in SOEs. This paved the way for establishing different policies for each group. Other important features of the amended Ordinance are the inclusion of public servants working at commune levels on the coverage of the amended ordinance, and the introduction of a pre-service period. Civil service management, especially in recruitment and promotion, has been also very much decentralized to ministries and provinces (Poon and Truong, 2007).

There has been steady and marked improvement in the public financial management institutions and technical systems. The most important reform is the revision of the State Budget Law which clarifies and better separates the roles of the NA, the Ministry of Finance and the Ministry of Planning and Investment. Other significant improvements in financial management include comprehensive decentralization through more explicit and coherent roles and powers to local government levels, increased delegation and allocation autonomy to spending units, and obligations with regard to the publication of budgets and audit reports.

In terms of improving the overall quality of delivery, significant progress has been made in providing public services to citizens and businesses. The introduction of the One-Stop-Shop (OSS, *dich vu mot cua*) model has reduced red tape and enhanced transparency. By the end of 2007, all 64 provinces had established OSSs in at least one of their departments, as had 98 per cent of all districts and 88 per cent of all communes (World Bank, 2006). IT has also been used to improve efficiency, add transparency and reduce corruption. A case in point is the application of an e-custom system.

The second phase of the PAR Master Plan for 2006–10 continues with some new activities, aiming to take ongoing reform to a higher level. The organizational reorganization will be continued to further streamline the structure of ministries (and departments at local levels). The strategy for the reorganization is to focus the government on a stewardship role. Further simplification of administrative procedures could involve the widening of the OSS model so as to overlap several levels of administration and the expanded adoption of internationally certified (ISO) standards. In the meantime, strengthening employment and pay policies remains a priority. Civil service pay is to be gradually aligned with market alternatives (ADB, 2005).

To sustain the reform momentum, additional measures should be introduced to further enhance government accountability. These measures include expanding the scope of judicially reviewable decisions, the piloting of administrative tribunals and creating an Ombudsman Committee (*Uy ban dan nguyen*) under the NA, which is specialized in handling complaints of wrongdoing by government officials. Towards this end, the government has issued regulations to manage complaints by citizens and enterprises against bureaucracy, harassment and the abuse of power. The government has also issued a further regulation to specify the rights and obligations of organizations and individuals with regard to requesting and providing information. The objective is to improve publicity and transparency in the operation of state agencies. Public service delivery agencies are now required to seek feedback from citizens and businesses on the quality of their services (World Bank, 2006).

It can be concluded that PAR made significant progress in the early years after it was launched. It is reported, however, that since then PAR has become slower and seems to have failed to function to lead a broader process of transformation of the executive branch of the state, including legal development and public financial reform (World Bank, 2006). One of the key reasons for the slow pace of change is that the scope of reform was beyond the authority of the Ministry of Home Affairs, which was entrusted with the task of monitoring the reform process. In addition, the lack of an effective reporting, monitoring and evaluation system also contributes to the frustration because nobody knows exactly where PAR is now. Whether the PAR process in Vietnam can regain its momentum and reach its predetermined targets remains to be seen.

The regulatory framework

The rapid economic growth in Vietnam has been on a par with the process of deep social and institutional transformation. Supporting this fast change requires improvements and adjustments in the legal framework. Despite some progress made, the current legal framework is still subject to numerous weaknesses and legal development has a long way to go (Buhmann, 2003).

Since the 1980s, Vietnam has made remarkable progress in developing its legal framework. Economic and civil relations have gradually become regulated by law and market practices instead of administrative orders of the former centrally planned economy. The legislative agenda has been very intensive since 2000. International integration, such as accession to the WTO, has resulted in the accelerated issuing of the most important legal documents needed for the conduct of business (see also Chapters 5 and 6). For instance, the number of laws passed by the NA increased from eight in 2004 to 22 in 2005 (World Bank, 2006).

The legal framework in Vietnam is complex and inconsistent. There are 26 types of normative document. The intense legislative activities since 2000 have produced about 200 decrees which, in turn, have probably led to 1,000 guiding circulars and decisions being issued by line ministries and local governments. A recent survey found that there were 134 legal documents regulating business investment, together amounting to 3,500 pages (Thanh, 2008).

There is a clear need to improve the enforceability and consistency of legal documentation. Such documents, when issued at different stages, by different agencies and at different levels in the transformation process, coexist and in many cases overlap. A strong case in point is in the area of investment. The LOI came into effect in 2006 with a clear aim to simplify the investment process and to remove all the remaining hurdles created by previous legal documentation regulating this area. Government officials, however, still refer to legal documents issued before the LOI when dealing with investors, thereby hampering the enforceability of the new law to the dismay of the investor community.

The legal system of Vietnam is far from complete in order to function well under the new conditions. One reason is the lack of a legal framework for the participation of citizen organizations in society. Another reason concerns the indirect investment of Vietnamese businesses in foreign markets. For example, Vietnamese businesses are unable to buy shares in foreign markets because there is no regulation in this area (Thanh, 2008). The need for new laws is urgent, yet because of limited capacity (especially knowledge) law makers in Vietnam often spend time debating which draft laws should be treated in order of importance (Son, 2008).

The government has identified two priorities for establishing legal institutions and systems to ensure the rule of law and a transparent, accountable government. The first priority is to reform the law-making process, by facilitating greater participation of citizens, enhancing the representation of legislative bodies and improving the skills of legal drafts people. The second priority is to ensure the constitutional and legal norms, by monitoring administrative regulations and reducing the number of forms of legal documentation. The government has also developed a Legal Systems Development Strategy leading towards 2020. This strategy identifies six key strategic areas: (a) building a responsive and clean government; (b) ensuring democratic rights and freedom of citizens; (c) drafting laws and building institutions to support the market economy; (d) facilitating the modernization and socialization of education, public health services and the implementation of social policy; (e) improving law on national security, social order and safety; and (f) facilitating the further integration of Vietnam into the regional and global economy (World Bank, 2006).

Management of civil servants

State personnel are grouped into 'public employees' at central government level, 'public servants' at local government level, and 'officials' at commune level. The estimated numbers for these three different groups are 1.5 million, 200,000 and 300,000 people respectively (MoHA, 2008). State personnel are also classified according to educational level: Group A for officers with university degrees or higher, Group B for officers with vocational qualification, and Group C for workers with no technical or professional education. Civil servants are graded into 'experts', 'principal experts' and 'senior experts'. Advancement up this grade scale is based mainly on seniority. As a general practice, it takes nine years to move from expert to principal expert level and six years to move from principal expert to senior expert grade. Officers at commune level are divided into 'elected' officers and 'appointed' officers.

It should be noted that the term '*can-bo*' ('cadres') is used to indicate all those who undertake a task of the government or of the organization (Van Tan *et al.*, 1977). In this sense, there is practically no difference between a 'party cadre' ('*can bo dang*') and 'state cadre' ('*can bo nha nuoc*'), since the state is led and supervised by the CPV, as explained earlier (Quang, 1981).

Generally speaking, the civil service is largely organized as a career-based system. Officers enter the civil service through a competitive recruitment process followed by a probationary period. Following successful completion of the probationary period, officers would generally expect to move up the grading scale. The achievement of a higher grade has great influence on salaries and career opportunities for leadership and managerial positions. For example, candidates for the position of department director must have reached principal expert level.

Given the complexity discussed above, the personnel management system for the CPV often overlaps with that of the government. Although there are practical benefits of this dual system, there are also disadvantages, such as duplication of effort and sometimes tension between the needs of the CPV (political imperatives) and the requirements of the bureaucracy (impartiality and technical competency).

Nevertheless, the policies and methods of recruitment have changed a great deal. For example, civil servants, including commune officers, are recruited and promoted through competitive examinations in accordance with the new regulations. The drawback of the reform in recruitment is that it mainly focuses on ensuring fairness, openness and objectivity. As the content of the examinations is not related to the jobs, there is no guarantee that the best candidates will be selected according to the requirements of the job. Also, the examination content tends to encourage candidates to learn by heart and mechanically remember knowledge, rather than understanding and making use of the knowledge creatively. Thus, there is a real need to introduce more robust recruitment techniques to link candidate qualifications to job specifications, as well as meeting the general requirements of a position. In particular, it is suggested that for senior appointments written and oral examinations should be supplemented with participative techniques, such as role playing, simulation of crisis situations, and speaking before the public for shortlisted candidates (MOHA, 2008).

In general, civil servants earn a fairly low level of salary compared with their counterparts in other countries. A new entry civil servant with a graduate degree earned a monthly salary of around US$100 in 2000. The government has made efforts to reform salary policy by increasing levels and creating a structure that is sufficiently differentiated to motivate and reflect personal capacity and performance (Painter, 2006). On average, the salary of civil servants increased by 55 per cent between 2002 and 2007 (Poon and Truong, 2007). This increase is very moderate, given the double-digit inflation rate reached in 2008 and the much higher salary levels in the private sector (Huong, 2008).

The major types of T&D and upgrading programme for civil servants consist of mandatory residential courses on politics and state management. These courses are designed to meet the general requirements of expert, principal expert and senior expert grades; hence the T&D content is not related to the practicalities of the work environment and the courses tend to resemble academic degrees. Foreign languages and computer application are also compulsory T&D courses. While efforts to change are under way, current T&D for state officials is largely ineffective. This is because the current training methods are overly focused on general theoretical and legal information in large lecture halls. In addition, within state agencies there is little or no culture of continuous learning. Long-term T&D activities – such as continuous professional development and post-training follow up in the form of mentoring and coaching – are largely missing.

The low salaries and unattractive working environments in the public sector prevent the government from acquiring high quality job entrants. For example, only 17 out of 300 outstanding students graduating from universities in Hanoi in 2003–05 chose to work for state agencies (Doan and Chau, 2006). State agencies are facing an increasing 'brain drain' that hampers the operation of government agencies and, in the worst case, seriously puts the whole government apparatus at risk. For instance, during 2003–07, 16,000 civil servants voluntarily left government agencies (Linh, 2008). The total turnover figure for HCMC is 6,400 (Huong, 2008). The most competent state employees leave for private and foreign companies where they are much better paid. In the past, those leaving were often job entrants and at low staff levels. Now managers, even senior managers, are the prime group who leave state agencies (see Case Study 7.3). Some government agencies – such as the State Bank of Vietnam, Ministry of Finance and the State Security Commission – are the worst victims of the 'brain drain' as the demand for skilled labour in the finance and banking area of the public sector has risen.

Little effort has been made to understand fully the working environment in the public sector in Vietnam and why civil servants are leaving. Among the efforts made is the study on public service careers by the National Institute of Public Administration that surveyed a sample of 500 civil servants working at the central and local levels (Linh, 2008). According to this survey, the main reasons for leaving state agencies include ineffective remuneration and lack of incentives and opportunity for development. The most popular reasons for working as a public servant are the job itself and job security. According to an online survey carried out by Vietnamnet (2008) of more than 37,000 readers in 2008, in order to attract and retain competent personnel in the public sector, the government needs to make the recruitment and promotion processes transparent (43.2 per cent of the respondents), increase salaries for public servants (42.3 per cent) and improve the working environment (14.5 per cent).

Given the slow progress in reforming personnel policy, maintaining a competent contingent of civil servants is a great challenge for the government, and further reforms are required to keep pace with new developments.

Fighting corruption

Corruption is both the outcome and symptom of weak governance (Ackerman, 2004). It is often considered among the top priorities on the government agenda for developing countries because corruption presents a serious threat to the development process. Corruption increases the costs of doing business, drains the capacity of a government and deprives the rights of disadvantageous people to basic public services. Unfortunately, corruption cannot be eliminated overnight by a quick-fix recipe. Constant, strong efforts are needed for lasting and sustainable achievement in combating corruption (World Bank, 2006).

Corruption poses one of the biggest challenges in that paying bribes is generally perceived as a 'habit' of the Vietnamese. Accordingly, 71 per cent of the residents in Hanoi and 67.5 per cent of their counterparts in HCMC admit that they are willing to bribe 'to get things done' (World Bank, 2004). A World Bank/IFC Enterprise Survey revealed that 67 per cent of companies surveyed reported to have made some form of facilitation payment (World Bank, 2006).

According to international organizations, the extent of corruption in Vietnam is comparable to that of other countries at a similar level of development (World Bank, 2004). In this regard, Vietnam ranks 123rd out of 180 countries surveyed in the Corruption Perception Index issued in 2007 (Transparency International, 2008). On a comparative basis, Vietnam's level of corruption is regarded as being as serious as that of many other ASEAN countries – for example, Thailand (84th), the Philippines (131st) and Indonesia (143rd) (Transparency International, 2008). Yet, few local companies consider corruption to be a constraint on their business activities in Vietnam, according to the Vietnam Development Report (World Bank, 2006). Companies may have learned how to live with corruption to the point that they do not see it as being a significant constraint. One possible explanation for the controversial perception is the long time institutionalization of the practice of bribes that is deep rooted (and generally tolerated) in Vietnamese society and throughout various forms of government.

Although varying to a considerable extent, corruption is perceived as common and existing at all levels and in all organizations (Overland, 2009). The most corrupt government agencies include land administration, customs, traffic police, tax administration and construction registers. It also appears that some government agencies, without being genuinely 'clean', are somewhat cleaner than others. Local administrators seem to fall into this category. They are considered the 'most friendly' and appear as less prone to ask for gifts (CPV, 2005).

The most common forms of corruption in Vietnam are soliciting bribes by creating obstacles, accepting bribes for favour, and using public means for personal benefit. Examples of the first form of corruption includes giving a 'tip' to police officers instead of paying a fine or giving money to government officials for having the business registration procedure completed. There have been some high profile cases of grand corruption (e.g., the PMU 18 in the North and PCI in the South) involving senior officials and large-scale embezzlement from ODA funds (Minh, 2007, 2008; Duy, 2009; Duong, 2009).

Officially, the government has acknowledged corruption as a serious problem. According to the report of the State Inspectorate, about 600 cases of corruption were detected and an amount of US$ 500 million was recovered in 2007 alone (Pham, 2008). Yet, given the scope and size of corruption as perceived by the general public, the efforts of the government to battle 'the number one enemy of the country' seemingly touches only the tip of the iceberg.

The most cited reason for corruption in Vietnam is the lack of legal regulation. Because of the lack of a legal framework, government officials can make decisions on an ad hoc basis. These decisions will be in favour of those who pay bribes. This scenario is most common in the bidding process for construction projects. The low pay of civil servants can also be another reason for corruption in Vietnam.

In any case, the government has shown strong political commitment to anti-corruption measures. In 2004, the government endorsed the ADB–OECD Anti-Corruption Initiatives for Asia and the Pacific. Subsequently, Vietnam signed the UN Convention against Corruption in 2003. In 2005 Vietnam passed the Law on Anti-Corruption that generally complies with the UN Convention and takes into account the principles of the ADB–OECD Initiative. The CPV has openly declared 'war' on corruption as it may undermine the party's legitimacy as the supreme authority in the country. The war on corruption has led to the imprisonment of a number of senior government officials (World Bank, 2006).

An effective anti-corruption strategy would help to discourage corrupt behaviour and identify those who are corrupt (World Bank, 2000). Legal and institutional frameworks aimed at curbing corruption and bribery have been strengthened. The NA is beginning to monitor anti-corruption initiatives. In recent years, the government has emphasized more positive, systematic approaches to reduce the scope of corruption, in contrast with the almost exclusively punitive measures previously employed. The new approaches include fostering transparency, minimizing bureaucracy and red tape, improving the accountability of government officials, etc. However, the independence of the institutions responsible for detecting and prosecuting corruption remains in question. This limitation significantly weakens the efforts to fight corruption in Vietnam as the key government agencies in charge of fighting corruption could also be the main sources of this problem.

Reform of SOEs

Restructuring SOEs has been one of the key public reforms in Vietnam. Before *Doi Moi*, the economy was entirely dominated by SOEs. Their performance was very poor, most of them were running at a loss and burdened with debts. The key themes for restructuring SOEs are to introduce profit-based accounting, replace output targets by profit targets, increase autonomy and abolish direct budgetary support. Yet, while gradually moving away from central planning, the state sector has made clear its intention to retain the leading role in the economy in most key industries (World Bank, 2004).

During the reform process, 12,500 SOEs in 1990 fell to 5,600 in 2001 and declined further to 2,100 by the end of 2006 (World Bank, 2006). The most popular forms of SOE restructuring is equitisation, although mergers and the liquidation of redundant and loss-making enterprises are more applicable in the earlier stages. Equitisation (*co phan hoa*) is the Vietnamese form of privatization, in which SOEs are transformed into companies (mostly JSCs, *cong ty co phan*) by issuing or selling a proportion of shares to the private sector, where the majority of the equity is meant to be offered to its own management and workers. About 2,000 SOEs were equitised in 2000–05. Larger SOEs were reorganized into general corporations (*tong cong ty*) that include several holding member companies as part of the government's overall reform campaign, known as the 'keeping the big and releasing the small' strategy (UNDP, 2006). The general corporations usually operate in strategic areas of the economy, such as oil exploration, electricity, telecommunications and shipbuilding. The relationships between the government, the general corporations and member companies are defined by the levels of investment and involvement of the state.

On the positive side, the restructuring effort has led to some improvements in the performance of SOEs. A survey of 550 equitised SOEs (UNDP, 2006) shows that 90 per cent had improved financial performance. In total, the turnover of the newly formed enterprises increased by 13 per cent and profits by 9 per cent on average. New investments and salaries also increased.

To push the reform further, the government established the State Capital Investment Corporation (SCIC) in 2005. This corporation operates in a similar way to the Temasek of Singapore (i.e., performing the role of investor and practising ownership rights over the state's assets in SOEs on behalf of the state). The largest general corporations report directly to the Prime Minister and the SCIC manages the remaining 3,000 or so SOEs. The establishment of the SCIC can be seen as a shift away from the direct management of state assets towards the management of investments. However, running SOEs at a profit still remains a great challenge to the SCIC.

The transformed SOEs, both equitised companies and general corporations, continue to face a number of problems. Most of the equitised companies are still managed by the same individuals as they were in the past. Although having significant advantages over private counterparts, most SOEs actually underperform in many respects. Inappropriate corporate governance structures, together with ineffective control systems, partly contribute to the poor performance of SOEs. Some attempts have been made to overcome this problem, such as allowing SOEs to hire CEOs externally instead of in the traditional way of direct appointment (Packard *et al.*, 2004), with a view to enhancing SOE competitiveness.

The strategic role of the general corporations has been seriously undermined as they diversify too much from their key, mandated business areas. Sizeable investments have been diverted into banking, real estate and financial services that boomed up to 2008. Official statistics from the Ministry of Finance show that the general corporations have invested about VND23,000 billion (about US$ 1.5 billion) in 'non-mandated' areas. In a typical case, the Vietnam Ship Building Corporation (Vinashin) made an investment equivalent to 110 per cent of its ownership capital in its non-core businesses such as banking, real estate and insurance (Minh, 2008). These 'out of line' investments actually added waves of chaos to the stock exchange market in the country in 2006–07 before the recession finally came in 2008. Real asset prices dropped by about 50 per cent and the shares of banks lost 50–70 per cent in just the first four months of 2008.

The focus of future SOE reform in Vietnam will be on the large corporations. On the agenda is to accelerate the equitisation of the general corporations and other large companies. After being equitised, the shares of the larger SOEs will be listed on the stock market. The holding company model will be used for large-scale corporations (e.g. energy, shipping, telecommunications, oil, coal, etc.), which cannot be equitised as a whole. The planned approach is to equitise their member businesses and transform the remaining ones into single-member or limited companies and, at the same time, to transform those corporations into group companies held by a holding company. According to this plan, about 950 SOEs will be equitised by 2010, when Vietnam will have 554 wholly state-invested companies, including 26 large-scale economic groups and corporations (UNDP,

2006). This is a very ambitious target because only 150 SOEs were equitised in 2007 (Tu, 2008).

Case studies

The following section presents case studies to illustrate the key issues of public management in Vietnam. These cases demonstrate how change is made in the public sector and the problems faced with regard to the quality of public service and public governance. The first case shows how a local authority experimented with a new management system. The second case is about a specific attempt to make SOEs become more effective. The individual manager cases illustrate the government's efforts to make its public services more effective, friendly and transparent. Those cases help to explain why reform in the public sector usually proceeds more slowly than in the private sector.

Case studies of organizations

Case Study 7.1: Performance management in HCMC

How can change be made?

One of the main purposes of a performance management system (PMS) is to improve effectiveness and efficiency. The key attribute of this system is to move the focus from activities and inputs to 'results' or 'outputs'. This system is particularly relevant when budget management is decentralized because it helps to identify priorities in resource allocation to meet the needs of the public in the best way (VIE/01/024, 2005).

HCMC is the largest municipality and the national economic hub of Vietnam. The recent development of HCMC mostly reflects the *Doi Moi* policy. HCMC contributes about a third of the national GDP. The annual growth rate of HCMC in 1998–2008 was around 10 per cent. However, HCMC is facing great challenges in sustaining its high growth rate. After a long period of strong economic growth, signs of slowdown have recently been seen. Foreign investors now prefer other neighbouring provinces, such as Binhduong, Dongnai or

Baria-Vungtau, claiming that the infrastructure of HCMC is now overburdened. HCMC's authorities seem to have great difficulties in dealing with problems such as poor urban planning, traffic jams and lack of skilled labour. These problems are becoming bottlenecks for the development of HCMC.

HCMC's administration suffered from several weaknesses in implementing its socio-economic development programmes:

(1) The traditional planning practice did not provide an effective process for breaking down overall socio-economic objectives into specific objectives, programmes and activities. As a result, programmes and activities were often not consistent with the corresponding objectives.
(2) Coordination, both vertical between levels and horizontal between functional agencies, was poor. This hindered socio-economic development greatly because it requires extensive cooperation between the various functions.
(3) There was a lack of an effective monitoring and evaluation mechanism that could help to assess the results of the programmes and the extent to which objectives were achieved.

It had been expected that the PMS would help HCMC to address these weaknesses.

In 2005, HCMC decided to develop a PMS with the aim of improving the effectiveness and efficiency of its administration. This effort was part of HCMC's public administration reform programme, which was supported by the United Nations Development Program (UNDP). The main support of UNDP was to provide international experts in this area.

The methodology adopted for implementing the PMS in HCMC was 'learning by doing'. Instead of taking a 'big bang' approach to introduce a complete system, the PMS would be constructed part by part. The system was started with small-scale pilots, followed by large-scale pilots and finally a full application. By the end of 2007, the initial pilots had been completed. The large-scale pilots were implemented in 2008 and full application in 2009 (Poon, 2005).

To implement the PMS, a steering committee was established. The committee was headed by a vice-chairman of HCMC's People's Committee with its members coming from key provincial departments. Two other implementing groups comprised one Core Team and five Department Action Teams. The Core Team was a group of six internal consultants who reported directly to the steering committee. The committee's main role is to support the Department Action Teams to implement the PMS. International consultants mainly worked with the

Core Team. Each department involved formed an internal Department Action Team which was responsible for implementing the PMS within the department. During the initial piloting of the PMS, the number of people participating in the Department Action Teams was 75.

For the initial pilots, three areas (urban management, economic development and social service development) were selected. Three objectives were set for the first areas; these included developing land resources, implementing site clearance for development projects and managing public land resources effectively. The second area had two objectives: to monitor private businesses in HCMC and to monitor private businesses registered in District 1. The third area also had two objectives that aimed to improve the quality of the investment for development of the grass-roots health care system in HCMC and Binh Chanh District. A typical PMS usually focuses on four dimensions: planning, Human Resource Management, financial management and organizational structure. However, the initial pilots covered only the planning aspect; the three other dimensions were not included because they were still largely regulated by the central government.

The design and preparation for the PMS took one year, from April 2006 to March 2007. Key activities during this period included selecting the intervening areas and agencies to be involved, identifying objectives, and setting up the organizational arrangements. During this stage, each Department Action Team prepared a comprehensive plan for implementing the PMS in its department. The plan included: (1) a review of the current status of the intervening objectives; (2) targets for the identified objectives; (3) key outputs of the objectives; and (4) assignment of tasks and allocation of resources. The implementation phase for the initial pilots took one year and the initial pilots ended in June 2007.

The results of the initial piloting of the PMS were encouraging, given its experimental nature. The achievement of the objectives was uneven. Some objectives were achieved at a fairly high level, while other objectives were at a quite low level. For example, the 'manage public land resource effectively' objective was more successfully implemented. The revenue from public land in District 1 in 2006 was VND58.9 billion, while the target was only VND10 billion. The 'development of land resource' objective felt short of its target: only 30 hectares of land was raised compared with the target of 258 hectares (HCMC, 2007).

The initial pilots of the PMS made a number of positive impacts on the administration of HCMC, including making the planning system more systematic, better clarifying tasks and responsibilities among functions, developing a more effective monitoring and evaluation mechanism, and improving overall coordination, especially within agencies.

HCMC is now piloting the PMS on a larger scale. More comprehensive socio-economic objectives are set and more agencies and districts are involved. If everything goes as planned, the PMS will be applied to the whole administration of HCMC. Whether HCMC can become a business hub of the South East Asia region in the future largely depends on its ability to initiate and implement breakthrough changes like PMS.

Sources: Adapted from HCMC (2007); Poon (2005).

Case Study 7.2: Hiring CEOs for SOEs
A mission impossible?

Top business managers, especially CEOs, have an important role in determining corporate performance. They are the ones who lead and drive the business. Their talent and individual performance strongly contribute to the business results of the organizations they manage. Competent top business managers often possess cutting edge business management skills. They also need to be motivated to make their best efforts in the interest of the business owners. Therefore, one of the key requirements of a good corporate governance system is to be able to ensure that companies are run by qualified and motivated top managers.

Most SOEs in Vietnam seem to lack competent top business managers. This is one the reasons for their poor business performance. Top managers of SOEs are largely selected or assigned based on their political credentials ('red' versus 'expert'). They usually have long tenure and high-ranking positions in the structure of the CPV. These people often possess an old-style business mentality and a working style that is partly a legacy of the past centrally planned system. They are often not familiar with modern business management practices. Top managers of Vietnamese SOEs usually lack the necessary capacity to run a large and diversified business in a market oriented economy.

Top managers of SOEs also lack the motivation to give their best efforts in maximizing benefits for their companies. The autonomy of CEOs is much more limited than that of their counterparts in PEs or in FIEs. They have to spend a significant amount of time seeking approval from higher administrative levels for their business decisions. SOEs do not have an effective remuneration system for top managers. The salary of SOE managers is much lower than that of their counterparts in other sectors. According to a salary survey, the average monthly salary of CEOs in FIEs was VND20.2 million, (about

US$1,150), in PEs is VND9 million (about US$530) and SOEs is VND7.4 million (about US$430).

In an effort to improve the performance of SOEs, the government finally allowed them to hire their own CEOs. If successful, the newly hired CEOs would work under contract with a more attractive remuneration package linked to their performance. This could be seen as a breakthrough because the government has maintained tight control over decisions over the top personnel of SOEs. In principle, the top managers of SOEs are still civil servants and have lifetime employment with the government. The aim of the government was to try this small-scale programme as an experiment; thereafter large-scale application would be made to SOEs.

In 2004, two SOEs (Vinamotor Corporation and Ship Building Corporation) were asked by the government to implement this programme. In 2005 three other SOEs (Vietnam Electrical Corporation, Constructional Glassware and Pottery Corporation and Song Hong Constructional Corporation) were added to the list. In theory, these companies can hire anyone, including foreigners, who are qualified for the job.

The outcomes of this experiment were disappointing. After four years of implementation, only Vinamotor Vietnam Electrical Corporation (VEC) had hired its own CEO. The remaining three have not been so successful. Vinashin and Song Hong Constructional Corporation have prepared their proposals for the government. The Constructional Glassware and Pottery Corporation did not even make a proposal and its last CEO was still appointed under the old procedure.

In the case of Vinamotor, the CEO post had been advertised widely in the local media for several months. A total of 10 candidates sent in their applications. Five of them were shortlisted, including an overseas Vietnamese. Vinamotor's management board finally selected Mr Tran Quang Thanh for the position. The company seemed satisfied with their choice. According to Vinamotor's HR Director, Mr Thanh met most of the company's criteria, such as being competent, trained overseas and having a track record of successfully managing a motor company. Mr Thanh's previous position was the CEO of Hoa Binh Motor, a JVE between Vinamotor and GM Daewoo. The new CEO of Vinamotor began his job in 2008 with a monthly salary of US$2,000.

The VEC case posed a serious question as to whether hiring CEOs was feasible for SOEs. VEC spent almost three years developing its proposal to the government for hiring its CEO. The proposal was revised at least seven times and there were three legal documents issued by the government to guide this process. VEC made a careful plan for the recruitment, which included the establishment of a selection panel. It also announced the position opening in most other relevant media channels. Several weeks after its announcements, the company had received only one application. Ironically, it was from the company's acting CEO. VEC finally signed the contract with its own CEO after his retirement.

The reasons for this disappointing result of the experiment include the lack of a legal framework to guide SOEs in implementing this task. In 2004, the Prime Minister asked the Ministry of Home Affairs to compile a regulation for CEO recruitment for SOEs. The Ministry has yet to complete this regulation. Another reason is a lack of qualified candidates because of the low level of development of the high-end labour market in Vietnam.

Vinamotor now has a competent CEO, but it is still uncertain whether he will be able to make significant changes to the company's performance. Many people believe that the newly hired CEO cannot do much. The existing corporate governance structure and working regulations do not give him the necessary leverage to lead and run the company in the way his CEO counterparts do in the non-state sectors. Many questions are still left open regarding the extent to which the CEO can make decisions, when he needs to seek the approval of the Board of Directors for his decisions, whether he works under the leadership of the CPV in the company, etc. In a recent interview, a Deputy Chairman of the Committee for SOE Reform and Development said he did not think the idea would work.

Sources: Adapted from Khaled (2007); Sjoholm (2006); Hong (2007); Ha (2008); Ngoc (2008); Vitinfo (2008).

Case studies of managers

Case Study 7.3: Mr Luong van Ly
A high-ranking official turned entrepreneur

On 16 March 2007, Mr Luong van Ly, the Deputy Director of the HCMC Planning and Investment Department (HCMC/PID), submitted his resignation, which was quickly approved. Together with Mr Ly, two other department deputy directors in HCMC and two deputy heads of section quit. As all of them were qualified in professional skills and foreign languages, and could easily find much better job opportunities outside the public sector. If they did not want to start their own businesses, they would be welcomed by FIEs or PEs where they would be offered much higher salaries and better working conditions.

The reason for Mr Ly's resignation was the unreasonable salary level. 'As a deputy director, I was paid about VND2 million (about US$120) plus VND500,000 (US$30) allowances a month. It is just not enough to support my family. And I don't really want to moonlight', he explained.

Of course low salary might be the prime reason, but other motives were equally important for such people to decide to terminate long public service careers. It is generally seen that public organizations often fail to provide their employees with a good career perspective and are not motivating enough for the talented to join in and work. More often than not, good relationships with superiors and seniority prevail over personal qualifications and performance in making decisions concerning promotion and appointment. Mr Ly noted further: 'I have worked for the government for quite a long period of time, but nothing really changed. Now I have only five more years to go before my nominal retirement, so it would be a waste to sit idle and watch the time passing by. If I join the non-public sector, I will learn new skills, acquire more experience, and meet new challenges to make my life more interesting and meaningful.'

At the time of his resignation, Mr Ly was 55 years old. It would not be the right age for someone to start a business or restart a new life, but Mr Ly argues against conventional thinking. He even believed that by quitting a public service job he might contribute more as a common citizen. He explained: 'During the period after the liberation, the country was in high need for rebuilding and development, so it was logical to join the state organizations. In the integration era, the private sector should take a more active role, and by choosing to be an entrepreneur, I will actually contribute more to the country's development process.'

Mr Ly is regarded as one of the most capable public officials in HCMC. He graduated in international law from Switzerland and is fluent in English and French. He had been in his position since 2001, with specific responsibility for the FDI Department in HCMC. Before this, he had a long stint as an experienced diplomat, working as Deputy Director of HCMC Foreign Affairs Department. His resignation was, therefore, a surprise to many as the first case of a high-ranking official to have done so, despite all the perks attached to the position.

After leaving his department, Mr Ly, together with few close friends, set up a consulting company for foreign investments (DNL Partners) and established himself as Chairman of the Board and CEO. In addition, he is also on the board of two other investment funds. DNL Partners provides one-shop services to potential investors in the areas of infrastructure, education, healthcare and high tech. Its competitive advantage is based on the practical experience and the relationships that Mr Ly had accumulated during his six years of working in the Planning and Investment Department. With only eight staff on board, the company received its first, yet sizeable, contracts with Indochina Land, Maxford Investment Management Ltd, and GS Engineering and Construction Corp.

Sources: Adapted from Anh (2007); Cuong (2008); Hai (2008).

Case Study 7.4: Mr Nguyen van Giau

A determined Governor of the State Bank of Vietnam (SBV)

The developments in the monetary market in 2008 has made his position at the SBV one of the most difficult to handle (and therefore unwanted) seats of the time, but Mr Giau himself thinks of it differently. On the contrary, thanks to his unconventional decision, Mr Giau has been praised as being the author of 'the most successful monetary policy ever'.

Being affected by the global credit crisis, most of the banks in Vietnam joined in the race to increase interest rates in an attempt to protect their asset base, which required the immediate intervention of the SBV to put the situation under control and restore public confidence. Mr Giau's direct action, in his position as Governor of SBV, was to send an urgent memo to all the commercial banks ordering them not to exceed the cap limit of 12 per cent.

At that time, many critics did not agree with his unpopular measure as it was not in line with 'free market' principles and might cause negative effects on the country's commitment to full integration, just one year after Vietnam became a member of the WTO. In retrospect, Mr Giau admitted that his unconventional decision indeed stirred a wave of protest from several prominent experts in the field and members of the government, but at the same time, earned the blessing of many others as being 'courageous' given the current economic and political situation of the country. Mr Giau argued that a natural reaction to the commercial banks' attractive offer would be for most clients to rush to withdraw their money from their current accounts, just to open new deposit accounts in order to enjoy the incredibly high interest rates. This would trigger an uncontrollable cash movement from one bank to another that would destabilize the country's economy at a time of crisis. Mr Giau added that it is natural that any policy to moderate interest rates should be contingent on the situation at hand and suitable to each period of the country's economic development. However, given the unusual and widespread nature of the global credit crisis of 2008, many experts in the field had to admit that both full liberalization and state intervention have disadvantages and, therefore, would not be the sole remedy for the crisis as it used to be in normal situations. In his view, it is more essential to decide when the state should intervene and where should be the limit for such intervention to keep the national interest in balance. For example, in order to curb inflation in the first month of the crisis, Mr Giau decided to cut back the volume of currency circulation on the market by increasing the interest rate to pull the money flow back to the SBV safe. For that, Mr Giau recalled: 'I myself and the Bank leadership had to endure heavy pressure from public opinion, commercial banks, and various critics in the party and government hierarchy. Yet, at the end, the Bank was able to withdraw a total of VND37,000 billion in cash and earned high credit from foreign financial analysts as a wise and successful move.'

According to Mr Giau's philosophy, serving the country is not only a duty, but also an honour. His success formula is threefold: national interest goes first; always be flexible and responsive to the conditions; and discuss and make decisions together with the staff.

Sources: Adapted from Thuy (2008); Ha (2009); Hoai (2009).

Challenges

After two decades of relatively high economic growth, Vietnam is expected to become a middle-income country at some time in the near future. Such a status involves a more complex economy that requires more competent, responsive public policies and a much higher level of cross-sectoral cooperation and networks. A more complex economy also means more stakeholders will be involved whose interests need to be addressed. This process actually entails a gradual change in the relationship between the state and society.

The overall goal for the public sector of Vietnam is to build an effective and accountable governmental machinery that effectively supports the country to successfully transform itself into a middle-income country and put it on the right track to become a developed country. The attainment of this goal greatly depends on how the country responds to several critical challenges, as elaborated in the following changes in the public sector.

Redefining the role of the government

The role of the government needs to be changed gradually when the economy becomes more developed. Its primary role of 'controlling' should be replaced by 'enabling' in order to create a favourable environment for all stakeholders in the economy to participate in and develop. This will require a strengthening of the rule-by-law principle. As such, the role of the government should be geared towards less 'doing' and more 'directing'. This change will lead to increased delegation and participation by non-state sectors into areas that were traditionally dominated by the public sector. The changing role of the government will also drive a wedge between regulation and ownership and between policies and public service delivery (United Nations, 2007).

Undoubtedly, the government has made significant efforts in changing its role. It has been trying to develop a more complete legal framework. The government has a 'decentralization programme' (*phan cap*) that aims to delegate decision-making authority to local authorities in every area. The central government now only approves very large and strategic important FDI projects; the remaining projects are decided by the provincial authorities. The government has also changed the way it manages the state public service delivery agencies. Public universities, hospitals and research institutes now enjoy much more autonomy. The government also promotes the participation of the non-state sectors in providing social services. This is a so-called 'socialization' (*xa hoi hoa*) of social services that primarily allows private institutions to provide social services, such as education and healthcare, for a fee. This strategy helps the government to reduce the burden of supplying social services to its citizens. The reform of SOEs also pushed forward the practice of ownership rights instead of directly controlling the businesses (Dung, 2006).

The efforts in changing the role of the government have made low progress as a result of inconsistent implementation. The legal framework was much improved but is still far from being complete. The decentralization campaign was not effective owing to a lack of capacity building and improvement of accountability. The reform of state service delivery agencies was slow and the efficiency of these agencies has not been greatly improved. There is still a controversial discussion on how the private sector participates in the provision of social services as this may conflict with underlying socialist values. The reform of SOEs was dragging also when the government found it was difficult to release its direct control over SOEs and, at the same time, effectively practise its ownership rights.

The reasons for the slow progress in changing the role of the government are numerous. To begin with, it can be incorrect solutions, as in the specific case of hiring CEOs for SOEs demonstrates. It can also be as a result of inappropriate implementation, as in the case of decentralization. Decentralization, without sufficient efforts to develop capacity and improve the accountability of those who are delegated, significantly reduces its effectiveness. Another reason is the fear of losing control. This is true in SOE reform. It is feared that the leading role of the public sector would be weakened if the government reduces its direct control over the SOEs too quickly. Whatever the reasons, this crucial process appears to be a great challenge to the reform of public management in Vietnam.

Balancing the competing demands of various stakeholders

One of the current challenges for the public sector in Vietnam is how to incorporate the demands and interests of various stakeholders, such as businesses and communities, in a manner that is complementary and balanced. This requirement is crucial because it helps to ensure that the development process will become more sustainable.

The recent boom in the private sector and economic growth requires much more utilization of resources, often at the cost of the community. For example, the process of industrialization and urbanization leads to the reduction of arable land used for agriculture. Many farmers who no longer have land for cultivation face several difficulties in their lives, in particular unemployment and social perils. Economic activities also pose threats to biodiversity and the environment. For example, in order to cope with the increasing demand for construction steel, many producers have to import scrap steel from other countries. Yet, this can lead to problems such as occurred in 2009 when thousands of containers of scrap steel were placed in custody at the Haiphong port as the country's environment protection agency claimed that the imported goods did not meet environmental criteria. The conflict of interests between business and community may be very direct in some cases. The people of the Son Tra peninsula of Danang City became furious when they found they no longer had access to their most beautiful beach. They were told that the beach was rented to an investor to build a spa resort (Chau, 2008).

Reform of the social service system that used to be sponsored by the state made some marginalized groups, such as the poor, more vulnerable. In the meantime, an effective social security system or 'safety net' has not yet been developed. The development of an unemployment benefit system has only been under discussion. Most poor people were not covered by the national health insurance system. It is not rare to find critically ill people receiving minimum care in public hospitals because they neither have money to pay fees nor health insurance. The increasing cost of school fees now make poor households struggle to afford education for their children.

Engaging the participation of civil society

The structure of civil society in Vietnam is very broad based, comprising a large number of organizations, associations and groups. There are six mass organizations – namely, the Fatherland Front, the Labour Federation, the Women's Union, the Youth Union, the Farmers' Unions and the Veterans' Association – together with other professional associations, Vietnamese NGOs and community-based organizations. However, the mass organizations are closely related to the CPV and hence have a minimum independent role.

The key reasons attributable to the less developed and insignificant impact of 'civil society' ('*xa hoi dan su*') in Vietnam include the lack of an awareness of the importance of the 'third' sector (i.e., non-party and non-state), the absence of a legal framework to enable civil society to operate, and the strong affiliation of many civil society organizations with the CPV and the state, which hampers independence. How civil society develops and contributes to public management largely depends on whether the mainstream political power and the state both want and allow the third sector to develop. It is a great challenge to create awareness of the important role of civil society organizations and an enabling environment in which they can develop.

Developing a competent contingent of civil servants

It has been pointed out that the quality of government policy, and by extension Vietnam's national competitiveness, depends on the quality of the civil service. In fact, building a competent and professional contingent of civil servants is one of the key components of PAR in Vietnam (Harvard University, 2008). However, the slow progress in reforming the civil service system proves to be a challenging task for the government.

Despite some improvements, the system for managing civil servants is not effective in attracting and retaining a capable workforce. Good practices of Human Resource Management – such as HR planning, job descriptions, recruitment, compensation and job performance – were not in place or, where they were in place, were often paid only lip service. Common values that are shared among civil servants are weak. The working environment in government agencies is not characterized by a high level of trust, transparency or accountability. To better serve the public as tax payers, who ultimately provide the source of income and the base of legitimacy for the state, a service/customer-oriented culture should be cultivated and practised in all governmental agencies.

Conclusion

Vietnam has made remarkable progress in terms of economic development in the last few decades and has emerged as one of the promising economies in Asia in transforming itself from a rigidly centralized system into a more flexible market mechanism. To fully integrate itself into the world economy, the government has made significant efforts to change the ways in which it used to run the economy. Radical and gradual reforms have also been made to overhaul the whole public management mechanism with a view to enhancing the country's competitiveness in the global arena. This process, however, has been slow and has resulted in a mixture of failure and success. More often than not, efforts at reform seem to be reactive rather than proactive, and have often failed to respond to the changing conditions in the external environment. As changes in public administration tend to be a consequence of the pressure created by the strong growth of the private sector, the public administration system itself has seemingly failed to initiate proactive change to accommodate the development of the ever growing non-state sector working for better wealth and the civil society longing for a better quality of life.

Notwithstanding this blurred situation, Vietnam's prospects for economic development appear to be promising. On the surface, the country is on the right track on the way to becoming a middle-income country. However, this will not happen automatically. Vietnam needs to fortify its foundations for the next stage of development and to avoid the middle-income trap elsewhere in the world, typically the widening of the gap between the rich and the poor, mismanagement, corruption and the abuse of power. To be more sustainable, the government needs to pay more attention to the quality of economic growth in the long run that covers not only economic development, but also socio-cultural and environmental considerations.

In conclusion, proper changes should be made to optimally utilize the available opportunities, given the current capacity constraints of the country. To do so, more aggressive and deeper institutional reforms are required to be made in the public sector to facilitate the socio-economic development process and capitalize on past achievements. Such reforms should be geared towards dealing with all three critical pillars – namely, the structure, the people and the culture of the public sector – to make it more effective and responsive to the increasing demands of the 'tax payers' and the ever challenging conditions in the global arena.

Bibliography

Ackerman, S.R. (2004) 'The challenge of poor governance and corruption', Copenhagen Consensus Challenge Paper. Available at http://www.copenhagenconsensus.com/Files/Filer/CC/Papers/Governance_and_Corruption_300404_(0.7MB_version).pdf

ADB (2005) 'Governance assessment with focus on PAR and anti-corruption', Strategy and Program Assessment, November, 2005.

ADB (2007) 'Country strategy and program 2007–2010', Vietnam.

Anh, P. (2007) 'Tam su cua nguoi tu quan lam doanh nhan (The story of an official leaving his position to join the private sector)', *VNExpress*, 4 April. Available at http://vnexpress.net.SG/Kinh-doanh/Kinh-nghiem/2007/04/3B9F4A76.

Binh, T. (2009) 'Phan quyen dia Phuong tai Viet nam va Dong A (Decentralization in Vietnam and East Asia)', *Dien dan Forum*, 17 January.

Buhmann, K. (2003) 'Reforms of administrative law in the PRC and Vietnam: The possible role of the legal tradition', *Nordic Journal of International Law*, 72, 2, 253–90.

Chau, H. (2008) 'Thanh pho phai "xin" lai dat lam bai tam cho dan (HCMC's Authority must claim back the beach for the people)', *VietNamNet*, 5 June. Available at http://www.vnn.vn/xahoi/2008/06/786815/

CPV (2005), 'Report on the prevalence of corruption and measures for anti-corruption in Vietnam', Communist Party of Vietnam, Central Committee on Internal Affairs, Hanoi, Vietnam.

Cuong, P. (2008) 'TPHCM: nguoi gioi quay lung khu vuc nha nuoc (HCMC: talents turn their back to public sector)', *VietNamNet*, 19 January. Available at http://vietnamnet.vn/chinhtri/2008/01/764852

Doan, L. and Chau, N. (2006) 'Nhieu thu khoa tu choi "moi goi" cua Hanoi (Several top graduates refused the "invitation" of Hanoi)', *Vnexpress*, 21 August. Available at http://www.vnexpress.net/GL/Xa-hoi/2006/08/3B9ED576/

Dung, H. (2008) 'Doanh nghiep nha nuoc van loay hoay tim CEO (SOEs are still struggling to hire CEOs)', *Vneconomy*, 13 March. Available at http://vneconomy.vn/61484P0C5/doanh-nghiep-nha-nuoc-van-loay-hoay-tim-ceo.htm

Dung, N. T. (2006) 'Nhin lai 5 nam sap xep, doi moi, phat trien doanh nghiep nha nuoc (A review of five years restructuring, reforming and developing SOEs)', *Nhan dan (People's Newspaper)*, 9 October.

Duong, T. (2009) 'Dien tien vu PCI tai Nhat ban' (The evolution of the PCI case in Japan)', *Tienphong Online*, 12 February. Available at http://www.tienphong.com.vn

Duy, T. (2009) 'Vu ong Huynh Ngoc Sy: chua the khoi to hanh vi nhan hoi lo (The case of Mr Huynh Ngoc Sy: He cannot be prosecuted yet for having accepted bribe)', *Tienphong Online*, 22 February. Available at http://www.tienphong.com.vn

Fforde, A. and Associates Pty Ltd (2003) 'Decentralisation in Vietnam: Working effectively at provincial and local government level . . .', Report prepared for the Australian Agency for International Development (AusAID), November, 92 pages.

Ha, K. (2008) 'Thue tong giam doc o doanh nghiep nha nuoc: Loay hoay nhu ga mac toc (Hiring CEOs for SOEs: No way out)', *Saigon Giai Phong (Saigon Liberation)*, 1 February, Available at http://www.sggp.org.vn/kinhte/2008/2/142180/

Ha, P. (2009) 'Thong doc Nguyen van Giau: nguoi ngoi ghe nong thoi lam phat (Governor Nguyen van Giau: holding the hot seat in the inflation time)', *Vietnamnet*, 26 January. Available at http://www.vietnamnet.vn

Hai, N. (2008) 'Khong co ai de cung chiu trach nhiem tap the! (Nobody is willing to take the responsibility collectively)', *VnEconomy*, 30 January. Available at http://vneconomy.vn/20090130102151969P0C5/khong-co-ai-de-cung-chiu-trach-nhiem-tap-the!.htm

Harvard University (2008) 'Choosing success: The lessons of East and South East Asia and Vietnam's future, a policy framework for Vietnam's socioeconomic development, 2011–2020'. Available at http://www.fetp.edu.vn/Research_casestudy/PolicyPapers/PP001_Choosing_Success_E.pdf

Hoai, N. (2009) 'Thong doc Ngan hang nha nuoc: "Toi da chiu rat nhieu ap luc" (The Governor of the State Bank: "I have been under lots of pressure")', *VnEconomy*, 23 January. Available at http://www.vneconomy.vn

HCMC (2007) 'Report on two years' implementation of the piloted Performance Management System', Ho Chi Minh City People's Committee.

Hong, A. (2007) 'Lanh dao doanh nghiep nha nuoc kho song bang luong (Top managers of SOEs find it hard to make a living with their salaries)', *Vnexpress*, 12 September. Available at http://www.vnexpress.net/GL/Kinh-doanh/2007/09/3B9FA279/

Huong, G. (2008) 'TP HCM: hon 6400 can bọ, cong chuc thoi viec (HCM City: more than 6400 civil servants quit their jobs)', *Tuoi tre (Youth Newspaper)*, 3 June. Available at http://www.tuoitre.com.vn/Tianyon/Index.aspx?ChannelID=3&ArticleID=260984

Huong, L. (2008), 'Cai cach tien luong: se khong khong che muc toi da (Salary reform: No ceiling)', *Dantri*, 30 August. Available at http://dantri.com.vn/c76/s76-248685/cai-cach-tien-luong-se-khong-khong-che-muc-toi-da.htm

Khaled, E. (2007) 'Does CEO duality really affect corporate performance?', *Corporate Governance*, 15 (6), 1203–14.

Linh, N.T. (2008) 'Cong chuc mong muon dieu gi? (What civil servants actually expect)', *Vietnamnet*, 1 August. Available at http://lanhdao.net/vn/chuyende/123676/index.aspx

Linh, X. (2008) 'Chi tang luong khong giu noi cong chuc (Salary increase only is not enough to retain civil servants)', *VietNamNet*, 12 August. Available at http://vietnamnet.vn/chinhtri/2008/08/798317/

Minh, D. (2008) 'Ong lon dau tu: hang chuc nghin ty dong bat on (Big guys invest: Thousands of billion dong invested unsecured)', *Vneconomy*, 23 April. Available at http://vneconomy.vn/60278P0C6/ong-lon-dau-tu-hang-chuc-nghin-ty-dong-bat-on.htm

Minh, Q. (2007) 'Vu PMU 18: khoi to 9 bi can (The case PMU 18: Nine suspects charged)', *Tuoi Tre (Youth Newspaper)*, 29 June. Available at http://www.tuoitre.com.vn/Tianyon/Index.aspx?ChannelID=6&ArticleID=207998

Minh, Q. (2008) 'Bui Tien Dung bi de nghi truy to toi tham o (Bui Tien Dung was charged with embezzlement)', *Tuoi Tre (Youth Newspaper)*, 27 May. Available at http://www.tuoitre.com.vn/Tianyon/Index.aspx?ArticleID=259749&ChannelID=6

Minh, T. (2008) 'Chinh sach tien te la thanh cong lon nhat cua nam 2008 (The monetary policy is the most successful one in 2008)', *VnEconomy*, 31 December. Available at http://www.vneconomy.vn

MoHA (2007) 'Report on the survey of the Civil Servant Census', Ministry of Home Affairs of Vietnam.

MoHA (2008) 'Report on the Five-year Implementation of the Ordinance of Civil Servants, Hanoi', Ministry of Home Affairs of Vietnam.

Ngoc, L. (2008) 'Thue giam doc cho doanh nghiep nha nuoc: kho kha thi (Hiring CEOs for SOEs: Not feasible)', *Thoi Bao Kinh Te Sai Gon*, 28 January. Available at http://www.thesaigontimes.vn/Home/doanhnghiep/quantri/2627/

Norlund, I. (2007) *Filling the Gap: The Emerging Civil Society in Vietnam*, Hanoi. Available at http://www.snvworld.org/en/countries/vietnam/ourwork/Documents/Filling%20the%20Gap-Emergng%20Civil%20Society%20In%20Vietnam.pdf

Overland, M.A. (2009) 'Corruption undermines Vietnam's stimulus program', *Time*, 23 February.

Packard, Tu Anh Le, and VICA Consultants (2004) 'The Diagnostic Audit of Vietnam's State Enterprises: Final Policy Paper'. Prepared for the Ministry of Finance, Finance Department for Enterprises, Hanoi, under print.

Painter, M. (2002) 'Public administration reform in Vietnam: Problems and prospects', *Public Administration Development*, 23, 3, 259–71.

Painter, M. (2006) 'Sequencing civil service pay reforms in Vietnam: Transition or leapfrog', *Governance*, 19, 2, 325–46.

Painter, M. (2008) 'From command economy to hollow state?

Decentralisation in Vietnam and China', *Australian Journal of Public Administration*, 67, 1, 79–88.

Pham, C. (2008) 'Chong tham nhung: khong vi nao do co so Dang phat hien (Anti-corruption: No case was detected by the party's system)', *VietNamNet*, 12 January. Available at http://vietnamnet.vn/chinhtri/2008/01/763805/

Poon, Y. (2005) 'Overall performance management framework for Ho Chi Minh City', Consultant Working Document (unpublished).

Poon, Y. and Do, T.X. (2007) 'Civil servant management in Vietnam: The challenges and the way ahead'. Report prepared for the Asian Development Bank (unpublished document).

Quang, T. (1981) 'Political development and leadership in the Socialist Republic of Vietnam (1975–1981), Doktoraal-Scriptie Politicologie, Vrije Universiteit, Amsterdam.

Scott, A.F. (2006) 'Probing system limits: Decentralization and local political accountability in Vietnam', *Asia Pacific Journal of Public Administration*, 28, 1, 1–24.

Sjoholm, F. (2006) 'State owned enterprises and equitisation in Vietnam', working paper, August.

Son, L. (2008) 'Quoc hoi du thao Luat ly lich tu phap (National Assembly discusses the Draft Law on legal profiling of citizen)', *Lao Dong (The Labourer)*, 11 November. Available at http://www.laodong.com.vn/Home/Ban-khoan-ve-tinh-can-thiet-phai-ban-hanh-luat/200811/114003.laodong

SRV (2008) Socialist Republic of Vietnam 'Government Web Portal'. Available at http://www.gov.vn (accessed 06 November 2008).

Thanh, T. (2008) 'Cai cach the che: nhin tu Luat dau tu (Institutional reform: The case of investment law)', *Saigontimes*, 10 April. Available at http://www.thesaigontimes.vn/Home/doanhnghiep/phapluat/4699/

Thuy, M. (2008) 'Chinh sach tien te la thanh cong lon nhat cua nam 2008 (The monetary policy was the most successful in 2008)', *Vneconomy*, 23 December. Available at http://www.vneconomy.vn

Transparency International (2008) '2007 Corruption Perception Index – regional highlights: Asia Pacific region', Berlin, Germany.

Tu, N. (2008) 'Lo cho co phan hoa (Worried about equitisation)', *VnEconomy*, 24 April. Available at http://vneconomy.vn/60276P0C5/lo-cho-co-phan-hoa.htm

UNDP (2006) 'The State as Investor: Equitisation, Privatisation and the Transformation of SOEs in Vietnam', Policy Dialogue Paper, 2006/03.

United Nations (2005) 'Unlocking the human potential for public sector performance – World Public Sector Report 2005', New York.

United Nations (2008) 'People matter: Civic engagement in public governance – World Public Sector Report 2008', New York.

Van Tan *et al.* (1977) *Tu dien tieng Viet* (Vietnamese Dictionary). Hanoi: Nha Xuat ban Khoa hoc xa hoi.

Vietnamnet (2008) 'State-owned corporations struggle to find qualified

CEOs', *VietNamNet*, 4 February. Available at http://english.vietnamnet.vn/reports/2008/02/767419/

Vitinfo (2008) '2000 USD cho muc luong cua tan tong giam doc Vinamotor (2000 US$ for the monthly salary of new Vinamotor's CEO)', *Tintuc*, 25 January. Available at http://tintuc.timnhanh.com/kinh_te/20080125/35A6F4BB/

VIE/01/024 (2005), 'Guideline for establishing a Performance Management System'. Document of Project coded VIE/01/024, sponsored by UNDP.

World Bank (2000) 'Anti-corruption in transition', New York.

World Bank (2004) 'Vietnam Development Report 2005 – Governance', New York

World Bank (2006) 'Vietnam Development Report 2007 – Vietnam aiming high', New York.

8 The changing face of women managers in small and medium sized enterprises in Vietnam

Anne Vo and Charles Harvie

- Introduction
- Key issues and new developments
- Case studies
- Challenges
- Conclusion

Introduction

Vietnam stands at an important crossroads in its transition from a planned to a market oriented economy. Since the implementation of economic reform, starting with *Doi Moi* in 1986, the economy has experienced rapid economic growth. Although the Asian financial crisis of 1997 slowed economic development, it has generally maintained relatively high rates of growth during its period of economic reform. From 2001 the country experienced a rapid recovery from the financial crisis and a return to high GDP growth rates. By 2007 the annual GDP growth rate had accelerated to 8.5 per cent, marking the seventh consecutive year of increase in this growth rate (GSO, 2008). The key sources of this have been the growth in output of the non-state sector, in particular private sector small and medium sized enterprises (SMEs), and foreign invested enterprises (FIEs) (Harvie, 2008a, 2008b).

Despite these impressive gains, much remains to be done. In 2007, the Vietnamese Gross National Income (GNI) per capita (GNI divided by mid-year population) was US$690. With this level of income Vietnam was classified as a 'low-income economy' (World Bank, 2007). While the FIE sector is a source of high-paying jobs, it tends to be focused in capital intensive industries, which generate relatively fewer jobs. Domestic private SMEs, which are more labour intensive and whose investment is more widely spread throughout the country, will be required to play the lead role in generating new jobs and increased investment. The WB has estimated that the manufacturing output of private SMEs will be required to grow by 18 to 20 per cent a year to generate the number and types of job that will be needed in Vietnam to achieve its socio-economic development plan covering the period 2001 to 2010 (World Bank, 2000).

If Vietnam is to achieve its economic and social objectives, it will be essential to harness the entirety of the country's entrepreneurial zeal. However, the ability of women to compete equally with men and to make a significant contribution to the development of the private sector is severely hampered by their lower education and lack of skills, and their lesser ability to capitalize assets as their names are not shown on currently issued land certificates (The World Bank Group, 2006). Entrepreneurial gender inequality, therefore, presents an important, but so far neglected, barrier to the further development of the private sector in Vietnam.

This chapter will examine gender issues in the development of private sector SMEs, with particular focus on analyzing the needs and constraints of women in SMEs. In doing so, the chapter will proceed as follows. The second part of the chapter presents key issues and new developments, along with the contextual (cultural, social, legal, economic) and gender dimensions of the development of Vietnamese SMEs. The third part presents case studies which focus on the experiences of organizations and female entrepreneurs working in indigenous SMEs in Vietnam. The chapter then identifies the challenges for the advancement of women in SMEs at two levels: family and institutional. Finally, the chapter closes with some conclusions.

Key issues and new developments

The country's period of rapid economic development is transforming its society from a number of perspectives, including that of gender relations. The movement towards a more industrialized society is presenting greater job opportunities for women, economically empowering them and increasing their importance as contributors to household income. This contrasts with their traditional child bearing, rearing, housekeeping and other family responsibilities. This tension is no less apparent in the context of entrepreneurial activities in SMEs. Many women have demonstrated the required acumen to be successful SME entrepreneurs and to further contribute to the rapid growth of the private SME sector. However, traditional responsibilities still constrain their ability to do so, which may work to the detriment of the country's further development over the longer term.

In this context the remainder of this section outlines, from a gender perspective, the cultural, social, legal and economic background of Vietnam (see also Chapter 1). It also discusses the impact of socio-economic transformation on gender relations in Vietnam and gender dimensions in the development of Vietnamese SMEs. The section emphasizes the importance of economic reform, initiated by *Doi Moi*, to the development of contemporary Vietnam. *Doi Moi* has been the most significant force of change, leading to the re-emergence and development of the private sector in recent decades and also bringing about noticeable changes in gender relations both at the state level and within households (see also Chapter 1).

Cultural and social background

Unlike most other South East Asian countries, Vietnam has a strong history of gender equality (see entries in Rowley and Yukongdi, 2009). Primitive beliefs raise women to the rank of 'goddesses' presiding over the cultivation of rice and other food crops. In many regions ancient temples still exist that were built in honour of women and bear the names of food crops, such as the temples for Lady Soya, Lady Mulberry, Lady Bean, and so on. The tradition of matriarchy was eroded during a thousand years of Chinese occupation, from 111 BC to the early tenth century. The Chinese brought Confucianism to Vietnam, which was later adopted as the official ideology of the Vietnamese feudalist state. This shift had a very strong effect on gender relationships (Le, 2005).

Confucianism stressed the supremacy of men over women, emphasizing the 'three obediences' ('*tam tong*') and 'four virtues' ('*tu duc*') that govern a woman's life. The 'four virtues' compelled women to comply with rigid propriety in behaviour, gestures, language and facial expressions. The 'three obediences' completed this obligation by binding women to their families and depriving them of their individual rights, according to a fundamental Confucian principle: a woman is to obey her father as daughter, her husband as wife, and her son as aged mother (Lebra, 1998: 211).

Although Vietnamese society has been under the strong influence of Confucianism, women historically enjoyed greater freedom compared to Chinese women (United Nations, 2000). This situation arose mainly because every century in Vietnam has been marked by popular patriotic wars against foreign aggressors and these long-lasting campaigns always called for the contribution and participation of women outside their households, especially during the wars with France (1946–54) and the US (1964–75). During the war against the US, women were also mobilized and called upon to assume tasks formerly assigned to men (e.g., the 'Three Ready' (*phong trao 'Ba San Sang'*) and 'Three Prepared' (*phong trao 'Ba Dam Dang'*) campaigns).

The contribution of women to the national war led to an improvement in their social status and validated the equality of sexes that was won in the revolution. Women replaced, and worked together with, men in agricultural, industrial, scientific and technical fields. The position of women was further strengthened after national reunification in 1975 under the communist regime (Le, 2001).

Legal background

Formal gender equality is widely regarded as one of the legacies of the socialist revolution and communist ideology. Immediately after the revolution against the French, a commitment to women's equal rights in Vietnamese society was declared. The first Vietnamese Constitution in 1946 states: 'All power in the country belongs to the Vietnamese people, irrespective of race, sex, fortune, class, religion . . . women are equal to men in all respects' (Government of Vietnam, 1946, Article 9). The Constitutions of 1959, 1980, 1992 and other legislation all further refined and highlighted the rights of women in the context of economic and political equality. Compared to countries where women had to fight for their rights, women in Vietnam were given them as part of government policy (United Nations, 2000).

However, the enforcement of these laws and regulations is questionable. Violations of such equality laws are widely recorded in both rural and urban areas. For example, in 1983 paid maternity leave in Vietnam was extended from 60 to 75 days. In 1984 paid maternity leave was further extended to 180 days. However, even in SOEs women are forced to return to work earlier, normally after 120 days, because of pressure by their companies, and women themselves fear that they might lose their job or be moved to worse positions in the same company after a full term of maternity leave (Vo & Strachan, 2009).

Economic background

After unification in 1975 Vietnam formally committed to the development of a socialist economic system. However, as early as 1977 it became clear that the economic strategy was not working. At the Sixth National Congress of the CVP in 1986, the government introduced a comprehensive reform programme, known as *Doi Moi*, with the objective of liberalizing and deregulating the economy. This resulted in a major turning point in the economic development of the country.

The results of the economic reforms were remarkable, with the annual GDP growth rate increasing gradually and sustainably after 1986. During the period 1992 to 1997, prior to the Asian financial crisis, Vietnam achieved an average annual GDP growth rate of 8.8 per cent, peaking at 9.5 per cent in 1995, the longest period of sustained growth in Vietnam's recent history (Vietnam Economic Times, 2003). The economy slowed in the late 1990s as a consequence of the Asian crisis, but subsequently experienced a sustained recovery until the onset of a global financial crisis in 2008. In 2007 annual GDP growth accelerated to 8.5 per cent, marking the seventh consecutive year of increase in the annual GDP growth rate (GSO, 2008).

One of the key focuses of *Doi Moi* was to allow the re-emergence of PEs in all areas of economic activity. At the heart of the Socio-Economic Development Strategy (SEDS) 2001–10 of the Central

Committee of the CPV was the aim of doubling the country's GDP from 2000 to 2010 (Communist Party of Viet Nam, 2000: 6). To achieve this growth, total investment was required to increase substantially from an average of 25 per cent of GDP during the 1990s to 30 per cent of GDP during 2000–10. With investment in SOEs expected to decline and FDI having stabilized at around US$1.3–1.5 billion annually since 2000, the private domestic sector will be required to contribute the additional 5 per cent of GDP investment and compensate for the expected decline in SOE investment (World Bank, 2002; Vietnam Consultative Group, 2005; Harvie, 2008a, 2008b).

Furthermore, according to WB estimates, the most cost effective means of generating off-farm employment is by promoting SMEs (World Bank, 1998). Each job generated in an SME is estimated to require a capital investment of about US$800 (VND11 million, in book value). In contrast, one job created in an SOE requires approximately US$18,000 (VND240 million). Empirical evidence from other countries also indicates that SMEs are more efficient users of capital under most conditions (World Bank, 1998: 29–30). A flourishing private sector, with an increasing number of SMEs, will be able to absorb not only new workers, but also labour displaced by the ongoing reform of SOEs, as well as contribute to export growth.

The government has shown solid support for the further development of the private sector, and SMEs specifically. New laws and regulations have been promulgated to ensure a more favourable legal framework for the development and integration of the private sector into the rapidly developing multi-ownership economy. In 1998 the Law on Promotion of Domestic Investment was revised, providing new incentives for the domestic private sector. However, the catalyst for change was the approval and implementation of the Enterprise Law in 2000. The Enterprise Law eliminated more than 100 different business licences that restricted entry into different sectors and substantially simplified business start-up, resulting in the registration of over 250,000 private enterprises over the period 2000 to 2007 (Ministry of Planning and Investment, 2008).

As a result of such change, the contribution of the private sector has become more significant and diversified. In fact, it has become the most dynamic component of the economy since 2000. Table 8.1

Table 8.1 Composition of GDP (%) and industrial production by ownership type (%)

	Total GDP (%)			Industrial production (%)		
	1995	2000	2005	1995	2000	2005
State sector	40	41	41	50	42	34
Non-state	53	48	47	25	22	29
Collectives	10	9	7	1	1	1
Private sector (domestic plus foreign)	51	51	52	49	58	65
Foreign invested sector	7	11	12	25	36	37
Domestic private sector	44	40	40	24	22	28
of which:						
Household enterprises/ farmers	36	32	30	18	12	9
Private SMEs	8	8	10	6	10	19

Source: Adapted from GSO (2007).

illustrates the changing composition of GDP and industrial production over the 10-year period from 1995 to 2005 by type of ownership.

This shows that PEs, primarily SMEs, have seen their share of GDP increase from 8 to 10 per cent. The domestic private sector's share of industrial production increased from 24 to 28 per cent with the big mover being domestic private sector SMEs, whose share of production increased from 6 to 19 per cent. The growth of private sector industrial output was in fact higher than that for SOEs and FIEs. The contribution of the private sector to employment has become even more pronounced. It has been the non-state sector, primarily private business enterprises and mainly in the industrial sector, that has dominated the generation of jobs – some 4.7 million new jobs or almost 83 per cent of the total over the period 2000 to 2006 (GSO, 2007).

Despite these advances, the domestic private sector remains small and fragile. It consists primarily of informal household enterprises, farmers and formal private SMEs which tend to be involved in low skill, low value-adding, low technology, finance constrained activities in agriculture, manufacturing and service sector activities aimed at the domestic market. Many of the enterprises lack capital, employ outdated technology, have unstable markets, produce poor quality but high price products, are subject to competition from illegal imports, have poor business skills, experience a shortage of land, use unskilled workers that are too costly to train, lack confidence in the government's commitment to a multi-ownership society and find difficulty in establishing links to large businesses and other SMEs (Vietnam Consultative Group, 2005).

New developments

Recent social economic changes have strongly influenced and redefined gender relations, at both the national and household levels. Much of the recent literature on gender in Vietnam speculates on the negative effects on women of the transition to a market economy. With the overnight dismantling of social and support provisions for women, the withdrawal of state subsidies, the downsizing of SOEs, the privatization of health and education and so on, the period since the introduction of *Doi Moi* has seen a period of deterioration in gender equality in Vietnam (see, for example, Beresford, 1994; Lofman, 1998; Le, 2001). At the household level, because state services have declined and there has been less social support for both the elderly and children, the burden of their care falls more heavily on female family members (Population Council, 1997). According to the 2002 Vietnam Household Living Standard Survey (GSO, 2002), the average hours spent per day on housework by women aged 15 and over is 2.5 times more than men in urban areas and 2.3 times in rural areas. As state subsidies diminish, families have had to pay the increasing costs of medical care and educational expenses. When faced with pressure to earn money, there is concern about women's conflicting roles. In contrast to men, women face a double burden when they work outside the home. Their role as carers of children is seen to conflict with their role as wage earners, whereas men do not experience this same tension (Le, 2001).

Yet, many trends post-*Doi Moi* are quite positive for women and gender relations. The expanding economy creates more work opportunities for women, especially within the newly developed non-state sectors. A majority of the jobs created through the reforms are held by women. A calculation based on the results of annual surveys carried out by the GSO reveals that the number of female workers finding employment opportunities in non-state enterprises and FIEs has increased very significantly, while it remained almost the same in SOEs (GSO, 2006). During the period 2000–04 the number of female employees working in the non-state sector increased by 122.7 per cent and in the FIE sector by 182.3 per cent, compared to only 0.38 per cent in the state sector (GSO, 2005: 127). These figures show that an expansion of private firms and enterprises with foreign investment capital has led to better employment opportunities for women.

However, not all newly created jobs are high paying and require skilled labour. The informal economic sector attracts labourers who have low educational standards, lack professional skills and have little capital. However, this sector still offers women an opportunity for upward mobility and improved economic wellbeing (Liu, 1995).

The recent trend for women to enter the wage labour market has narrowed the earnings gap between men and women, and thus altered the traditional gender division of labour. In their in-depth research of gender relations at the household level in Go Vap District, an urban community in HCMC, Long et al. (2000) argue that women's entry into the labour market has increased their autonomy and improved gender equality in the home. The reasons for these changes include the fact that younger women have more opportunities in the labour market while older women may be the major wage earners of the household income, particularly if their husbands have retired from the public sector. The financial contributions of women are becoming increasingly critical in meeting the rising expectations of higher standards of living. Working women also have an opportunity to expand their own knowledge, skills and experience. These trends lead to improvements in equality and result in greater empowerment of women, giving them more voice in the home vis-à-vis men.

Gender dimensions in Vietnamese SME development

While Vietnam has one of the world's highest female labour force participation rates, and women as well as men have both contributed to and benefited from economic growth, inequalities persist in the process of economic development. These inequalities are presented here in three main categories: educational level; participation in the workforce; allocation of time and workloads.

Educational level

Women's participation in all levels of education (except professional and secondary education) and their highest level of education achieved is lower than that for men (see Figure 8.1). Most of the attainments in women's education are achieved at the secondary (lower and upper) school level. Overall, only 2.7 per cent of women go to college/university, compared to 4.2 per cent of their male counterparts. These figures suggest clear gender differences in schooling and education in Vietnam.

In research on educated women in Vietnam, Le (2005) points out that their development can be described by a triangular-shaped chart that has no top vertex. This is as a result of women's responsibilities as daughters, wives and mothers – burdens that leave them with little time to further their education. Furthermore, with the limited financial resources of most families, it is only considered natural that male family members be given priority for further education.

In a subtle way, education emphasizes gender differences by stereotyping gender roles in textbooks. Men and women are portrayed in stereotypical 'traditional' male and female roles that they fill in the

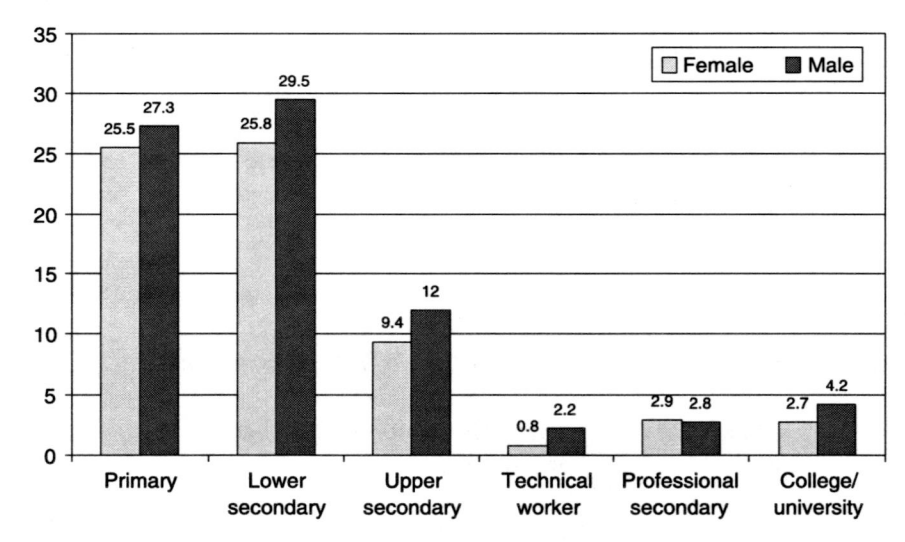

Figure 8.1 Highest education level achieved by population aged 15 and over in 2002 (%).

Source: Adapted from GSO (2002: 37)

community. Such stereotyping can limit the potential that male and female students have by naturalizing, as opposed to challenging, gender differences (NCFAW and GSO, 2005). Stereotyping also perpetuates attitudes and behaviour that reinforce gender inequalities in the workforce, society and home (The World Bank Group, 2006).

Allocation of time and workloads

The central feature of the sexual division of labour in Vietnam is captured by one of the principles of Confucianism, which dictates that men are primarily outside the home and women are primarily inside the home (Leung and White, 2004). Furthermore, a Vietnamese custom imposes that childbearing, rearing and education are the responsibility of women, with men playing a minor role. Thus, 'A bad mother is the cause of a spoilt child; a bad grandmother is the cause of a spoilt grandchild' (Vietnamese proverb).

With the burden of having to balance work and home obligations, Vietnamese women usually work very long hours. While women contribute equal amounts of time to income generating activities, men do not share equally in housework, leaving women with an unequal share of the work burden overall (World Bank, 2006). According to a Vietnam Women's Union assessment of gender equality in Vietnam, women work an average of 13 hours per day compared to only 9 hours for men (SRV, 2005). Legislation seems to reinforce the situation as the Labour Code 2002 and associated regulations relating to leave to care for a newborn baby or sick child are only available to mothers.

Participation in the workforce

The participation of women in the labour market is very high in Vietnam. Their integration into the labour market is supported ideologically by equal employment opportunity law and is promoted by the country's poor economic situation, in which an average family can barely live on a single income. In 2005 the population of Vietnam was over 83 million, of which 50.9 per cent were female and 49.1 per cent male (GSO, 2005). The number of women of working age (between 15 and 55) who participated in the labour force was 21.7 million, compared to 22.7 million men (MOLISA 2006: 19) as shown in Figure 8.2.

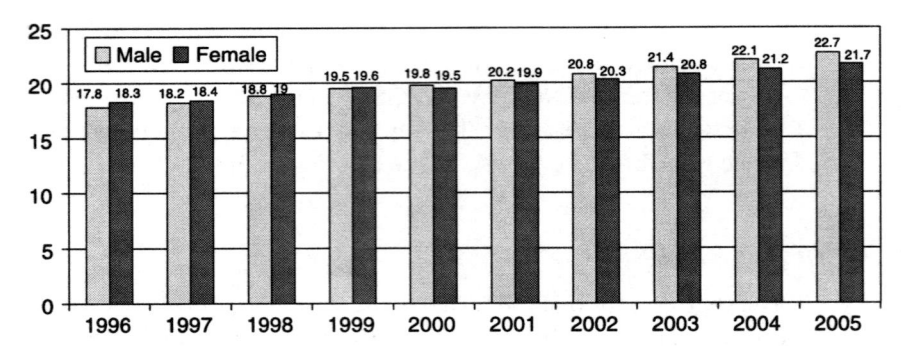

Figure 8.2 Labour force participation rates (million people).
Source: Adapted from MOLISA (2006: 18)

Despite this high proportion of participation, women are under-represented in higher-status occupations, and over-represented in lower-status ones. The main sectors in which women are concentrated are agriculture and forestry, light industry (especially textiles and garments), hotels and restaurants, banking and finance, education and training, social affairs, and as housemaids. Meanwhile, men dominate in the areas of communications, chemistry, science and technology, sport, culture, heavy industry, energy, construction and diplomacy, and international affairs (GSO, 2002; MOLISA, 2006).

According to the MOLISA (2003), female workers receive less remuneration for their work. They also suffer a higher chance of unemployment. The official overall unemployment rate in 2005 was 2.14 per cent, but men had a 1.99 per cent rate, while women had a 2.29 per cent rate (MOLISA, 2006: 60), as seen in Figure 8.3 below. Moreover, women cannot move as quickly and freely in the labour market as men. They generally require employment opportunities within close commuting distance of their households (Le, 2005). Women are also restricted by domestic demands, such as childcare and housework (Vo and Strachan, 2009). Therefore, women are more inclined to accept jobs that are below their skills level and/or are low paid.

The career progression of Vietnamese women also provides evidence of gender inequalities at work. Women with higher levels of education are able to secure employment in white collar occupations. However, women generally do not hold decision-making positions. For example, women account for only 4 per cent of the general directors

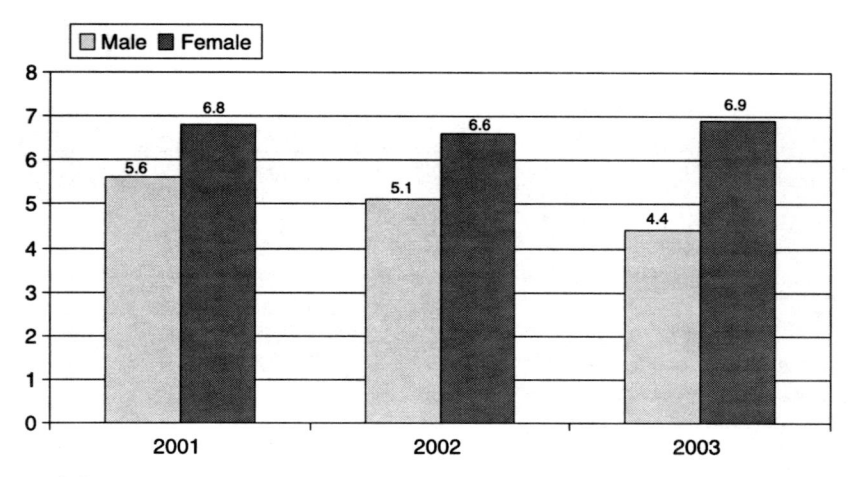

Figure 8.3 Unemployment rate in urban areas by sex, 2001–2003 (%).
Source: Adapted from GSO (2005: 19)

and deputy-general directors in Vietnam (NCFAW and GSO, 2005: 69). Women struggle to break through the 'glass ceiling' to gain equal opportunities in the workplace and acceptance from both male and female colleagues. These issues are compounded by the Confucian belief that still pervades a society in which women are thought to deserve little authority, show less commitment, have lower intelligence and are less experienced than men (NCFAW and GSO, 2005).

As far as the private sector is concerned, Vietnamese SMEs owned by women comprise about 25 per cent of the total of 160,000 SMEs in Vietnam and 40 per cent of the more than three million household businesses (VCCI, 2008). Enterprises owned by women are under-represented in production and over-represented in trade, especially retail sales. Within the production sector the main sub-sectors in which women are concentrated are food and beverages, and textiles and garments. Meanwhile, men dominate in the areas of agriculture and forestry, construction, vehicle sales, maintenance, repair, transport and communications, business and financial services. This gender difference reflects the stereotyping of gender roles in society. Such stereotyping can limit the potential that female entrepreneurs have in terms of gaining access, and overcoming barriers, to establishing and running businesses in certain industries. The gender differentiation is illustrated in the Table 8.2.

Table 8.2 Types of non-farm household enterprise operated by men and women in rural and urban areas (%)

Type of enterprise	Rural Male	Rural Female	Rural Total	Urban Male	Urban Female	Urban Total
Production						
Agriculture and forestry	9.6	3.1	6.4	0.6	0.0	0.2
Aquaculture	15.0	2.9	9.0	8.0	0.0	3.3
Mining	2.4	1.0	1.7	0.3	0.0	0.1
Food and beverage processing	10.9	13.7	12.3	4.0	4.5	4.3
Textiles, garments and leather products	3.2	9.7	6.4	5.5	9.4	7.8
Wood and paper products	9.8	8.2	9.0	5.8	1.2	3.1
Other production / processing	5.1	0.1	2.7	6.7	1.1	3.3
Construction and utilities	4.6	0.2	2.4	2.7	0.2	1.2
Trade						
Vehicle sales, maintenance, repair	1.2	0.0	0.6	2.5	0.3	1.2
Wholesale and agent sales	14.7	2.3	3.5	2.2	2.7	2.5
Retail sales	14.8	51.5	32.8	20.0	59.9	43.7
Services						
Hotel and restaurant	0.4	3.7	2.0	4.6	11.7	8.8
Transport and communication	8.1	0.6	4.4	19.8	0.9	8.5
Business and financial services	2.6	0.2	1.4	3.0	1.2	1.9
Education, health, cultural services	2.8	0.4	1.6	4.3	2.9	3.5
Sanitation and personal services	4.9	2.4	3.7	10.2	4.1	6.6
All production	60.6	38.9	49.9	33.5	16.3	23.3
All trade	20.7	53.8	36.9	24.7	62.9	47.4
All services	18.7	7.3	13.1	41.8	20.8	29.4

Source: Adapted from Desai (2000: Table 4.10)

Women tend to own smaller enterprises, with lower asset values, hire fewer employees and achieve lower turnover (except in the services sector) and profits. In both rural and urban non-farm enterprises, male-owned enterprises have a larger value of total business assets than those owned by females. In rural areas non-farm enterprises owned by females have a value of total business assets that are 70 per cent of that of male-owned enterprises, while in urban areas the ratio is even lower at 52 per cent (Desai, 2000: Table 3.5). The best enterprise earnings are associated with those in trade, where male-owned non-farm household enterprises earn profits of VND 4,950,000 (US$353.5) per year in rural areas and VND10,985,000 (US$784.5) per year in urban areas. By comparison, female-owned firms earn VND3,600,000 (US$257.1) per year in rural areas and VND7,040,000 (US$502.8) in urban areas (Desai, 2000: Table 4.12). According to Akram-Lodhi and Staveren (2003: 11), on average, profits in female-owned non-farm household enterprises, which include SMEs, are about 70 per cent of those made by their male counterparts.

There have been continuous efforts from government agencies, institutions and international organizations to strengthen the entrepreneurial and technical skills capacity of Vietnamese women. For example, the VCCI, by itself or with other domestic and international partners, frequently organizes courses that aim to equip women with basic business and management knowledge. Examples of these are set out below.

1 In 1998, in collaboration with the ILO, the VCCI introduced the 'Start and improve your business' T&D project in Vietnam. The T&D project was developed to address the shortage of basic business management skills in the micro and small enterprise sector. The programme achieved certain outcomes in that almost 97 per cent of the participants stated that their business performance had improved considerably, and nearly 49 per cent confirmed that their personal income for private spending had increased (Barwa, 2003: 18).
2 In 2007, the VCCI worked with BP Vietnam to organize the 'Towards success' programme, which invited senior and experienced female entrepreneurs to share their experiences of initiating a business and providing advice to less experienced women. As a result of this programme, a network of consultants was set up and developed.
3 In 2008, the VCCI cooperated with the APEC Digital Opportunity Centre and later signed a cooperation deal with the Corporation for Financing and Promoting Technology (FPT) in Vietnam to organize an e-commerce T&D course for women.
4 Along with the VCCI, other government agencies, such as FULL (VWU), also conducted a series of T&D courses on gender knowledge and gender mainstreaming in policy formulation to support the development of female-owned enterprises and the private sector.

The sorts of activity outlined above have no doubt contributed to enhancing the business competence of SME female entrepreneurs and their participation in production and business. However, being separate endeavours and highly dependent on one-off funding opportunities, the effects of these programmes have been limited. Therefore, a systematic approach coordinated at the macro level is still needed.

Case studies

This section offers portraits of two successful SMEs and their female owners. The women entrepreneurs' candid stories shed light on the life of women SME entrepreneurs in Vietnam, the opportunities and challenges they have faced on their journey to achieve financial freedom and personal development in contemporary Vietnamese society.

Case studies of organizations

Case Study 8.1: Garment Company (GC)

In 1994, Ms A and a business partner established GC as a small garment manufacturing company with 20 old sewing machines, 18 employees and an initial capital of only VND30 million (less than US$3,000). In the beginning the GC was located in the partner's house and occupied an area of 250 square metres, where the majority of workers were Ms A's relatives recruited from her home town.

In the first two years, GC's total revenue fell short of the owners' expectations because production during this period consisted mainly of small and irregular orders. As a result, the volume of production was unstable. In order to reduce their dependence on small orders, Ms A and her partner actively sought customers via the relationships and connections that they had established with local suppliers and customers during the time they worked for previous employers. GC also started using intermediaries, offering them a commission of the sale value. Thanks to GC's active customer-seeking policies, the number of orders rose rapidly. In 1998 the business partner who had invested in the company withdrew her capital. As a result, Ms A offered both her house and the company as collateral for a bank loan to buy out her business partner and become the sole owner. In 2000, in order to meet demand, Ms A rented an area of 400 square metres to expand production capacity, and employed 16 additional workers, raising the number of workers to 34.

From 2002 onwards, GC witnessed a strong growth in business. Because of the increased production scale, and having established trusted relationships with suppliers, Ms A was able to place direct orders with suppliers, which significantly cut input costs. Revenue and profit grew quickly. Ms A also participated in some international trade fairs and exhibitions in HCMC, with the purpose of advertising and promoting her products to foreign customers. Thanks to this effort the number of orders, both locally and internationally, continued to increase. GC is now producing and exporting men's, women's and children's clothing to European and American markets. In order to meet the stringent quality demands of overseas markets, GC has implemented comprehensive quality management systems that have resulted in low defect rates. GC performs rigorous inspections of its entire production processes, from the quality of the raw materials through to the packaging of the finished products. The total capital of the company is now VND415 million (about US$26,000), while the number of workers has increased to 63 people.

Source: Author's interview (December 2007)

Case Study 8.2: Printing Company (PC)

Back in the early 1990s Ms B realized that, as a result of *Doi Moi* and a boom in consumption in Vietnam, the SOEs who monopolized the printing industry would not be able to meet the resulting demand, especially for printing books, business cards, greetings cards and invitation cards. Thus, in 1993, Ms B set up the PC with a capital of VND65 million (less than US$7,000), the majority of which was obtained from the bank, employed eight local unskilled workers, and located the business in Ms B's house. The competition strategy of PC was to satisfy the demands of small customers, to whom large printing firms charged a very high premium for small orders.

During the period 1993–96 PC's profits were relatively low owing to the lack of manufacturing experience and the burden of bank interest. In 1997 PC products were subjected to fierce competition from other SMEs. To stave off the competition, Ms B made a decision to obtain a bank loan to improve technology and to move the business to a larger location with an area of about 500 square metres. As a result, the new products were of a much higher quality, with which very few of the other SMEs could compete. In 1999, noticing the demand for flexible packaging, paper packaging and high quality labels, Ms B decided to expand PC's business into this area. At that time PC grew very fast; the workforce increased to 20 workers and three sales people.

In 2002, PC once more expanded its scale and activities. The company started trading in products of pre-press, printing, packaging, inks and chemicals. The number of workers increased to 35. Besides the original unskilled workers who were trained by the company, over the years PC recruited skilled workers from vocational education schools and engineers from universities.

The company is now producing and developing reliable and high quality printing and packaging products that can meet the demand of large industrial firms. In addition to the local market, PC has expanded its customer network to other provinces.

Source: Author's interview (December 2007)

Case studies of individual managers

Case Study 8.3: Ms A, Owner, GC

Ms A was born in 1971 in Hue City (central Vietnam), the fifth child in a poor family of eight children. Growing up in a large family with many children meant that she learned to take care of herself very early in life. Because of the family's poor economic situation Ms A left school at Grade 10, which made it impossible for her to find a good job in her home town. Thus, Ms A went to HCMC hoping to find better job opportunities. Thanks to an introduction from a relative, she obtained a job as a worker in a small family firm producing clothes, where she worked hard and was very productive. Furthermore, after a few years, her honesty earned Ms A the trust of the owners of the firm and she was made responsible for dealing with customers and their orders, from which she developed and honed her communication and customer service skills. Ms A was sometimes sent to other towns to find materials or new contracts. This was the time in which Ms A learned about the production process, the industry itself and built important relationships with some key customers.

In 1994 a former customer who had known Ms A for years asked her to become a partner in establishing a new clothes manufacturing business, and this opportunity became a significant turning point in her life. Ms A saw this request as a rare chance to start a business of her own, in which the majority of the necessary capital investment came from the other business partner while she could use the knowledge she had gained from her previous job. Thus, Ms A readily agreed. In 1998, after five years in business together, her business partner withdrew her capital and Ms A became the sole owner of GC.

When asked about the challenges and difficulties she has experienced as an SME entrepreneur, Ms A's first comment was about her conflicting roles as an entrepreneur and a mother of two young sons. Ms A's position on the role of women within her house is a traditional one: 'In my family, I take care of the housework. We have three generations living under the same roof: my husband's old parents, ourselves and our two young kids. We also have one of my brothers and a cousin from my husband's side living with us. I need to make sure that the house is clean, food is in the fridge, meals are on the table, and the kids study well at school. It is hard work but this is my responsibility. My family has always come first.'

Prioritizing one's work over family obligations for women is seen to interfere with family harmony and happiness. Even if they are half of a dual career couple, women are expected to fulfil household chores and take care of the children, whereas men do not experience this same tension. The inequitable division of labour within the household puts a double burden on career-oriented women. Ms A spends much more time doing housework than her husband. On average, she spends around four hours per day on housework, while she estimates that her husband spends less than one hour per day.

Ms A recognizes the importance of family support to her success in running her business. Financial help from her husband's family was crucial to the continued survival of her firm, especially in the difficult times when her business partner withdrew from the business and when she decided to expand the business and buy new equipment. Family members also provide Ms A with childcare services. Interestingly, Ms A considers that female entrepreneurs are supported by their family if they do not face direct resistance from their families in running their business. This is not considered as family support to male entrepreneurs, as it is taken for granted.

Ms A believes that her successful business has had a positive impact on their family life. While voicing concerns about the lack of time devoted to her family and children, Ms A emphasized the importance of her contribution to the household income. Ms A is now the major wage earner of the household, and she also sends money to her parents to help with the family expenses and education of her younger siblings. These facts give her voice more 'weight' with the men within her home and a sense of empowerment in society.

Source: Author's interview (December 2007)

Case Study 8.4: Ms B, Owner, PC

Ms B graduated from the Economics University of HCMC in 1987. She started her working career as a marketing staff member in a SOE that specialized in the production and supply of printing products, flexible packaging, paper packaging and high-grade labels. In 1991 Ms B moved to another company in the same industry where she worked as an Assistant Marketing Manager, and where her scope of responsibility was much greater and her salary was significantly higher. After working in this position for the next two years, Ms B decided to leave her job and start her own business in the same industry.

Ms B discussed candidly the challenges she encountered in starting and running her own business. Ms B first mentioned the difficulty of obtaining capital to open a business. One of the main ways in which assets can be capitalized is by using land (in rural areas) or house ownership (in urban areas) as collateral to access loans. Although traditional inheritance practice in Vietnam dictates that land and houses can be passed down to males and females, in practice women are less likely to be registered as land users and/or house owners. Most of the certificates issued are in the name of the man only. As Ms B said: 'Although my family is well off, I had no assets to my name, except a motorbike. Therefore, the business must be registered under my father's name, who at that time was 65 years old. This led to a lot of annoyances and inconvenience in terms of paperwork later on.'

Ms B admitted that understanding the law and keeping up to date with the changes are a challenge to her. Communication from the government to SMEs about new laws and their implications to SME business activities is non-existent. Legal regulations are often complex, ambiguous and sometimes contain gaps that local authorities can abuse for their own benefit. Furthermore, frequent changes in the regulations provide an unstable legal environment. Ms B said: 'There are many laws! Far more than what I can remember . . . I do not understand tax regulations, and I especially have no idea about the tax rates. I ended up having to bargain with tax officers about the amount of tax I had to pay.'

Ms B is also concerned about upgrading her firm's technology. She mentioned that the government's policies supporting the enhancement of technology for SMEs have many weaknesses. For example, no research and development organization has been created specifically for SMEs and the existing promotion centres were established mainly to meet the requirements of international assistance projects rather than to satisfy the need to support SMEs.

Ms B confirmed that she mainly obtained market information via personal contacts and not through formal channels. These contacts include friends, business partners, current customers and trade fairs. Only the larger and more dynamic SMEs tend to contact formal organizations like the SME Club, the VCCI and the various trade associations for such information, because the average SME can neither digest nor effectively use the large quantity of statistical data and general information available from these sources. The lack of reliable and useful market information often leads to a situation in which local firms export their products with lower prices than the competition or miss out on good business opportunities. Ms B stated that the opportunity to obtain market information for female entrepreneurs is considerably less than that for their male counterparts as in the Vietnamese business environment, and especially that of SMEs, market information is mostly exchanged in informal social settings. Thus, as Ms B put it: 'To have market information, one needs to socialize a lot. In the majority of cases, that happens in bars and restaurants after work. That alone reduces our chances [of obtaining market information] significantly. And if we do [go out drinking and socialising], our virtues are questioned by our family and the society. In many cases, I had to beg my husband and/or my brother to accompany me.'

Furthermore, women entrepreneurs have more problems in terms of mobility than their male counterparts. They are more hesitant to travel between the provinces and overseas to obtain market information and find new market opportunities. Restricted by domestic demands such as childcare and housework, women generally need opportunities to be within close commuting distance of their household and business. Therefore, they are more inclined to accept business that is 'convenient' rather than endeavouring to expand their customer base.

Although Ms B agreed that there is a certain societal prejudice against businesswomen, being a strong character she did not allow it to prevent her from fulfilling her dream of financial independence and success. Ms B described her work as an integral part of her identity, and believed

> that her work has given her a sense of fulfilment and self-realization. She thinks that society has become more tolerant of women in business: 'Twenty years ago, the idea of a young woman establishing her own business would be unthinkable . . . The older generations complain about the new generation deteriorating ethical values, but they have no choice but to accept the changes [in gender roles].'
>
> Source: Author's interview (December 2007)

The case studies tell the stories of the working lives of two female entrepreneurs, and voice their opinions and concerns on gender issues. *Doi Moi* has provided a strong impetus to the advancement of women, giving them more favourable conditions and opportunities to contribute actively to national economic and social development. The role and position of women in the family and community have been enhanced. However, there is still a long way to go for Vietnam to achieve gender equality. Women who wish to be successful in SMEs still encounter many challenges in the family, society and in business. This next section discusses these challenges further.

Challenges

The key challenge for gender equality in SMEs is still to counter the old paradigm of male chauvinism, which has existed for thousands of years. Male dominance has been 'shaped and reinforced over so many generations that it is deeply rooted in people's minds and exists as a social stronghold resistant to opposition' (Nguyen, 1997: 29). Efforts have been made to eliminate gender prejudices and change the perception of the roles of women and men. Vietnamese laws proclaim that in the family the husband and the wife are equal in all aspects. In reality, however, domestic work and taking care of family members are still considered the 'natural duties' of women. The old system of a labour division based on gender is still maintained in the majority of Vietnamese families, which has led to limited school opportunities, a disproportionate burden of unpaid housework and has hindered women in taking up employment opportunities outside their family (Long *et al.*, 2000; Vo, 2008).

In terms of doing business, perhaps the more pressing problems that female entrepreneurs face are access to finance and their lower educational and training levels. As far as access to finance is concerned, one of the main ways in which assets can be capitalized is through the use of land or house ownership as collateral to access loans. However, a recent survey found that of women who were denied financing, 20 per cent said it was because they lacked collateral (MPSDF, 2006). Although the Land Law does not discriminate against women and allows joint land titling between husbands and wives, most people simply follow the tradition, and it is most common for titling to be solely in the husband's name. This creates problems for women when they need to provide collateral for accessing loans. Not until 2003 did a revision of the Land Law decree that all new Land Use Certificates must include the names of both the husband and wife. Although this is a step in the right direction, the law does not require the previously issued titles to be changed (The World Bank Group, 2006).

As far as T&D and education are concerned, while technical and higher education levels are low in Vietnam for both women and men, women are disadvantaged in comparison to men. Increasing the access women have to appropriate career and skills development opportunities is fundamental to ensuring that they can compete equally and have the same opportunities as men to contribute to the economy. To ensure a more level playing field for both female and male SME entrepreneurs, different institutions need to provide SMEs with tailored policies to address their specific needs, such as the provision of skills T&D, business development services, etc. The World Bank Group (2006) suggests that the government needs to allocate resources for T&D and skills development to promote the participation of women in employment, especially ethnic minorities, migrants, those in rural areas, and the young working in the informal sector.

The government depends on organizations concerned specifically with gender issues, such as the VWU and the National Committee for the Advancement of Women in Vietnam, for the successful implementation of government policies associated with women. Although they have done a good job of ensuring that attention is paid to gender issues, VWU and NCFAW have a very limited role with respect to the actual implementation of gender policies, which need to be done by other institutions (The World Bank Group, 2006). A stronger institutional framework and closer cooperation amongst different institutions is needed for an integration of gender equality in the development of SMEs.

In 2006 the government passed the country's first Law on Gender Equality (LGE). The law includes provisions to stipulate gender equality in the fields of the economy (Article 12), employment (Article 13), education and training (Article 14), science and technology (Article 15), culture, information, physical exercises and sports (Article 16), public health (Article 17), and in the family (Article 18). Furthermore, the LGE codifies the state's accountability for gender equality. There are clear provisions on the responsibilities of the government, state agencies, other agencies and organizations, families and citizens in ensuring gender equality in society (Chapter IV).

The best aspect of the new LGE is that each provision is closely followed by measures to ensure and promote the occurrence of gender equality. There are provisions for inspection, oversight, handling and punishment of violations of the gender equality law (Chapter V). Moreover, the LGE calls for the establishment of a new State Management Agency on Gender Equality (Article 9), which is responsible for advocating and supervising the implementation of gender equality laws within government agencies and overseeing the implementation of the law. Before the LGE was passed, no national agency was accountable for gender equality results. The new State Management Agency will provide an opportunity for the government to more effectively mainstream gender at the executive level and to uphold gender equality in Vietnam.

The new LGE is a move towards achieving gender equality in both public and private life in Vietnam. However, turning the LGE into practice presents considerable challenges (The World Bank Group, 2006). Decisions on some controversial issues, such as the retirement age for women, the need to ensure equality between children of both genders, etc., have still been put on hold. In addition, other issues need to be addressed, such as the need to pay attention to different classes of worker (e.g. female farmers), support for the provision of skills training, increasing the value of household work to encourage shared responsibility between men and women, providing incentives for regulated private sector provision, and so on.

Enhancing the chance of success for female entrepreneurs should also go hand in hand with developing the private sector. To advance the development of SMEs, Vietnam requires a regulatory framework based on the rule of law. The present system, consisting of vague and frequently changing regulations and excessive bureaucracy, results in increased risk and costs of doing business and represents a drain on the resources and time of private entrepreneurs that would otherwise have been available for investment or for management of the business (Harvie, 2008a). A transparent legal and regulatory framework for the private sector, therefore, has to be established, to ensure a more level playing field for both the state and private sectors. Ministries and agencies involved in industry, planning, education and T&D – such as the Ministry of Industry, Ministry of Planning and Investment, and universities – are still geared towards support of the SOEs. These organizations need to shift their focus towards the private sector and SMEs in order to enhance the general economic environment. This shift requires a fundamental change in social and administrative attitudes and a focusing upon an improvement in the image of the private sector in the country. Given the many years of discrimination against PEs and private entrepreneurs, stronger and more frequent government endorsement of private business is required.

Further impetus to these requirements has been provided by the global financial crisis since 2008 and difficult times ahead for the Vietnamese economy. The crisis has impacted severely on Vietnam, a highly open economy that has become heavily dependent upon trade and foreign investment in the wake of earlier market liberalization reforms. Foreign capital flows have become essential to sustain its high rates of economic growth, inflows of technology, exports and balance of payments. Consequently, the spectre of a global recession and credit crunch can only bode ill, at least in the short term, for the foreign invested sector and for the country's fledgling private sector more generally. SMEs, in particular, face traditionally greater difficulties in accessing finance, and these are likely to be further compounded. Given Vietnam's need to develop private sector SMEs, any constraint in accessing finance will have a substantial impact on new business development and the growth of existing private SMEs, and will have a deleterious impact upon overall economic growth and employment generation. A credit crunch will not only make lending by banks more limited, it will also require the provision by borrowers of greater collateral to risk averse and cash-strapped financial institutions.

In this context, women entrepreneurs are likely to face both greater challenges and opportunities. In terms of challenges, they are likely to face disproportionately greater difficulty accessing finance for their existing fledgling and marginally profitable and new enterprises, as has been the case in the past, resulting in (a) the need to generate funding from personal and family savings, (b) exacerbation of the existing collateral related issues, and (c) a major disincentive for the establishment of new female-owned SMEs. An economic downturn will result in greater business insolvency in general, and require displaced SME entrepreneurs to seek employment in related or other sectors of the economy. Given the important contribution that women make to family income, displaced women entrepreneurs will be required to return to a weakened wage labour market as a matter of urgency.

Despite these problems, there are possible opportunities for women entrepreneurs in the future. Women-owned SMEs have a higher density in the non-traded sectors of the economy, such as the services and retail sectors, which are likely to be less affected by global developments. This may, therefore, present opportunities for women entrepreneurs already operating in these sectors. In addition, women may receive greater support from their spouses and family to establish or maintain their SMEs in recognition of the importance that their income contribution makes to the family well-being. This could also contribute to the breaking down of the stereotypical roles of men and women in Vietnamese society.

Conclusion

This chapter has presented an overview of women in SMEs in Vietnam. The unequal division of labour characterized by the aphorism 'men live outside in society, women inside the family' still moulds thinking and behaviour. In general, women are still at a disadvantage in terms of educational level, participation in the workforce and allocation of time and workloads. *Doi Moi* has had some positive influences on gender relations by changes in the labour market and increasing labour mobility. Having more chance to enter the labour market, women have narrowed the earnings gap with men, thereby altering the traditional gender division of labour and affecting individual lives and relationships.

This chapter argues that female Vietnamese SME entrepreneurs are attempting to combine their new role as (another) breadwinner with the traditional role of daughter, wife and mother. The main challenge that women entrepreneurs must overcome in order to achieve recognition and financial success is the stereotypical perception of women's unsuitability to own and run a business, which is widely held in Vietnamese society. However, there are emerging signs that the younger generation of women have taken up new perceptions and attitudes towards gender relations and the balance of family and working life. In terms of business-related issues, both female and male entrepreneurs face a number of problems in managing their businesses. In particular, they are facing problems with access to land, access to finance, an understanding of the legal framework and laws relating to business, access to technology and use of IT, access to markets and government support. However, female entrepreneurs have even more problems with access to finance, access to market information and opportunities.

This chapter has also pointed out that even though the Vietnamese government has successfully created an institutional context for the advancement of women's rights, public administration is primarily concerned with the formal and legal aspects rather than with the actual implementation of gender strategies and policies. In order to attain the long-term goals of the SEDS, support by the government for the further development of the private sector and SMEs will be essential, involving levelling the playing field between SOEs and private companies, enhancing the general business environment in Vietnam and ensuring the full utilization of the country's entrepreneurial capability irrespective of gender.

Bibliography

Akram-Lodhi, A.H. and Staveren. I. (2003) 'A gender analysis of the impact of indirect taxes on small and medium enterprises in Vietnam'. Paper presented at the International Association for Feminist Economics Annual Conference on Feminist Economics, University of the West Indies, Cape Hill Campus. Barbados, 29 June.

Barwa, S.D (2003) *Impact of Start Your Business (SYB) Training on Women Entrepreneurs in Vietnam*. Vietnam: ILO Office.

Beresford, M. (1994) *Impact of Macroeconomic Reform on Women in Vietnam*, Hanoi: UNIFEM.

Communist Party of Viet Nam (2000) 'Socio-economic development strategy (SEDS) 2001–2010 draft', Hanoi.

Desai, J. (2000) 'Viet Nam through the lens of gender: Five years later. Results from the Second Viet Nam Living Standards Survey'. November. Hanoi: FAO. (Unpublished document.)

General Statistics Office (GSO) (2002) *Vietnam Household Living Standard Survey*, Hanoi: Statistical Publishing House.

Government of Vietnam (1946) *The Constitution of Vietnam*, Hanoi.

GSO (2005) General Statistics Office, *Vietnam Gender Statistics in the Early Years of the 21st Century*, Hanoi: Women's Publishing House.

GSO (2006) General Statistics Office, *Statistical Yearbook of Vietnam*, Hanoi: Statistical Publishing House.

GSO (2007) General Statistics Office, *Statistical Yearbook 2006 (NGTK)*, Statistical Publishing House, Government of the Socialist Republic of Vietnam, Hanoi, Vietnam.

GSO (2008) General Statistics Office, *Statistical Data*. Hanoi: Statistical Publishing House. Online. Available at http://www.gso.gov.vn/default_en.aspx?tabid=468&idmid=3> (accessed 26 February 2008).

Harvie, C. (2008a) 'SME development strategy in Vietnam', in C. Harvie and B.C. Lee (eds.) *Small and Medium Sized Enterprises in East Asia: Sectoral and Regional Dimensions, Studies of Small and Medium Sized Enterprises in East Asia*, Volume IV, Chapter 9, pp. 200–39. Cheltenham, UK: Edward Elgar.

Harvie, C. (2008b), 'Vietnam's economy', in *Europa World, The Far East and Australasia 2009* (40th edn), November, pp 1290–1304. London and New York: Routledge.

Le, T.N.T. (2001) *Employment and Life of Vietnamese Women during Economic Transition*. Hanoi: The Gioi Publishers.

Le, T.N.T. (2005) *Images of the Vietnamese Women in the 21st Century*. Hanoi: The Gioi Publishers.

Lebra, T.S. (1998) 'Confucian gender role and personal fulfilment for Japanese women', in W.H. Slote and G.A. De Vos (eds.) *Confucianism and the Family*. State University of New York Press.

Leung, K. and White, S. (2004) *Handbook of Asian Management*, Birkhäuser.

Liu, Y.C. (1995) *Women's Labour Participation in Vietnam's Emerging Market Economy: Are Women Worse Off?* Hanoi: AusAID/NCDS.

Lofman, D. (1998) *The Women of Tuong Duong: Situations, Voices, Problems, and Solutions: A Gender Case Study*, Hanoi: Oxfam Hong Kong.

Long, L.D, Le, N.H., Truitt, A., Le, T.P.M. and Dang, N.A. (2000) 'Changing Gender Relations in Vietnam's Post Doi Moi Era', The World Bank

Development Research Group, Poverty Reduction and Economic Management Network.
Ministry of Planning and Investment (2008), National Business Information Centre, Agency for SME development, Government of the Socialist Republic of Vietnam, Hanoi.
MOLISA (2003) Ministry of Labour, Invalids and Social Affairs, *Statistical Data of Employment and Unemployment in Vietnam 2003*. Hanoi: Labour-Social Publishing House.
MOLISA (2006) Ministry of Labour, Invalids and Social Affairs, *Statistical Data of Employment and Unemployment in Vietnam 1996–2005*. Hanoi: Labour-Social Publishing House.
MPSDF (2006) Mekong Private Sector Development Fund, *Women Business Owners in Vietnam: A National Survey*. Hanoi: International Finance Corporation.
NCFAW and GSO (2005) National Committee for Advancement of Woman and General Statistics Office, 'Emerging gender issues in Vietnam during economic integration'. Executive Summary of Empirical and Secondary Research by Mekong Economics, Hanoi.
Nguyen, K.C. (1997) 'Women's movement and the Vietnamese women's role through historical periods', *Asian Women*, (5) 69–81.
Population Council (1997) *Production, Reproduction and Family Well-Being: The Analysis of Gender Relations in Vietnamese Households*. Hanoi.
Rowley, C. and Yu, Vukongdi. (eds.) (2009) *The Changing Face of Women Managers in Asia*. London: Routledge.
SRV (2005) Socialist Republic of Vietnam, *Vietnam Achieving the Millennium Development Goals*. Hanoi.
The World Bank Group (2006) 'Vietnam country gender assessment'. Online. Available at http://www-wds.worldbank.org/external/default/WDSContentServer/WDSP/IB/2007/01/24/000310607_20070124141846/Rendered/PDF/384450ENGLISH0VN0Gender01PUBLIC1.pdf (accessed 26 February 2008).
United Nations (2000) *Gender Briefing Kit*. Vietnam: Hanoi.
VCCI (2008) Vietnam Chamber of Commerce and Industry, 'Vietnamese businesswomen: Taking initiative in business management'. Online. Available at http://vibforum.vcci.com.vn/news_detail.asp?news_id=13067 (accessed 18 August 2008).
Vietnam Consultative Group (2005) 'Vietnam Development Report 2006', joint donor report to the Vietnam Consultative Group Meeting, Hanoi, 6–7 December.
Vietnam Economic Times, 26 May 2003.
Vo. A. (2008) 'Gender issues in the age of economic transformation: The case of Vietnam', in C. Rowley and V. Yukongdi (eds.) *The Changing Face of Women Management in Asia*. London: Routledge.
Vo, A. and Strachan, G. (2009) 'Gender equity in a male-dominated industry: The case of the steel industry in Vietnam', in M.F. Ozbilgin and J. Syed,

(eds.) *Diversity Management in Asia.* Cheltenham, UK: Edward Elgar Press.

World Bank (1998) 'Vietnam: Rising to the challenge'. Economic Report of the World Bank Consultative Group Meeting for Vietnam, Hanoi, 7 December. New York: World Bank.

World Bank (2000) 'Vietnam 2010 – Entering the 21st century: Pillars of development', World Bank Report, Washington, DC.

World Bank (2002), 'Vietnam Development Report: Implementing Reforms for Faster Growth and Poverty Reduction', World Bank Report, prepared for the Consultative Group Meeting for Vietnam, Hanoi, December 2001.

World Bank (2005) 'Country classification – data and statistics'. Online. Available at http://web.worldbank.org/wbsite/external/datastatistics/0,,contentmdk:20420458~menupk:64133156~pagepk:64133150~pipk:64133175~thesitepk:239419,00.html (accessed 26 February 2008).

World Bank (2006) 'Gender analysis of the 2004 Vietnam household living standard'.

9 The changing face of Vietnamese management revisited

Chris Rowley and Quang Truong

- Introduction
- Major findings revisited
- Implications and future trends
- Conclusion

Introduction

Vietnam underwent rapid economic change and development in the post-*Doi Moi* period and with WTO membership. In this context an objective of this book was to shed new light on the strategic changes and management practices of organizations and businesses. Much of what we know about Vietnamese organizations has mainly focused on their corporate and business strategies. Less is known about the changing roles of managers in Vietnam and the specific operational and managerial issues they face both internally and externally. Therefore, this book has also focused on this gap and adding detail to the changing face of management in Vietnam.

The previous chapters in this book have provided analysis of a broad range of the critical practices, functions and issues facing Vietnamese organizations and companies. This is in areas of Human Resource Management, marketing, finance and strategy and also FDI, public sector management, women managers and SMEs. This final chapter first summarizes the major findings in the key management and business areas and then discusses their implications along with some possible future directions.

Major findings revisited

The following key developments, findings and conclusions were discussed in the previous chapters. Chapter 2 on Human Resource Management concluded that in the coming years Vietnam faces many challenges in its development. While Vietnam will not face substantial HR shortages in labour-intensive industries, it will find it difficult to increase the 'value-added' content of products and services to enable competition in the global arena. Vietnam's capabilities for future success are, to a great extent, dependent upon its ability to manage and further develop its HR, not only in terms of quantity but also, critically, in terms of quality. Subsequently, these high-quality HR will be an important driver of Vietnam's competitiveness and sustainable growth.

Chapter 3 on marketing concluded that international firms could continue to play a role in transferring know-how and marketing skills. However, T&D was required for marketing HRs, especially in the face of increasing competition. Also, local firms would be challenged to move beyond their typical short-term thinking and adjust approaches to give the marketing function more suitable organizational positions, to play roles in corporate strategy with a longer-term perspective and in designing an IMC strategy. Business constraints worldwide with the post-2008 global financial crisis would also impact, especially in export industries, and marketing spending may also decline. Vietnam began to experience high inflation from 2008 and a degree of uncertainty entered the market place with firms commensurably adjusting their marketing and revenue expectations.

Chapter 4 on finance concluded that Vietnam's currency system – such as price and exchange rate stability with pegging to the US dollar, and maintaining a low value – means that measures to tackle inflation are limited. A policy change allowing for a moderate appreciation of the VND against the US dollar could be a solution, together with limiting capital inflows and introducing moderate taxes on capital gains and property. In the longer term, a fully independent central bank could be introduced. To reduce banking sector risks, efforts to lower non-performing loan ratios, tightening loan classification standards and upgrading capital requirements to international levels all need to be improved. In addition, changes to the supervisory regime are necessary. Establishing a sub-national debt system is advisable, with commensurate legal framework shifts to support it. Finally, while a number of measures had already been introduced to overcome stock market problems, it is important to control inflation in order to keep stock markets attractive for investors.

Chapter 5 on strategy concluded that, in order to survive competition and the post-2008 global financial crisis, great efforts and cooperation from both the government and the business community will be required to upgrade the level of competitiveness of both the workforce and products. Such an integrated strategy could help to resolve the key issues identified as the lack of strategic planning and implementation, the dilemma of 'quality' versus 'quantity' for sustainable growth, equal treatment of all economic sectors, quality of public services and corruption. The focus of future strategy should be to create synergetic impacts (government, educational and T&D institutions and industry) and comprehensive transformation with due emphasis on Human Resource Management and HRD and more effective use of 'internal strength' (*noi luc*). A shift in the way of thinking and doing business is seen as important to effectively match responses with changing conditions in the world.

Chapter 6 on FDI concluded that, like many other emerging countries, Vietnam can no longer hope to be an attractive country for FDI across all business sectors. Instead, the country needs to find its market niche in the global marketplace. Further liberalization should be given careful consideration, especially in the infrastructure and energy sectors, as these could benefit from higher levels of openness to FDI. However, economic and business risks – such as inflation, corruption, poor infrastructure and the post-2008 global financial crisis – could deter foreign investors and alter capital inflows.

Chapter 7 on public sector management concluded that Vietnam requires effective and accountable governmental machinery that supports transformation into a middle-income country and developed country status. Within this the government's primary role of 'controlling' should be replaced by 'enabling' in order to create a favourable environment for all stakeholders in the economy to participate and develop. The new role would help the government to better reconcile the demands and interests of various stakeholders, such as businesses and communities, in a manner that is more complementary and better balanced. Indeed, the participation of the civil society could be employed as a means to improve the accountability and transparency of government agencies. It was finally concluded that all the changes should be implemented by a professional and effective civil service.

Chapter 8 on women managers and SMEs concluded that although an institutional context for the advancement of women's rights has been created, paradoxically, the government's ability to influence gender relations has declined. Therefore, the state's capacity to promulgate equality has also fallen. Public administration is primarily concerned with the formal and legal aspects of gender strategies and policies, rather than with the actual implementation. In order to attain the country's long-term development goals, support from the government for the further development of the private sector and SMEs is needed. This development involves levelling the playing field between SOEs and PEs, enhancing the general business environment and ensuring the full utilization of the country's entrepreneurial capability irrespective of gender.

Implications and future trends

The implications from the key findings of this book and predictions of future trends are myriad and are summarized in Table 9.1. They are listed in terms of focus – both present and future, and general and specific – from each of the substantive chapters and the areas and issues of management and business in Vietnam.

Deeper integration into the world economy and the post-2008 global recession has brought more challenges for Vietnam, at least in the short term. Like other economies in the world, Vietnam has been affected by the crisis. As a result, the country's main sources of economic growth of the early 2000s, such as FDI, remittances of overseas Vietnamese and exports, have drastically reduced, with the exception of ODA. It is expected that disbursed FDI capital would only reach US$2.2 billion in 2009, compared to US$7.6 billion in 2008, and with a total registered value of US$20 billion for 2009 compared to US$64 billion in 2008, representing a drop of about 70 per cent (Huong, 2009). Remittances from overseas Vietnamese

Table 9.1 Implications and future trends

General	Present Focus	Future Focus
Objective	Growth	Sustainability
Measurement	Quantitative	Qualitative
Areas/Issues		
Human Resource Management	• Non-strategic • Unprofessional	• HRs as competitive advantage • Quality HRs • T&D
Marketing	• Low price and quality products • Low brand recognition	• Quality focus • Brand management • CRM • Value chain
Finance	• High number of JSB • Privileged treatment of SOEs	• Consolidated banking system • Capital markets (stock exchange)
Strategy	• Unbalanced economic structure • SOEs in leading role • Export-oriented	• Private sector/SME • Domestic markets • High value added content • 'Made-in-Vietnam' brand
FDI	• Large projects • Unviable (economically, environmentally)	• Better investment environment • High local content • 'Green' projects
Public sector management	• Slow equitisation process • Limited PAR	• Good governance • Social responsibility
Women managers and SMEs	• Gender equity	• 'Level playing field' (social, economic, political) • Entrepreneurial roles

would be much lower than the 2008 level of US$8 billion (Huong, 2009)

Critically, total export values are forecast to fall sharply, especially in industries like garments and footwear, as a result of tumbling global demand (Thinh, 2009). This scenario provides enough reasons for the government and other organizations to re-adjust projected growth from 6.5 per cent down to 5.5–5 per cent (government), 5 per cent (WB), 4.75 to 4.5 per cent (IMF), or even a scant 0.3 per cent (The Economist) in 2009 (Johnston, 2009). Nevertheless, despite this downward trend, Vietnam is still one of just four Asian countries (along with China, India and Indonesia) expected to continue to expand in 2009 in the face of the global crisis (Huong, 2009).

As Vietnam is now facing a strategic dilemma, as discussed in many chapters in this book, perhaps a more appropriate focus for future development should be on a more sustainability and inward orientation. Such a shift in strategic direction could include continuing existing efforts, such as enhancing governance in the public sector, reducing corruption, improving infrastructure, deepening financial market reform, improving regulatory attractiveness for domestic and foreign investments in combination with reform in Human Resource Management and HRD at all levels (e.g., basic education, vocational T&D and higher education), SOEs and cluster development (Porter, 2008).

Indeed, one area of development can be seen in the figures. These show that one area, Human Resource Management, is vital – for example, the challenges, at both macro (national) and micro (organizational) levels, and responses in terms of HR resourcing, rewards and development, and the use of Human Resource Management as a competitive edge.

Thus, in terms of the management of people (Quang *et al.*, 2008), this is a key aspect of Vietnam's future. Indeed, this requirement has been seen more broadly, such as in South East Asia (Rowley and Abdul-Rahman, 2008) and parts of North East Asia (Rowley and Paik, 2008). The role of key elements of the workforce, such as women, has also been seen as critical in both Vietnam and Asia more widely (Rowley and Yukongdi, 2009).

Table 9.2 HR challenges in Vietnam

- Inefficient use of human capital
- Overall low quality of labour
- Serious shortage at mid-end and high-end
- Lack of professionalism and business ethics
- HRM low awareness/'best' practice in local enterprises
- Unbalanced expats versus locals relationships
- Low international/cross-cultural experience
- Industrial relations

Table 9.3 Human Resource Management challenges and responses in Vietnam

HRM Areas	Current	Solutions
Acquiring	• Recruitment and selection procedure not standardized	• HR planning and HRIS • Job analysis and description • Based on qualifications and job requirements
Utilizing	• No structured orientation • Placement and appointment based on relationships	• Socialization programme for recruits (corporate culture) • Best match job/qualifications • Define core staff – use outsourcing
Developing	• Lack of or inappropriate T&D programme • No career planning • Promotion based on seniority and relationship	• Reserve budget for T&D • Career development for all • Job rotation • Development plans for potential managers
Retaining	• Pay not linked to performance • Reward policy not in line with strategy • Inappropriate working environment	• Pay for performance and PAS • Incentives linked to business indicators • QWL • Regular employee survey

Source: Adopted from Quang (2006)

Table 9.4 Human Resource Management as a competitive edge in Vietnam

1. Proactive search for and acquisition of qualified personnel, especially in state and private sector
2. More attention on retaining employees to protect scarce human assets
3. Using training and development as leverage to build competitive edge
4. Building HRM professionalism toward a fully-fledged centre of competence and a strategic partner in the organizations
5. Emphasizing the task of management development to ensure organization's capability for long-term survival and growth
6. Allowing 'horizontal' buy-in of high-level executives or professional positions, by third nationals or overseas Vietnamese
7. Establish triangle linkage among state agencies, education and training institutions and industries to ensure sustainable development

Conclusion

Vietnam needs to continue to examine further its economic structure, and management and business practices, and make adjustments to cope with the new conditions. One way to do this is to develop a long-term, visionary strategy with focus on repositioning Vietnam strategically in the global context, developing and exploiting its 'internal strength' (HRs and domestic markets), enhancing its quality level of delivery, and building a new generation of managers and quality-based workforce. Since the country is now entering a new phase of development with special emphasis on 'quality of growth', the next generation of HRs will not only need new competencies, concern for community and the environment, but also be able to turn obstacles into opportunities (Stoltz, 1997) in order to be competitive in the global arena.

Finally, our book, part of the innovative *Working in Asia* series, has covered a broad area of Vietnamese management, both by key functions and issues. In doing this, the chapters covered the context, practice and challenges in their areas as well as giving 'voice' to managers and organizations. It has shown the 'face' of Vietnamese management, like the country itself, to be both fascinating and changing.

Bibliography

Athukorala, P.C. (2009) 'Economic transition and export performance in Vietnam', ASEAN Economic Bulletin, 26, 1, 96–114.

Huong, Lan (2009) 'Kinh te Viet Nam chi tang truong 0.3% nam 2009 (Vietnam's economy will only grow 0.3% in 2009)', *Dan tri*, 16 March.

Johnston, T. (2009) 'Vietnam growth slowest in a decade', *Financial Times*, 26 March. Available at http://www.ft.com/cms/s/0/0f26c85a-19db-11de-9f91-0000779fd2ac.html.

Leung, S. (2009) 'Banking and financial sector reforms in Vietnam', ASEAN Economic Bulletin, 26, 1, 44–57.

Pincus, J. (2009) 'Vietnam: sustaining growth in difficult times', 26, 1, 11–24.

Porter, M.E. (2008) 'Vietnam's competitiveness and the role of the private sector'. Conference, 1 December, Ho Chi Minh City, Vietnam.

Quang, T. (2006) 'Human resource management in Vietnam', in A. Nankervis, S. Chatterjee and J. Coffey (eds.) *Perspectives of Human Resource Management in the Asia Pacific*, pp 231–52. Sydney: Pearson Education Australia.

Quang, T., Thang, L.C. and Rowley, C. (2008) 'The changing face of human resource management in Vietnam', in C. Rowley and S. Abdul-Rahman (eds.) *The Changing Face of Management in South East Asia*, pp 185–220. London and New York: Routledge.

Rowley, C. and Abdul-Rahman, S. (2008) *The Changing Face of Management in South East Asia*. London and New York: Routledge.

Rowley, C. and Paik, Y. (2008) *The Changing Face of Korean Management*. London and New York: Routledge.

Rowley, C. and Yukongdi, Y. (2009) *The Changing Face of Women Managers in Asia*. London and New York: Routledge.

Stoltz, P.G. (1997) *Adversity Quotient: Turning Obstacles into Opportunities*, New York: Wiley & Sons, Inc.

Thang, L.C., Rowley, C., Quang, T. and Warner, W. (2007) 'To what extent can management practices be transferred between countries: Human Resource Management in Vietnam', *Journal of World Business*, 42, 1, 113–27

Thinh, P.D. (2009) 'Xuat khau tiep tuc giam (Exports continue to fall)', *Thoi bao kinh te Sai Gon*, 11, 5 March, 10 & 64.

Vo, T.T. and Nguyen, A.D. (2009) 'Vietnam after two years of WTO accession: what lessons can be learnt?', ASEAN Economic Bulletin, 26, 1, 115–35.

Vuving, A.L. (2008) 'Vietnam: Arriving in the world and at a crossroads', *Southeast Asia Affairs*, 375–93.

Index

Abdul-Rahman, S. 258
access to finance 240, 242–3, 245–6
Ackerman, S.R. 197
acquisitions 168–9
active support policy 151–3
ADB–OECD Anti-Corruption Initiatives for Asia and the Pacific 199
advertisements 54, 83; *see also* marketing
AFTA 137, 140
age structure 12
agricultural exports 136
agriculture 9, 10, 131, 213
Akram-Lodhi, A.H. 235
Amata 179–80
An, T. 31
An Phuoc Garment Company (APG) 142–3
ancestor worship 11
Anh, H. 34, 43
ANZ Bank 58, 78–9
APEC 140
APEC Digital Opportunity Centre 235
ASEAN 161
Asia Pacific Breweries 168
Asian Development Bank (ADB) 140
Asian financial crisis 128, 131, 134, 135, 225
assessment centres 31
asset purchase acquisitions 169
automatic teller machines (ATMs) 111
automotive industry 163

balance sheets, banks' 110

Bank for Agriculture and Rural Development (Agribank) 99
banking system 16, 98–100, 125; case studies of banks 108–11; challenges 118–19
Bao Veit 113
Baughn, C.C. 51, 59, 60, 84
beauty salons 56
Berjaya Land Berhad 160–1
best practices 19, 59, 85
BIDV 99
BIG-C 76
Binh, Truong Gia 80–1
BP Vietnam 235
'brain drain' 196–7
brands/branding 60–1, 64–5, 76, 82, 137–8, 148–9
Brazil 158
bribery 197–9; *see also* corruption
British American Tobacco 167–8
Buhmann, K. 192
build-operate-transfer (BOT) projects 166
business cooperation contracts (BCCs) 165–6
business expansion service group 171–3
buyer behaviour 67–70, 86

cabinet (executive) 6, 7, 189
Canada 161
Canler, E. 95
Cao Dai 11
capital requirements 116, 118

career progression 232–3
caring work 228, 231
cars 56
case studies 19, 20; FDI 171–6; finance 107–15; Human Resource Management 37–43; marketing 72–81; public sector 202–10; strategy 141–51; women SME entrepreneurs 236–42
central bank *see* State Bank of Vietnam (SBV)
central bank independence 117
Central Committee of the CPV 6, 189
central planning 8, 130–1
Central region 4
Chau, H. 213
Chau, N. 196
Chevron 173–4
chief executive officers (CEOs), hiring for SOEs 201, 205–7
child-rearing 231
China 12–13, 67, 69, 117, 137, 158; melamine scandal 64, 75; occupation of Vietnam 223
Ching Luh Vietnam Co. 36–7
civil servants 18, 190; developing a competent contingent of 214; management of 194–7
civil society 213–14
climate 4–5
coffee franchises 146–50
Cohen, M. 153
collateral 240, 243
collectivism 13, 67–8
commercial banks 98
communication 64, 68
communism, collapse of 131
Communist Party of Vietnam (CPV) 6, 7, 131; Central Committee 6, 189; and civil servants 194, 195; and government 188–9; 'war' on corruption 199
competitiveness 13–14, 21, 45–6, 129–30; Human Resource Management as a competitive edge 257; productivity improvement 139–40; quest for 137–41, 153; role of private sector 140–1; SCV's strategy 114–15
complaints 191–2
conditional sectors 164
Confucianism 223–4, 231, 233
Constitution 188, 224
Constructional Glassware and Pottery Corporation 206
consulting services, HR 45
consumer psychology 67–70, 86
contexts 3–13; cultural 10–13, 223–4; development of SMEs 223–8; economic 8–10, 11, 50–1, 52–4, 225–8; geographical 3–5; historical and marketing 52–4; political 5–8; religious 10–13; social 10–13, 223–4
corporate governance 141
corporate social responsibility (CSR) 15, 41, 59, 77, 83–4
corporate tax rate 183
corruption 18, 159, 197–9
Corruption Perception Index 197–8
costs 177
credit control 116
credit crunch 245–6
credit funds 98
cultural context 10–13, 223–4
culture 174; differences between north and south 65–6, 68; issues in marketing 67–72
currency 94–8, 125, 252; challenges 115–18
customer relations management (CRM) 19, 61, 83
Czinkota, M.R. 57, 83

Dai-Ichi Life Insurance Company of Vietnam (DIIVN) 176
dairy products 74–5, 76–7
Dao, T.T.L. 51, 59, 60, 84
De Angelis, M. 101, 102, 103, 119
De Burca, S. 68
De Mooij, M. 57, 68
De Sterlini, M.L. 163
debt: non-performing loans 118–19, 133; SOEs 133; sub-national 100–3, 119–22

decentralization programme 211, 212
decision-making, household 56–7
Decree No 11 181–2
democratic centralism 6
deputy Prime Ministers 7
Desai, J. 180, 234, 235
development, economic 5, 8–9, 215
Development Assistance Fund 99
Diethelm, W.H. 171
distribution 54–5
DKSH 171–3
DNL Partners 209
Doan, L. 196
documentation, legal 193
Doi Moi (renovation) 8–10, 24, 50, 242; impact on the economy 128, 130–1; and the private sector 223, 225–6
dollar, US 94–5, 97, 117
DOMESCO Group 145
double exchange rate system 95
Duc, H. 138–9
Duc, N.V. 36, 37
Dung, N.T. 211
Dung Quat Oil Refinery 173
Duoc Hau Giang (DHG Pharma) 144–6
Dutch Lady 72–3, 74–5, 76

ease of doing business 13–14
economic context 8–10, 11, 50–1; marketing 52–4; SMEs 225–8
economic development 5, 8–9, 215
economic growth *see* growth, economic
economic structure 13, 132–7
education 69
educational level 230–1, 243
Electricity of Vietnam (EVN) 145, 173–4, 177
employee relations 35–7, 180–2
employee satisfaction 31–2
'enabling' role of government 211, 253–4
energy sector 170–1, 173–4, 177
Enterprise Law 133, 140, 163, 165, 226
entrepreneurship 152
entry modes 164–7
equitisation 9–10, 52, 133, 200, 201–2; SOCBs 99
Erasmus, E. 67–70

ethnic groups 10–11, 12
Euromonitor 72
events management 63–4
exchange rate 94–5; regime 116, 117
experts 194
export-orientation 135–7
exports 8, 9, 82, 137, 255
external challenges/internal response analysis 30–7

family 56–7, 67–8
Farmers' Unions 6, 213
fast moving consumer goods (FMCG) 76–8
Fatherland Front 6, 7, 213
finance 16, 93–127, 191, 252–3, 255; access to 240, 242–3, 245–6; banking system 16, 98–100, 108–11, 118–19, 125; case studies 107–15; challenges 115–24; currency and monetary policy 94–8, 115–18, 125, 252; stock exchange 103–7, 122–4, 125; sub-national debt 100–3, 119–22
financial companies 98
Flockhart, S. 112–13
footwear industry 136, 139
foreign banks 98, 100; HSBC 112–13; SCV 114–15
foreign companies: influence on marketing 58–9, 61–2; listing on the stock exchange 105; marketing 84–5; wholesalers 54–5
foreign direct investment (FDI) 2, 17–18, 58, 61, 158–86, 253, 254, 255; case studies 171–6; challenges 177–82; constraints on implementation 159; economic structure 132, 134–5; entry modes 164–7; flows of 169–71; implications of WTO membership 17, 161–4; industrial parks 179–80; labour productivity 177; labour relations 180–2; legislation to attract 131; modes of 167–9; real estate 178; registered and implemented capital 159, 160, 161; size of inflows 159–60; sources of 160–1; and Vietnamese stock market 105

foreign invested enterprises (FIEs) 15, 17, 132, 134–5, 221–2, 228–9
foreign markets, investment in 193
foreign workers 27, 44; limit on 183
FPT Corporation 28, 59, 65, 74, 80–1, 235
France 224
franchising 146–50
free capital movement 117
free trade agreements (FTAs) 25
Fujii, T. 176

garment industry 136, 139
garment manufacturing company: case study of organization 236–7; case study of owner 238–40
GDP 8, 9, 10, 53, 128; composition of 226–7; impact of *Doi Moi* on growth 221, 225–6; year-on-year growth 96
gender equality 228–9; challenges 242–6; cultural context 223–4; legal context 224–5; persistent inequalities 229–36; *see also* women managers
general corporations 200, 201
General Confederation of Labour 6, 36, 37, 213
general obligation financing 103
geographical context 3–5
Giau, Nguyen van 209–10
global economy, integration into 24–5, 128–30, 151–3, 187
Global Equipment Services (GES) 167
global financial crisis 10, 86–7, 225, 245–6, 254–6
good governance 19, 152
government 6–8; active support policy 151–3; CPV and 188–9; 'enabling' role 211, 253–4; redefining the role of 211–12; support needed for developing private sector and SMEs 247, 254; T&D programmes for female entrepreneurs 235
growth, economic 2, 24, 46, 187, 225–6; annual growth rate 50–1, 53, 221; trends 96, 128, 129, 158, 225
growth competitiveness comparison index (GCI) 138

Hanoi 65–6, 148, 170; North Red River new residential area 178
Hanoi stock exchange 103
HASTC 103
health care 69
health insurance 213
high-tech industry 10
historical context 5, 52–4
Ho, N. 43
Ho Chi Minh City (HCMC) 65–6, 148, 170; PMS 202–5; resignations from civil service 207–9
Ho Chi Minh City stock exchange 103, 104; issues in improving trading conditions 107
Ho Hung 150–1
Hoa Hao 11
Hofstede, G. 13, 56
holding company model 201–2
Hong Kong 117
Hong-Phiet, Nguyen thi 40–2
house ownership 240
household enterprises 133–4, 234–5
household goods 57–8, 76–8
households 56–7, 68
Housing Bank of Mekong Delta (MHB) 109–12
HSBC 112–13, 114
human resource management 15, 19, 24–49, 252, 255, 256–8; case studies 37–43; challenges 43–5; civil servants 214; employee relations 35–7; function 27–9, 44–5; labour market development 25–7; managers 42–3; marketing staff 81–2; motivation 34–5; practices 30–7; recruitment 31–3; training and development 26, 27, 31, 33–4
Hung, L.N. 12
Huong, G. 196
Huong, L. 254, 255, 256
Huu-Nghi 2 Garment Co. Ltd 40–2

IBM 59, 72, 73–4, 76
immigration 27
immobile assets 183
importers 55

imports 8, 9, 136
'Impossible Trinity' 116–17, 125
incentives: industrial parks 179; securities trading 103–4
income statements, banks' 110–11
independence of central bank 117
India 158
individualism 13
Indonesia 198
industrial parks 177, 179–80
industrial production 226–7
industrialization 152
industry 9, 10, 137
inflation 36–7, 53–4, 96–7, 98, 124; challenges for currency and monetary policy 115–18
informal sector 229
infrastructure 101–2, 159
integrated marketing approach 81
integrated marketing communication strategy (IMC) 81, 83
integration into the global economy 24–5, 128–30, 151–3, 187
intellectual property rights 163
interest rates 115, 117, 209–10
'internal strength' 152–3, 253
International Labour Organization (ILO) 235
International Monetary Fund (IMF) 107, 123
internet 12, 84
internship programme initiative 39–40
investment 226; FDI *see* foreign direct investment; Law on Investment 163, 164, 168, 193; legislation to attract 131
investment promotion offices 167
inward orientation 154, 256
Ishii, S. 24
IT sector 73–4, 78

Japan 12–13, 146, 149; FDI in Vietnam 69–70, 161
Jeffries, I. 104
Johnston, T. 255
joint stock banks (JSBs) 98–9, 99; SeABank 108, 109–12
joint stock companies (JSCs) 165, 200

joint venture enterprises (JVEs) 84–5, 167–8; JVE banks 98, 99, 100
Jung, A. 94

Kamoche, K. 35
Kao corporation 77
Keller, E.A. 171
KFC 70
King-Kauanui, S. 25, 29, 33, 35
Korea, South 12–13, 69, 160, 161, 162; Korean-owned facilities and strikes 180
Kotabe, M. 57, 83
Kotler, P. 61, 81, 83
Kumho Asiana 160

Labour Code 231
Labour Federation 6, 36, 37, 213
Labour Law 36
labour market: development 25–7; FDI and 177, 183; female participation 228–9, 231–6
labour press 37
labour relations 35–7, 180–2
Lai, L. 152
Lall, S. 183
Lan, P. 139, 153
land 57, 179–80, 240
Land Law 243
Land Use Certificates 240, 243
languages 12
Law on Anti-Corruption 199
Law on Competition 168, 169
Law on Enterprise (LOE) 133, 140, 163, 165, 226
Law on Foreign Investment (LFI) 105
Law on Gender Equality (LGE) 244
Law on Investment (LOI) 163, 164, 168, 193
Law on Promotion of Domestic Investment 226
Law on Real Estate Transactions 168
Law on Securities 102, 105; implementing regulations 123
Le, T. 224, 228
Le, T.N.T. 223, 230, 232
Lebra, T.S. 224

Lee, J. 97
legal context 192–4; gender equality 224–5; sub-national credit market 119–22
Legal Systems Development Strategy 194
legislation: encouraging development of private sector 131; law-making process 193; relating to acquisitions 168–9; *see also under individual laws*
Leung, K. 231
'level playing field' 19–21, 44, 141, 151–2
LG Household and Health Care Ltd 77
life expectancy 12
limited liability companies (LLCs) 165, 167
Linh, L.U. 34
Linh, X. 46, 196
listed companies, number of 104; *see also* stock exchanges
literacy rate 12
Loan, T. 44
local content requirements 163
local government 6, 7–8, 189, 211; tiers 8
localization 59
Long, L.D. 229
Lunar New Year festival 181
Ly, H. 28
Ly, Luong van 207–9

magazines 83
male dominance 223–4, 242
managerial case studies: FDI 174–6; finance 112–15; Human Resource Management 40–3; marketing 78–81; public sector 207–10; strategy 146–51; women SME entrepreneurs 238–42
market information 241
market-oriented economy 8–10, 13, 27, 130–1
market research 71–2
marketing 15–16, 50–92, 252, 255; branding and public relations 64–5; case studies 72–81; challenges 81–5; culture and 67–72; events management and promotions 63–4; historical context in pricing and products 52–4; influence of foreign companies 58–9, 61–2; north-south differences 65–6, 68; professionalism 60–5, 85, 85–6; sectors and segments 56–8; Trung Nguyen 150; wholesale and distribution 54–5
Masina, P. 178
mass marketing tools 83
mass organizations 6, 7–8, 213
Massmann, O. 168
maternity leave 225
matriarchy 223
Matthaes, R. 66
Mayeda, A. 119
McDonald's 150
melamine scandal 64, 75
mergers and acquisitions 168–9
Metro 54–5
Mexico 122
Meyer, K.E. 83
Michalet, C.A. 183
Millennium Development Goals 24
Minh, Q. 159, 201
minimum wage 34
Ministry of Agriculture 52
Ministry of Construction 52
Ministry of Defence 52
Ministry of Finance 124
Ministry of Home Affairs 190, 192, 207
Ministry of Labour and Social Affairs (MOLISA) 36, 231, 232
Mizuno, T. 149
modes of FDI 167–9
monetary policy 94–8, 125, 209–10; challenges 115–18
money stock 116, 210
motivation 34–5
MS Trade Finance LLC 72
My, Nguyen Thanh 150–1
My Lan Chemicals (MLC) 150–1

Napier, N.K. 66
National Assembly (NA) 6–7, 189, 190, 193, 199

National Committee for the Advancement of Women in Vietnam (NCFAW) 243
national treatment 100
natural resources 4
Neal, C. 68
Neelakantan, R. 63
Nestlé 72–3, 74–5, 76
Nettra 168
Neupert, K.E. 51, 59, 60, 84
newspapers 37, 83
Ngan, Dang Thi 167–8
Ngoc, T. 31
Nguoi Lao Dong 137
Nguyen, K.C. 242
Nguyen, N.T. 24
Nguyen, T.D.K. 63
Nguyen, V.T. 66
Nhan, N. 36
Nielsen market research company 71
Nike 181
non-performing loans (NPLs) 118–19, 133
non-state sector 132, 133–4, 221, 228–9; *see also* private sector, small and medium enterprises (SMEs)
north-south differences 65–6, 68
Northern region 4

Odessa 121
official development aid loans 101
officials (communes) 194
Ombudsman Committee 191
one-stop shops (OSSs) 191
open market operations 116
Ordinance on Cadres and Civil Servants 190
Ordinance on Foreign Exchange (OFE) 94, 95
organizational case studies: FDI 171–4; finance 108–12; Human Resource Management 38–40; marketing 73–8; public sector 202–7; strategy 142–6; women SME entrepreneurs 236–8
'out of line' investments 201

outsourcing 27
Overland, M.A. 198
overseas Vietnamese professionals 27, 44
ownership: banking system 98–100; Human Resource Management practices and 27, 28

pack behaviour 123
Packard, T. 201
Paik, Y. 258
Painter, M. 195
pay *see* salaries/pay
People's Committees 7–8, 189
People's Councils (PCs) 6, 7, 189
performance: evaluation 34–5; marketing 86–7; SOEs 200
performance management system (PMS) 202–5
permanent secretariat 6
Peterlik, R.-U. 56
Petrolimex 173
Petrovietnam 173–4
Pham, C. 198
Phan, L. 138
Philippines 122, 198
Phuong, Nguyen thi 43
Phuong, Thanh Phung 71–2
Pieper, R. 27
Pierre Cardin Group 142–3
pilot projects 120
policy lending institutions 98
politburo 6, 189
political context 5–8
Poon, Y. 190, 195, 203
Porter, M.E. 57, 256
poverty reduction 24, 187
practical experience 119–20
President 7
price-to-earnings (PE) ratios 122–3
pricing 52–4
Prime Minister 7
principal experts 194–5
printing company: case study of organization 237–8; case study of owner 240–2

private sector 9, 14, 133–4, 245; economic context 225–8; government support needed for development of 247, 254; Human Resource Management 28, 29; role in competitiveness 140–1; *see also* small and medium enterprises (SMEs)
privatization *see* equitisation
Procter & Gamble 77
production sector 233, 234
productivity 139–40, 177
products 52–4
professionalism 19, 152; Human Resource Management 38–9; marketing 60–5, 85, 85–6
promotions 63–4
property development company 38–9
public administration reform (PAR) 18, 189–92, 214
public employees 194; *see also* civil servants
public relations 64–5
public sector 18, 44, 187–220, 253–4, 255; balancing stakeholders' competing demands 212–13; case studies 202–10; challenges 210–14; fighting corruption 197–9; management of civil servants 194–7, 214; PAR 189–92; participation of civil society 213–14; redefining the role of government 211–12; reforms 189–202, 215–16; regulatory framework 192–4; state-owned commercial banks (SOCBs) 98, 99, 109–12, 118–19; state-owned enterprises *see* state-owned enterprises (SOEs)
public servants 194; *see also* civil servants

Qiao, H. 96, 121–2
quality improvement 137
Quang, T. 7, 8, 13, 27, 29, 31, 33, 34, 35, 36, 131, 152, 169, 180, 188, 194, 256, 257
Quangnam VBL Ltd 168

Ralston, D.A. 13, 66
real estate 178
recruitment: civil servants 195; Human Resource Management and 31–3
regulation: FDI 159, 163; financial sector 119, 123–4; private sector 245; public sector 192–4; and sub-national debt 102
relational capital 169
religious context 10–13
remittances 159, 254–5
representative offices (ROs) 164–5
reserve requirement ratio 116, 118
retailing 53
retention of civil servants 196–7, 207–9
retraining 43
revenue-based financing 103
risk, financial sector 118, 120–1
Romania 121–2
Rowley, C. 256, 258

salaries/pay: civil servants 195, 208; motivation and 34–5; SOE managers 205–6
sales, focus on 60
Schiller, M. 174–5
scrap steel imports 213
Securities Law *see* Law on Securities
securities-related credit exposures 124
securities trading 103–4
segments, market 56–8
senior experts 194
service sector 9, 10, 234
share purchase acquisitions 169
Shipbuilder Strategic Marine (SSM) 174–5
short-term deposits 101
Siber, H. 171
Singapore 160, 161, 162, 200
Singapore International Arbitration Centre 166
skilled labour shortage 43, 62, 159
small and medium enterprises (SMEs) 18–19, 32–3, 140–1, 221–50, 254, 255; case studies 236–42; challenges 242–6; contexts and development of 223–8;

employee compensation 34–5; gender dimensions in development of 229–36; marketing 86
social context 10–13, 223–4
social security 213
social services 211, 212, 213
Société Générale 108
Socio-Economic Development Plan (SEDP) 187
Socio-Economic Development Strategy (SEDS) 225–6
Son Tra peninsula 213
Song Hong Constructional Corporation 206
south-north differences 65–6, 68
Southeast Asia Commercial Bank (SeABank) 108, 109–12
Southern region 4
spending on advertising and marketing 54
SSC 105, 124
stakeholders' competing demands 212–13
Standard Chartered Vietnam (SCV) 114–15
Starbucks 150
'Start and improve your business' project 235
starting up a business 13–14, 240
state agencies, reorganization of 190
State Bank of Vietnam (SBV) 98, 119, 124; Directive 3 124; governor Giau 209–10; monetary policy 115, 116, 117, 125; new regulations of January 2007 123; supervision of SOCBs 98, 119
State Budget Law 191
State Capital Investment Corporation (SCIC) 119, 200
State Management Agency on Gender Equality 244
state-owned commercial banks (SOCBs) 98, 99, 118–19; MHB 109–12
state-owned enterprises (SOEs) 16–17, 132–3; declining investment in 226; employee compensation 34; equitisation 9–10, 52, 99, 133, 200, 201–2; government role and reform of 211, 212; hiring of CEOs 201, 205–7; marketing 52–3, 84, 86; restructuring 9–10, 199–202; stock market and 104–5, 106; strategic partnerships and equitisation 166–7
state service delivery agencies 211, 212
State Trading Commission (STC) 105
Staveren, I. 235
steel 213
stereotyping 230–1, 233, 247
stock exchanges 103–7, 125; challenges 122–4
Stocking, B. 66
Stoltz, P.G. 258
Strachan, G. 225, 232
strategic competencies 21
strategic mismatch 10, 11, 21
strategic sectors 164
strategy 16–17, 128–57, 253, 255, 256; advent of *Doi Moi* 130–1; case studies 141–51; challenges 151–3; economic structure 132–7; marketing and 85; quest for competitiveness 137–41
strikes 36–7, 180–2
subcontracting market 27
sub-national debt 100–3; challenges 119–22
subsidiary banks 100
Sud, A. 114–15
Sumitomo Group 160
supermarkets 76–7
supervision, banking 98, 119
sustainability 256
Swierczek, F.W. 13
Swinkels, R. 24

Taiwan 161, 162
takeovers 168–9
Tan Thuan Export Processing Zone 181
Techcombank 113
telecommunications 12, 167
Temasek 200
Terutomo, O. 168
Thailand 137, 158, 177, 198
Thang, L.C. 13, 27, 31, 34

Thanh, T. 193
Thanh, Tran Quang 206, 207
Thanh, Trinh Quang 172
Thinh, P.D. 255
Tho, T.V. 137, 138
Thu Huong, Vo thi 43
Thuy Dam 58, 78–9
Thuy, L.X. 167, 169
Tien, Cam 42
time, allocation of 231
Tinh, Pham Van 179
TNS 71
Tokyo 146, 149
'Towards success' programme 235
trade 158; exports 8, 9, 82, 137, 255; imports 8, 9, 136; trade balance 136–7
Trade Related Investment Measures Agreement (TRIMS) 163
trade sector, SMEs and 233, 234
trade unions 6, 35, 36–7, 182, 213
training and development (T&D) 19; civil servants 196; FDI and 179; Human Resource Management 26, 27, 31, 33–4; marketing 62–3, 84; women 235–6, 243
Tran, A.N. 37
Tran, D. 167
Tran Duc Kien 163
Tran, L.T. 26
Tran The Tuong 150–1
Tri, V.N. 131
Trung Nguyen cafés 146–50
Truong, D.L. 104
Truong, Q. 24, 190, 195
Trustee Swiss Group 160
Tsang, E.W.K. 85
Tu, N. 202
Tu Tam 175, 176
Turk, C. 24
turnover 62, 196

Ukraine 121
unemployment 25, 26, 27, 232, 233
Unilever 31, 58, 59, 65, 72, 74, 76–8
United Nations Convention against Corruption 199

United Nations Development Programme (UNDP) 203
United States (US): Bilateral Trade Agreement with 135–6, 137; dollar 94–5, 97, 117; war against 224
unlawful strikes 36, 180–2
UNZA International 77

Van, H. 31
vertical integration 149
Veterans' Association 213
Viet Nam Brewery Ltd 168
Viet Nga, Nguyen thi 145–6
Vietcombank 99
Vietinbank 99
Vietnam Chamber of Commerce and Industry (VCCI) 56, 63, 102, 235
Vietnam Electrical Corporation (VEC) 206–7
Vietnam General Confederation of Labour (VGCL) 6, 36, 37, 213
Vietnam Ship Building Corporation (Vinashin) 201, 206
Vietnam–US Bilateral Trade Agreement (VNUSBTA) 135–6, 137
Viettel 168
Vinachem 77
VinaGame 39–40
Vinamotor Corporation 206, 207
VN Index 103, 106, 124
Vo, A. 225, 232
Vu, Dang Le Nguyen 146–50
Vungtau 170
VWU 243

Wagner, W. 94
wars 224
White, S. 231
wholesalers 54–5
women 180; participation in the workforce 228–9, 231–6
women managers 18–19, 221–50, 254, 255; case studies 236–42; challenges 242–6; contexts 223–8; gender dimensions in SME development 229–36; HR managers 42–3
Women's Union 6, 7–8, 213

Work Plan 102
workforce 25–7; female participation 228–9, 231–6; imbalanced 26, 43
workloads 231
World Bank 141, 222, 226, 243
World Economic Forum (WEF) 138
World Investment Report 159–60
World Trade Organization (WTO) 16, 25, 164, 182, 187; and Human Resource Management 30; implications of WTO membership for FDI 17, 161–4; and marketing 55, 64; rules on telecommunications 167; and strategy 130, 137

Yin, S. 65
Yoong, C.K. 43
Youth Union 6, 7–8, 213
Yukongdi, Y. 258

Zhan, J. 168

ROUTLEDGE INTERNATIONAL HANDBOOKS

Routledge International Handbooks is an outstanding, award-winning series that provides cutting-edge overviews of classic research, current research and future trends in Social Science, Humanities and STM.

Each *Handbook*:

- is introduced and contextualised by leading figures in the field
- features specially commissioned original essays
- draws upon an international team of expert contributors
- provides a comprehensive overview of a sub-discipline.

Routledge International Handbooks aim to address new developments in the sphere, while at the same time providing an authoritative guide to theory and method, the key sub-disciplines and the primary debates of today.

If you would like more information on our on-going *Handbooks* publishing programme, please contact us.

Tel: +44 (0)20 701 76566
Email: reference@routledge.com

www.routledge.com/reference

Routledge
Paperbacks Direct

Bringing you the cream of our hardback publishing at paperback prices

This exciting new initiative makes the best of our hardback publishing available in paperback format for authors and individual customers.

Routledge Paperbacks Direct is an ever-evolving programme with new titles being added regularly.

To take a look at the titles available, visit our website.

www.routledgepaperbacksdirect.com

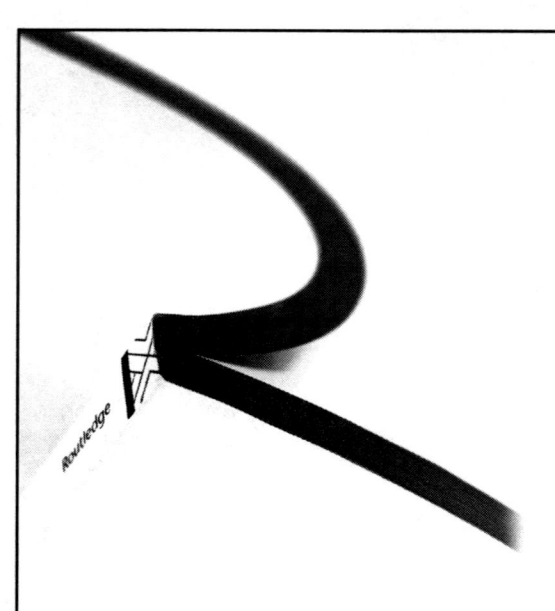

Routledge
Taylor & Francis Group

ROUTLEDGE Revivals

Are there some elusive titles you've been searching for but thought you'd never be able to find?

Well this may be the end of your quest. We now offer a fantastic opportunity to discover past brilliance and purchase previously out of print and unavailable titles by some of the greatest academic scholars of the last 120 years.

Routledge Revivals is an exciting new programme whereby key titles from the distinguished and extensive backlists of the many acclaimed imprints associated with Routledge are re-issued.

The programme draws upon the backlists of Kegan Paul, Trench & Trubner, Routledge & Kegan Paul, Methuen, Allen & Unwin and Routledge itself.

Routledge Revivals spans the whole of the Humanities and Social Sciences, and includes works by scholars such as Emile Durkheim, Max Weber, Simone Weil and Martin Buber.

FOR MORE INFORMATION

Please email us at **reference@routledge.com** or visit:
www.routledge.com/books/series/Routledge_Revivals

www.routledge.com

Routledge
Taylor & Francis Group

eBooks – at www.eBookstore.tandf.co.uk

A library at your fingertips!

eBooks are electronic versions of printed books. You can store them on your PC/laptop or browse them online.

They have advantages for anyone needing rapid access to a wide variety of published, copyright information.

eBooks can help your research by enabling you to bookmark chapters, annotate text and use instant searches to find specific words or phrases. Several eBook files would fit on even a small laptop or PDA.

NEW: Save money by eSubscribing: cheap, online access to any eBook for as long as you need it.

Annual subscription packages

We now offer special low-cost bulk subscriptions to packages of eBooks in certain subject areas. These are available to libraries or to individuals.

For more information please contact webmaster.ebooks@tandf.co.uk

We're continually developing the eBook concept, so keep up to date by visiting the website.

www.eBookstore.tandf.co.uk